tactics for
teaching
the disadvantaged

tactics for
teaching the disadvantaged

william f. white

Professor, Educational Psychology
The University of Georgia

mc graw-hill book company   *New York   St. Louis   San Francisco*
Düsseldorf   Johannesburg   Kuala Lumpur   London   Mexico
Montreal   New Delhi   Panama   Rio de Janeiro   Singapore
Sydney   Toronto

tactics for
teaching
the disadvantaged

Library of Congress Catalog Card Number
72–137132
07–069685–3

1 2 3 4 5 6 7 8 9 0   MAMM   7 9 8 7 6 5 4 3 2 1
This book was set in Primer by Brown Bros. Lino-
typers, Inc., and printed on permanent paper and
bound by The Maple Press Company. The designer
was Paula Tuerk; the drawings were done by John
Cordes, J. & R. Technical Services, Inc. The edi-
tors were Nat LaMar and Paula Henson. Annette
Wentz supervised production.

CONTENTS

nine
Information-systems Approach in Programs for the Deprived

ten
Preservice and In-service Training for Teaching Disadvantaged Children

Bibliography

Name Index

Subject Index

PREFACE

Although there are many serious problems in the field of education, none are more urgent than the problems involved in teaching of economically deprived children. Each year the number of disadvantaged children has been growing in both metropolitan and rural areas. In seven of our large metropolitan areas, 50 percent of the children enrolled in school come from homes that are economically deprived. Hardly a school district in any region of the country can state that it does not have an economically deprived group of children that demands special and immediate attention.

Adding to the large number of deprived students, desegregation procedures have highlighted and exposed the shockingly poor quality of education among economically deprived children. Attention has been focused on the needs and performance of each individual at every economic level in a manner that has not been known before in our history. The effects of desegregation place the weight of accountability upon school boards, administrators, teachers, specialists, and parents to guarantee quality education for each child, especially for children with "limited experience."

The important inference to be drawn from the surveys, research, and governmental concerns of the past six years is that deprived children are finally being identified. The problem has been competently stated. Characteristics of economically deprived groups have been described over and over again. The elimination of the causes of deprivation must take place, and the 1970s must produce the treatment. Some excellent work in the late 1960s has been accomplished in the physical, emotional, and cognitive dimensions of the life space of children which can serve as guides to the effective procedures for the next five years. Project Follow Through, for example, with its complex program of model sponsorship and local development has provided comprehensive programs for implementation. No matter what information we have from the past, new tactics for teaching the disadvantaged must be developed which are significantly different from traditional approaches we have used with advantaged children. The "old methods" have not worked with deprived children. Creative strategies in teaching must be developed which utilize sound teaching and learning theories and, at the same time, are able to be continuously evaluated in a scientific manner. *Tactics for Teaching the Disadvantaged* was written to present some of the creative attempts at new strategies as well as to give evidence of successful contemporary programs toward economically deprived children.

Probably the outstanding variable that teachers, administrators, parents, and taxpayers must face is that, compared with the money needed to teach those children who are advantaged, it will cost more to teach deprived children effectively. Programs that are merely aimed at the academic improvement of deprived youngsters without consideration for comprehensive services are doomed to fail. The psychosocial deficits in economically deprived youngsters range from those concerning nutrition and health to those involving parental images and community relationships. When one forgets medical and dental controls as well as parental stability and community acceptance, and merely considers the reading and writing variables in the classroom, one is likely to use the pattern of the *advantaged* child's life-style to fulfill a *disadvantaged* child's needs. Instructional strategies will have to include tactics for teaching the whole child. Above all, a different kind of teacher is required to be effective with disadvantaged children. Too many teachers of advantaged children have been miserable failures for economically deprived youngsters. The issues and advances in the quality and characteristics, pre-service and in-service training of the effective teachers of the disadvantaged are strongly emphasized in this book. Throughout the book, the teacher of the disadvantaged child is perceived as a very special kind of teacher with special skills and specific accountability.

Continuous information about each child and the total program will permit a new perception of the disadvantaged child. The old method of measuring the progress of students on the basis of standard pretests and posttests impede the understanding of disadvantaged children. There is entirely too much emphasis on performance rather than on learning. A design in which continuous information on specific criteria (physical, affective, and cognitive) is fed back to teachers, students, and administrators will permit new and realistic decisions about an individual's skills and competencies as well as about the style of teaching that is going on in the classrooms of the disadvantaged. One of the most harmful procedures in evaluating the teaching of disadvantaged children has been the demand on the part of boards of education to consider standardized test scores as the sole criterion of student achievement and effective teaching. This entire book is devoted to the elimination of this invalid and punitive principle.

A definite attempt has also been made in this book to be research oriented toward the responsibility for the education of disadvantaged children—and yet not to merely provide a text for researchers. The merit in reading this book will lie in the fact that it will allow teachers to perceive deprived children more objectively and that it provides examples of some of the tactics employed by those who have been successful in the teaching of disadvantaged children.

William F. White

**tactics for
teaching
the disadvantaged**

one

Characteristics of disadvantaged children and adults

There should be nothing mysterious about the word *disadvantaged*. The term is not a label for a profound, insightful principle in either education, psychology, or sociology. All sorts of labels have been attached to that particular population which has not had the opportunity for a modern full life: "culturally disadvantaged," "culturally deprived," "socially disadvantaged," "poor children," "educationally disadvantaged," "undereducated," "slum dwellers," "prisoners in the ghetto," "poor migrants," and the "inner-city," or "rural," "isolated" children. The difficulty is found only in varied definitions which have failed to describe disadvantaged youth and adults in terms of specific behaviors. Operationally, the clearest meaning in discriminating disadvantaged from advantaged children can be obtained by using a specified scale of economic deprivation or minimal annual family income. In recent years, the criteria for the severity of economic deprivation have been popularly established by the federal guidelines on poverty. The roots of poverty carry us back to our Puritan heritage, to a social syndrome which emerged from an industrial civilization, to the harmful effects of slavery, and to a laissez faire creed of business economy (Seligman, 1968). What constitutes poverty is relative, and determining it is very complex; there-fore, characteristics of poor children and adults will depend upon one's working definition of the term *poverty*.

In 1964, the report of the President's Council of Economic Ad-visers (CEA) suggested that the criterion of poverty refers to those persons and families whose basic needs exceed the means to satisfy them. Using a minimum yearly income level of $3,000, 11 million children in the United States were identified as povertous. The CEA concluded that 20 percent of the nation lived in poverty. Of these, 22 percent were identified as black and 74 percent as white. It was not surprising to find an inverse rela-tionship between the formal level of education and the CEA indices of poverty. The poor were found in all sectors of the nation and in all age groups. Poverty was identified by low earn-ings, low productivity, discrimination, low bargaining power, lack of mobility, and inadequate minimum-wage protection.

POVERTY INDEX

There were many leaders in the country who could not perceive a singular income level of poverty for all people. Although every-one noted the difficulty in establishing any amount of money as a discriminator of what it means to be poor, it was agreed that there must be some minimal amount of purchasing power below which the essentials to living as dignified human beings could not be provided. Mollie Orshansky of the Department of Health, Education, and Welfare conceptualized poverty as determined by standards of consumption within a family and the varying numbers of adults and children in a family. Based on the Orshansky concept, the "poverty index" of the Social Security Administration and the Office of Economic Opportunity (1964) was born. The poverty guideline which has been representative for most federal programs is presented in Table 1-1.

WHAT DOES CULTURALLY DISADVANTAGED MEAN?

When deprived children are identified merely as *culturally dis-advantaged*, there is the danger that they will be regarded as an

TABLE 1-1   *Criteria of Family Income for Eligibility to Participate in OEO Programs**

Number of persons in family†	Annual family income, in dollars	
	Nonfarm households	Farm households
1	1,800	1,500
2	2,400	2,000
3	3,000	2,500
4	3,600	3,000
5	4,200	3,500
6	4,800	4,000
7	5,400	4,500
8	6,000	5,000
9	6,600	5,500
10	7,200	6,000
11	7,800	6,500
12	8,400	7,000
13	9,000	7,500

* *OEO Instruction* 6004–1a, Office of Economic Opportunity, January 30, 1970.

† For families with more than thirteen members, add $600 for each additional member in a nonfarm family and $500 for each additional member in a farm family.

inferior type of schoolchild and as a lower class of human being. There are many professional people who speak about racial equality and preach a gospel of civil rights and the need for blacks and minority groups to occupy status positions in society. However, how frequently we read proposals for federal monies, writings of political candidates, and emotionally tinged editorials about what should be done to "lift up" the culturally deprived. From the omnipotent position of the middle class, white, Protestant, Anglo-Saxon superculture, advice is given on how the black, the Indian, or the Puerto Rican can best fit the correct, or "advantaged," culture. As long as professionals look down on the minority groups and play the role of the benevolent caretakers of the poor, assuming the authoritarian role of having the answer for the lower class and the status position of having the advantage, deprived children are not going to improve their scholastic position very much. The "pecking order" of the advantaged and disadvantaged society will still be strongly with us. Equality of educational opportunity will continue to be a myth, and programs for deprived children will be momentary efforts at charity. Teachers, more than any other group of professionals, must know and understand the culture of poverty. By *culture,* we mean "the whole way of life that is created, learned, held in common, and passed on from one generation to another by the members of a particular society. Culture is the sum total of ways of behaving that a group of people builds up and expects its members to acquire, share, and live by."* If the term *culturally disadvantaged* is used, the culture should not be declared inferior or evil. The broad semantic meaning of the term permits too many value judgments about who is disadvantaged. At most, it is a dangerous term in dialogue with teachers of deprived children. *Disadvantaged* is a relative term. Scholarly, scientific men such as Robert Havighurst (1964) speak of the socially disadvantaged child as one who has a disadvantage relative to some other child for some kind of social life. The child is handicapped in growing up to lead a competent and satisfying life. Generally, the handicaps are well defined in family descriptions as well as by psychosocial group characteristics. The socially disadvantaged, the culturally disadvantaged, the deprived, etc., are defined by most writers and investigators with a host of language, learning, and background variables.

TEACHERS AND THE DEPRIVED

The difficulty for teachers is mainly that their backgrounds are dissimilar to the severely povertous groups that they may be teaching. Teachers become confused by the sophisticated jargon and the multitudinous factors describing the deprived children in their classrooms. Many teachers of the disadvantaged are reluctant to discuss the characteristics of poor children because they fear they may not be knowledgeable about all the academic variables that are being reported in voluminous reports. Two directives should help to clear up the difficulties with the multi-

---

* *From* A cultural history of Western education, *by R. F. A. Butts, 1955, p. 1. Used with permission of McGraw-Hill Book Company.*

varied characteristics of the semantically confusing labels of deprived children: (1) Deprivation can be identified by the "poverty index." This may not be the ideal criterion, but it is the clearest definition of the degree to which children and adults are limited by their experiences. (2) Teachers should not expect a unique, homogeneous pattern of behavior among poor children. There are marked differences among children in groups identified as culturally disadvantaged, socially disadvantaged, educationally disadvantaged, or economically deprived.

THE DISADVANTAGED AND SCHOOL

Public schools have continued to show awareness of the many meanings attributed to the word *disadvantaged*. Children can be disadvantaged if their parents do not give them enough time, enough love, and an adequate image for imitative behavior. School personnel are constantly trying to cope with children who suffer from a deprivation of love within the home. Mentally retarded, as well as physically handicapped, children are considered disadvantaged and in need of special education. The school, again, attempts to provide a different program and procedure for these children. Although there has been a great debate about the worth of special-education classes for the mentally retarded (Blackman & Heintz, 1966), many excellent school programs have provided special education for exceptional children (Gallagher & Hunt, 1966). The major task of the public schools in the 1970s will be to provide educational opportunities for the deprived students who have failed to "make it" under the traditional curriculum and instruction. The community schools in Boston, New York, and Washington offer examples of parents rising up to denounce traditional concepts and to invest total responsibility for schools in parents.

School administrators in big cities recognize that Reissman's (1962) prophecy was not fantasy when he stated that by 1970, there will be 1 deprived child in every 2 among the fourteen large metropolitan areas. In 1963, Martin Deutsch stated that 40 to 70 percent of the elementary-school students represented minority groups. The inadequate preparation of the economically de-

prived children to perform successfully in our academic environment and their need for compensatory education have been
documented by such outstanding scholars as Ausubel (1964),
Deutsch (1964), Hunt (1964), and Bloom, Davis, and Hess
(1965).

Children who belong to economically deprived parents are
characterized by identifiable deficiencies in cognition, affect, and
physical development. Teachers, administrators, and other school
professionals must be able to recognize those deficits in the
physical, cognitive, and affective dimensions of disadvantaged
children. If these youngsters are to be brought into the mainstream of educational opportunities, care should be taken to
avoid the misunderstandings that are associated with labels,
clichés, and inaccurate descriptions of the behavior of the disadvantaged.

In discussing the characteristics of disadvantaged children
and adults, we must begin with the premise that there is no
scientifically demonstrated view that disadvantaged groups differ
from more advantaged populations in innate abilities. Jensen
(1968), however, argues that a failure to give due weight to the
biological basis of individual and group differences may hinder
efforts to discover what is best in the instructional procedures
of the classroom:

If the results of heritability studies such as those of Burt, of
Newman, Freeman, and Holzinger, and of Shields, are accepted as
valid, as I believe they must be until contrary evidence is forthcoming—it almost inevitably follows that some of the variance in
intelligence among social classes must be genetic. [Jensen, 1968,
p. 15.]

The differences and comparisons pointed up in this chapter
appear to be the result of learned behavior. Whatever an individual's genetic potential may be, cognitive (thinking) and
affective (feeling) development occur primarily in response to
a variable range of stimulation. While deprivation and restriction of the range of stimulation bring about selective retardation
in educational development, the variety and quantity of experi

ences among privileged youngsters provide the effective stimulation for a full intellectual and emotional development.

COGNITION OR THE INTELLECTUAL PROCESSES

There are many aspects of the thinking, reading, language, intelligence, and scholastic achievement of deprived children which must be discussed if improvements are to be made in the teaching of the disadvantaged. Children reared in the impacted metropolitan slum areas or in rural, isolated districts will be deprived in any one or in all of those cognitive processes. It would be erroneous to infer that there is one universal effect of being deprived. Whenever deprived children are examined for intelligence, language, or achievement, individual differences can always be observed. Deprived children are not homogeneous in cognitive abilities. There will be varying levels of mental ability in any group of disadvantaged youngsters. If teachers could be trained to view children as having "limited experience" rather than as being culturally disadvantaged, teacher expectations would be heightened and more learning would take place. The amount of limited experience varies among poor children, and therefore cognitive abilities are varied and uneven in each child as well as within groups. Perhaps the most discouraging universal fact about the mental functioning and achievement of economically deprived children is that all measures for assessing those constructs have only questionable validity among disadvantaged populations (Houghton, 1964; Klineberg, 1963; Yourman, 1964).

Furthermore, in making comparisons between advantaged and disadvantaged groups on data from tests, we must keep in mind that mean differences and variance of group scores are telling us very little about individual abilities and potentialities. There is no such thing as an average person. Group differences are essentially abstractions, and they sometimes predispose us to stereotypes, which are harmful to the individual. When the issues and advances of the deprived are discussed, let no one lose sight of the individual, to whom we are trying desperately to give full opportunity to develop to a degree unheard of in prior educational methods and procedures.

Thinking   Martin Deutsch and his coworkers at the Institute for Developmental Studies (1964) pinpointed the observation which many teachers have reported that economically deprived children are inferior to more affluent children in abstract functioning and in the classification of visual stimuli. Numerous research studies support the statement that the thinking patterns of deprived children are different from those of advantaged children. It should be clearly stated, however, that this does not mean that deprived children cannot think; it means only that they think in a different mode. If any characterization can be made of children born and raised in poverty, it must be the slowness with which they shift to abstract thinking levels. The transition to the use of signs and symbols in interpreting things perceived is much less frequent and less automatic in disadvantaged children than in children from homes where there is more stimulation from oral language, pictures, printed materials, tools, music, and toys. The total quantity and quality of concepts generated by deprived children appear to be lower than among their advantaged peers. The causes of the reduced number of concepts and the predominantly concrete style of conceptualization in deprived children are still debatable. Probably the most significant contribution of educational psychology to our understanding of the conceptualization processes of deprived children has been Ausubel's (1964; 1965) conclusion that a delay in learning certain language forms by the disadvantaged slows down their passing from concrete to abstract modes of thinking. Ausubel has suggested that the transition "normally" begins during the junior high school period. Children passing through this "stage" are no longer limited to intuitive, concrete, and particularized thought processes but can formulate precise, abstract, and universal concepts. In the disadvantaged group, the transition is much slower, Ausubel (1965) feels, because deprived children lack the abstract terms to manipulate relationships and because they lack adequate practice in relating abstractions to each other with the benefit of concrete-empirical props. Since the use of concrete operations is much slower than classifying in abstract categories and since the deprived children lack the facility with the formal language, they are slower in school and tend to be retarded in most verbal interaction situations. It is extremely difficult to speak about thinking processes without discussing verbal ability. Although there is considerable academic debate about cognition as determined by word knowledge and use, teachers are convinced that children who are deficient in language are extremely restricted in conceptualizing.

Children with parents earning less than the economic deprivation index are highly predicted to be relegated to concrete operations. Their concepts will be restricted to the immediate, the instinctual, and the present. Teachers interacting with deprived children observe most frequently that the students need to see concrete applications of what is learned to immediate sensory satisfaction. When disadvantaged children are asked to think about things that are *possible,* teachers observe that students "cut out," becoming distracted and inattentive. Only an exceptionally small number of the deprived have the anchorage in successful experiences or the hope (emotion) of making a leap into the "unknown." Guessing the solutions to complex problem-solving tasks appears to be beyond the skills of the deprived in early as well as in middle childhood. Many teachers and psychologists involved in evaluating programs for the disadvantaged assert that deprived children can and will solve simple problem-solving tasks. Called upon to classify objects into meaningful groups, deprived children more than likely will group the objects but will describe the groupings by functional, present, and utilitarian concepts. Seldom will very young children group objects and recognize their clustering with symbolic or abstract references. For example, when asked to group a knife, fork, spoon, plate, bicycle bell, hammer, screwdriver, nails, two sugar cubes, and two crackers, deprived children are frequently observed to refer to the knife, fork, spoon, and plate as "for eating." Very seldom would young children group the knife, fork, spoon, bell, hammer, screwdriver, and nails and label the grouping as "made of metal." Many young deprived children would not even be able to label the items, much less classify them into abstract categories. Perceiving the abstract dimensions and identifying with abstract terminology appear to be very different for most deprived children.

Differences from middle class homes   Many teachers and parents have noticed how different the thinking patterns of children from deprived homes are from those from "middle class" homes. When deprived children talk about imaginary playmates, parents frown upon such activity and even punish children for talking about the world of fantasy and make-believe. In fact, deprived children might be accused of "lying" or of being "off their rockers." Middle class parents permit and encourage a great deal of role playing and dialogue with imaginary creatures. Nursery schools consistently reward imaginative play. Toys and adult costumes are used to stimulate such activity. Books, films, and bedtime stories are filled with the unreal and the fantastic. How often do we hear the economically advantaged parent ask his child, "What do you want to be?" or "Where would you go if you had all the money you wanted and could go anywhere?" Parents who facilitate this level of thinking are bringing their children into a dimension far removed from the present, immediate, and instinctual.

ABSTRACT FUNCTIONING IN PARENTS

The tendency of a mother to use abstract language has been found to be a better predictor of her child's abstract functioning than the verbal IQ of the mother or even the child's own IQ (Hess & Shipman, 1965; Olim, Hess, & Shipman, 1965). This appears to be a powerful variable in teaching the disadvantaged child. Parent participation can be suggested as the basic means to develop abstract abilities in parents of children in early childhood. More and more schools are bringing parents into the learning program of each child. On the theory that thinking levels are primarily determined in the home, interaction between the home and the school will be the pattern in the 1970s. Since the disadvantaged child starts with fewer cognitive resources than in advantaged homes, compensatory programs will focus more and more on reconstructing cognitive resources and developing cognitive skills in parents as well as on the stimulation of children in the classroom.

REVERSING THE CUMULATIVE MENTAL DEFICIT

Size, shape, and form are relatively difficult concepts for most disadvantaged youngsters at preschool and kindergarten ages. Limited in communication skills, the younger children in deprived areas are slower to identify different shapes and to make comparisons of various heights. This does not mean that deprived children cannot perceive and learn abstract concepts, but they will be slower in acquiring and retaining those concepts than their more advantaged peers. Something can be done about it. The direction of mental processes in deprived children can be reversed, and the level of ability can be raised. Deficits in problem-solving tasks can be overcome. Some of the early-childhood methods currently used in improving the ability to shift cognitive modes are discussed in Chapter 2. Dr. Lassar Gotkin, for example, uses *matrix games* to develop classification modes, verbal labeling, and semantic dialogue. More important than all the data suggesting deficits in a language system and slowness in abstract volitional shifts is the extent of the modification of thinking that is possible among the disadvantaged. Limiting effects from the restriction of experience in deprived children are being reversed by instructional programs combined with parent participation, comprehensive services, and self-evaluating programs. The price in time and money is high, but the empirical evidence is emerging.

Teachers and administrators must avoid unrealistic expectations about the behavior of disadvantaged children, for the deficits in intellectual development tend to be cumulative in nature. Any child who has limited experience in early childhood is less able to profit from new and varied types of stimulation. Ausubel (1965, p. 11) states:

Hence, it is evident that the possibility for complete reversibility of environmentally induced retardation in verbal intelligence decreases as children advance in age. This is not to say, of course, that later enrichment is entirely to no avail; but in my opinion, some of this failure in developmental actualization is irreversible and cannot be compensated for later, irrespective of the amount of hyperstimulation that is applied.

With an optimal learning environment, Ausubel (1965) insists that most of the retardation can be not only arrested but also reversed. One of the most important means by which the cumulative mental deficit of deprived children can be turned around into an incremental acceptable direction is by the ameliorative use of instructional materials and audio-visual aids. This does not mean that gimmicks are going to eliminate the intellectual gap between deprived and nondeprived children. The use of "listening centers" (tape recorders and earphones), video tapes of classroom behavior, the abacus, schematic models, and colorful diagrams has been extremely valuable in working with the disadvantaged child's deficits in intellectual development. The effective teacher is the key to the change in deprived characteristics. Instructional tools and audio-visual aids have proved extremely helpful in the teacher's difficult role. Ausubel (1965) is quick to warn teachers that aids and techniques are merely ways of facilitating transfer along a continuum toward higher abstract functioning. It would be discouraging if teachers induced a permanent dependency on concrete-empirical props. Deprived children should not be forced into a mold of merely using concrete props and physical manipulation. The appropriate starting points for many deprived children are those supports, but in continued development of the conceptualizing ability, teachers must provide for learning of a cognitive style that implements abstract concepts.

THE DISADVANTAGED-TEACHER SYNDROME

Too frequently, we observe the dedicated teacher of disadvantaged children who has learned "the disadvantaged syndrome."

The teacher herself adopts a fairly consistent concrete level of functioning, depending almost totally on props for all teaching strategies. The expectations these teachers have of their children's performance becomes very limited, and the classroom stratagem is relegated to a stereotyped, inflexible style that will keep deprived students shackled to beginning-level modes. Teachers of the disadvantaged need training in their strategies as much as the students need improvement of their cognitive functioning.

GENERAL SCHOLASTIC ABILITY, OR THE IQ

Investigators using individual and group IQ tests have almost always found that mental ability in children with limited experience is significantly lower than in children with advantaged backgrounds. One hopeful sign is being observed in teaching the disadvantaged. The mystique of the IQ test and the overemphasis on the value of IQ scores are being removed from discussions about children and how they learn. It would be much better for everyone involved in working with the development of youngsters if we were to put aside the many-splendored label of the IQ and merely call the intelligence score a general school ability measure. The more teachers are aware of the following basic principles, the more effective they will be in relating intelligence levels and abilities to deprived youngsters:

1. Every intelligence test is based on a special theory (or theories). Since intelligence is only an inference about behavior, the author of the intelligence test is merely proposing, or assuming, that certain behavioral responses made by the testee are indications of intelligent behavior.
2. An IQ score from an individual or group-administered intelligence test is only a score of a particular person, at a particular time, at a particular place, on a particular instrument. These scores can and actually do change over time and circumstances. For example, it can be expected that between the ages of ten and eighteen the IQ scores of 50 percent of youth will change 15 points or more; 33 percent will change 18 or more points. The IQ score, while relatively stable, is not fixed.

3. IQ tests are not measuring some hidden potential of mental processes. Intelligence tests identify present abilities to deal with verbal symbols and abstractions. The focus is predominantly upon convergent processes, i.e., upon the logical, unique solutions to problems. The divergent processes are not measured by traditional IQ tests. Alternative solutions, imaginative thinking, wild and silly answers, or creative responses are not acceptable to the meaningfulness of the IQ.

4. Economically deprived children come to school with a limited variety of experiences and low verbal articulation. The very things which the intelligence test either assumes or rewards positively are deficient in the deprived child. A variety of stimulation from person and thing concepts, combined with verbal mediation, will sharpen the mental processes and build more efficient cognitive structure to cope with problem-solving tasks.

5. Our goal of achieving equality of educational opportunity will not be accomplished by adding more studies which only place emphasis on differences in global or omnibus test scores. As Jensen (1968, p. 23) asserts, the global IQ scores reflect only an "undifferentiated composite of abilities having unknown weightings in the total test scores."

If intelligence test scores are used to make inferences about the deprived children in the myriad of funded programs, teachers and psychologists will have to discriminate much more carefully about test validity than we have done in the past. More than twenty years ago, Allison Davis (1948) severely criticized intelligence tests, systematically demonstrating that IQ tests penalize lower class children. On the basis of many studies, Davis and his colleagues demonstrated that a large proportion of items in a variety of IQ tests were biased against children from the very low social strata of society. In some tests, the cultural bias was as high as 90 percent. Furthermore, Davis concluded, the norms from many of the tests had been constructed on children with middle class backgrounds. Perhaps most important of all has been the clear indication of the higher motivational index among children from more advantaged homes. Even if parents of deprived children want their children to have a "good education," the frustration of parents in providing the necessary means is quickly observed and learned by deprived children. The defenses against classroom advancement and learning opportunities can be witnessed by the "why try"

expressions of children who are economically deprived and by
their failure to attain academic competence.

One of the components in the intelligence tests, *digit span,*
which provides part of the total IQ score has been observed to be
less culturally biased than vocabulary. Few studies, however,
have used the digit span as a control variable in research dealing
with the disadvantaged. Figure 1-1 shows the discrepancy between black and white children at various ages when their scores
on vocabulary and digit span were compared. Future research
may find data about digit span a potentially valuable criterion in
studies with the disadvantaged.

More recent studies of intelligence levels among children point
up the fact that intelligence is a result of the interaction of the
individual with his environment. Research about the characteristics of deprived children indicates that the conditions of life in
slums and in rural, isolated areas are meager for developing
children in terms of stimulation levels, as compared with conditions for more advantaged children.

Slum life provides a minimum range of stimulation and minimum
opportunity to manipulate objects or to experiment with them in an
orderly manner. Monotony of input limits expressiveness of the output and ability to perceive precise relationships or other abstract
qualities, such as size, shape, distance and time. In addition, the

FIGURE 1-1   *Percentage of Negro and white children, six to
ten years of age, passing the vocabulary and digit-span tests
of the Stanford-Binet (Kennedy, Van de Riet, and White,
1963).*

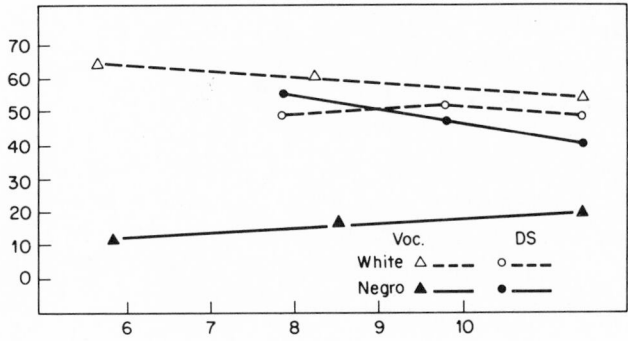

lack of adult mediation reduces further the child's opportunities to link experience with its interpretation, i.e., the ability to convert objects and events into verbal symbols, to perceive causal relationships, and to form abstractions. [Taba & Elkins, 1966, p. 7.]

Since the correctness of the responses to intelligence test questions is determined by cultural standards assumed by those who devised the test (Siegel, 1963), scores from IQ tests place the deprived child in context only with the white, middle class, Anglo-Saxon world. Little wonder the school dooms the individual to the class of his birth! Kennedy, Van de Riet, and White (1963) conducted a study of 1,800 black elementary-school children in five southeastern states. The children, drawn from rural, urban, and metropolitan areas in the South, were observed to have an average IQ of 80.7 with a standard deviation of 12.4. With students clustering more closely around the mean, it appeared consistent with prior studies that the average score for the black sample was lower than the 16th percentile on Terman and Merrill norms. The unique conclusion that should be emphasized is that the mean IQ score was highly correlated with socioeconomic status. The mean for upper class blacks was 105, whereas the mean for deprived black children was 79. Deprivation in living conditions, not race, appears to be the determiner of lower IQ levels. This does not mean that there will not be a discrepancy between intelligence test scores of black and white subjects; Horton and Crump (1962), in working with black and white children, concluded that socioeconomic status and parental education determined the test performances of both black and white children. The issues involved in the question of black-white differences in intelligence test performances have been debated for more than thirty-five years. Otto Klineberg (1963) summarizes the studies dealing with a new look at an old problem.

For teachers of the disadvantaged the most pressing question is: Can children with retarded levels of the intelligence quotient modify their abilities and close the gap on their advantaged peers? There are enough controlled studies of IQ differences to be optimistic about the improvement of general scholastic ability under well-planned and well-executed instructional programs. Teachers and psychologists should not be misled by much of the data that have been reported in a large number of early-childhood programs (e.g., Head Start and Follow Through). Frequently, IQ tests are administered to children at the beginning of the year and then again at the end of the school year as pretest and posttest measures. Marked increases in IQ are being reported. It should be noted that many deprived children have never taken a formal test at the time of the first testing. Further, fear is generated from the middle class values which are evident in the tests. This fear depresses the performance of the majority of economically deprived. The situational demands only increase the anxiety. The highly dispersed and questionable validity of test scores in the beginning of the year are generally compared with the end-of-the-year performance. Too much emphasis has been placed upon the changing of IQ scores among disadvantaged children. If intelligence tests have to be used, it might be better to administer IQ tests about halfway into the child's first year of school (January or February) to obtain a more stable index of the child's general ability. Above all, the IQ test score should be carefully interpreted; it should not become a pigeonhole criterion for specific mental functioning. The IQ should be regarded as a general scholastic ability measure over time and situation.

To "screen" disadvantaged children on traditional standardized IQ tests and compare them with middle class children opens the door to many questions of validity. Anastasi (1958) and Lesser (1965) offer some evidence for matching the cultural and racial backgrounds of tester and testee. There are many psychologists who are seeking diagnostic types of inventories in assessing the disadvantaged rather than making criteria out of the global IQ score.

At early-childhood levels, the Screening Test of Academic Readiness (Ahr, 1967), the Lee-Clark test (1962), the Metropolitan Readiness Test (Hildreth, Griffiths, and McGauvran, 1964), the Caldwell Preschool Inventory (1967), the Early Childhood Preschool Inventory (1967), and the Illinois Test of Psycholinguistic Ability (1968) are being used in many programs to bring feedback on individual differences in cognitive abilities. In Chapter 9 is a discussion of these tests and of their import in thinking and achieving. We are now going beyond the classroom variables and finding strong evidence for causes of intellectual deficiency in the intrafamily and interpersonal interactions of children's development (Deutsch, 1966). The comprehensive services and parent participation component in Project Head Start and Follow Through are some of the means by which extra classroom variables are being tested.

There are numerous studies over time which point up major intellectual gains in programs for deprived youngsters. In 1952, Bogur brought about a significant increase in the total IQ scores of both black and white children by training the children for five months in perceptual discrimination. The California Test of Mental Maturity and the Otis-Alpha were the criterion tests on which the gains were shown. Marked increases in IQ were reported over a six-year period in a program aimed at reversing the deprivation effects in elementary-school children (Clark & Clark, 1959). More recently (1967), the Research and Development Center at the University of Georgia maintained an instructional program for 110 economically deprived children at Gainesville, Georgia.* In conventional integrated kindergarten classrooms with twenty-seven students in each of four classes, the mean IQ of 89 on the Stanford-Binet for the total group changed to a mean of 97 by the end of the school year. From the data, it is evident that the instructional program with the deprived is most promising.

Elizabeth Starkweather (1968) reported significant intellectual changes in two special-treatment kinds of classes as compared with a control group (Figure 1-2). A public school enrichment program ($N = 33$) and a Montessori enrichment program ($N = 36$) were compared on the Peabody Picture Vocabulary Test (PPVT), the Caldwell Preschool Inventory (CPI), and the creativity measures. PPVT is primarily a measure of vocabulary, in which the subject points to the best picture describing a word. The CPI is essentially an achievement test, which was developed for use in Head Start research. It purports to measure

---

* The early-childhood instructional approach used in Gainesville, Ga., is described in Chap. 2 by the Georgia early stimulational model.

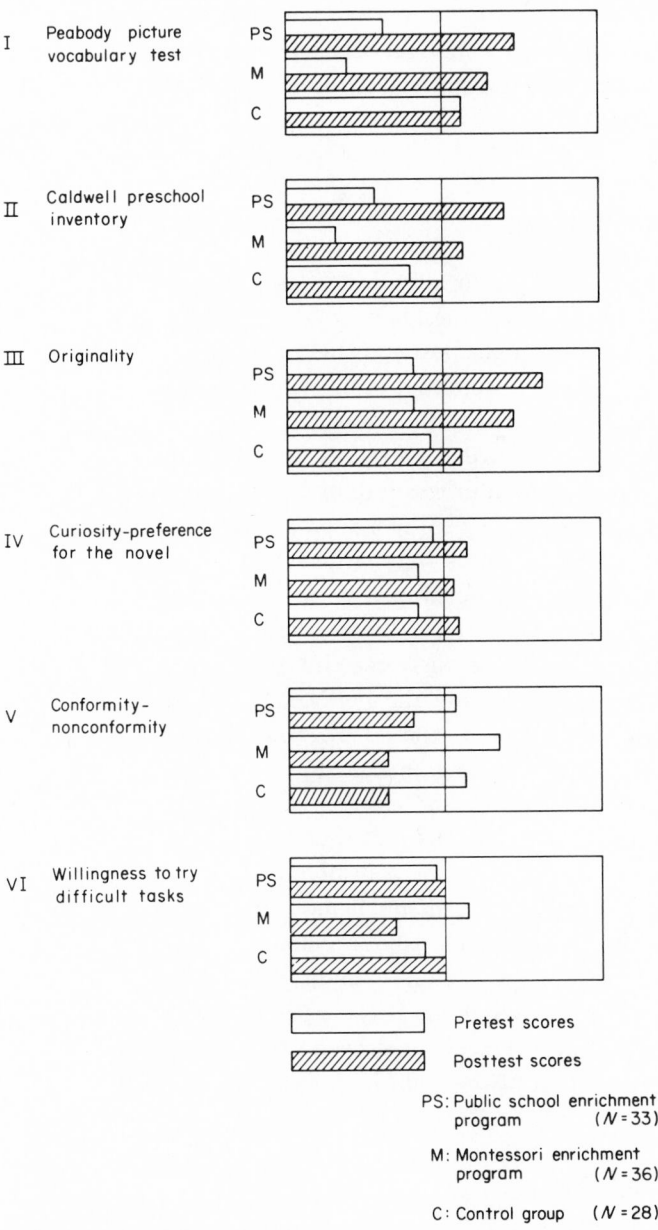

FIGURE 1-2   *Bar graph showing median ranks for pretest and posttest scores obtained by three groups of preschool children.*

personal-social responsiveness, associative vocabulary, numerical concepts, and sensory concepts. Data on the PPVT lend support for a change in verbal ability in the public school enrichment program and the Montessori program as opposed to the control class, in which there was no gain.

TRANSFER OF STUDENTS AND IQ CHANGE

Rentsch (1966) compared changes in intelligence, as measured by the Otis Test of Mental Ability, of students who were transferred from inner-city schools in Rochester, New York, to predominantly white, middle class, suburban schools under the open-enrollment plan with those of students who did not transfer. Transferred pupils had higher recorded IQ scores prior to their participating in the open-enrollment program than did those who remained. Apparently, children who were more competent in IQ tests chose to transfer. After the scores were adjusted, however, transferred students at every grade level except the fifth grade attained significantly higher scores than those who were not transferred. And even the fifth-grade transferred children showed a higher adjusted mean score than did the nontransferred. In reading and arithmetic achievement, the fifth grade showed marked gains over their peers who remained in the inner city. Although the data in this study are impressive, care must be given in the interpretation to point to the fact that control over class size and teacher variables was not considered. It would seem that transferred children changed much more in intelligence performance than did students who remained in the ghettolike schools, but these same children might have made the same overall increase in mental ability if class size had been reduced or if a different kind of teacher had been employed or if teacher aides had been a part of the classroom structure.

SCHOLASTIC ACHIEVEMENT LEVELS

When one examines the multitude of ESEA Title I and Title II projects, e.g., seventeen programs in the city of Buffalo, New

York, funded at over 5 million dollars, the question of the worth of these programs becomes essential. Which programs succeed in reaching proposed objectives of classroom achievement? Frequently, comparisons of total scores on standardized achievement tests are not found to be significant. In general, however, the conclusions from experimental programs with deprived children are most promising. Although some programs have failed, in no manner does it warrant Jensen's (1968) conclusion that compensatory education has been tried and apparently has failed. The most disappointing aspect of many of the programs is the failure to control the determining effect of many variables. Too often, the program is designed and implemented so quickly that control is set aside in the sincere interest to do something for deprived children. If the problem is poorly stated and the hypotheses are only semantic attempts at doing something constructive, poor evaluations must be expected. When one cannot define the behavioral objectives, the project has to be a hit-and-miss affair.

ACHIEVEMENTS IN TITLE I

From 1965 to 1968, more than 4 billion dollars was allocated for use in areas with a high index of the economically deprived. More than 6 million children of ages five to seventeen in the United States were included in the category of the deprived. The single largest type of program in Title I during 1966–1967 focused on reading improvement. In New York State, 254,000 children in grades 1 to 6 shared in specialized, remedial types of reading programs. Each local evaluator estimated the effectiveness of his program using four categories: (1) marked improvement, (2) some improvement, (3) no improvement, and (4) adverse effects. Table 1-2 describes the distribution of all programs by level of improvement and type of measuring device.

Over 300,000 New York State elementary- and secondary-school students participated in various kinds of reading activities. From conclusions, it was found that 36 percent of the programs showed *marked* improvement in students' skills, with

TABLE 1-2   *The Distribution of All Programs by Level of Improvement and Type of Measuring Device, 1966–1967**

| Levels of improvement | Types of measuring devices, % | | | |
	Subjective	Objective	Standardized tests	Total
Marked	16	5	15	36
Some	28	7	28	63
None	0	0	1	1
Adverse	0	0	0	0
Total	44	12	44	100

* State Education Department, *Closing the gap*, The University of the State of New York, Albany, N.Y., 1968, p. 27.

74 percent of those successes being determined by standardized test data (Figure 1-3). At least 63 percent of the total group were reported to have made "some" improvement, which was determined primarily (68 percent) by standardized tests. Based on the criteria each particular program used in an evaluation, 98 percent of the programs reported *some* or *marked* improvement in the reading behavior of children. The results appear to be quite interesting since the criterion of standardized tests has been so prominent in the reading programs. Where no improvement was reported, subjective judgments were dominant in the assessment. Level of improvement in reading programs by percentage of measuring devices is reported in Figure 1-3. In five reading centers in Tonowanda, New York, gains in reading ability of students ranged from 1½ to 3 years. Success in the program seemed to point to in-service teacher training just as strongly as to development of the reading behaviors in the children. The remedial reading program in Rochester, New York, is attempting a new total approach to reading in a school, in addition to aiding children with specific reading difficulties. From the data of the 1967–1968 program, it can be stated that 90 percent of the 734 elementary-school students receiving intensive aid improved significantly in reading behavior.

Junior high school students in Rochester, New York, who had failed to respond to conventional teaching methods became the

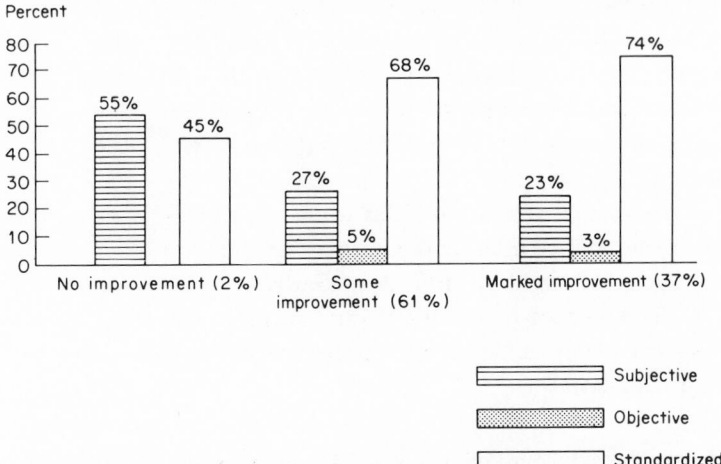

FIGURE 1-3   *Level of improvement in reading programs by percentage of measuring devices used, 1966–67. (From New York State Education Department. Closing the gap, 1968, p. 29.)*

target of an experimental program (1968–1969). Emphasis was placed on small classes and supplementary teaching materials. Teachers in this program originated the design and provided the entire administrative procedures. Each day the teachers had one hour free from instructional responsibilities to discuss the problems and coordinate the lessons for the total program. A neighborhood aide visited the homes of the students in the program. Results indicate that this was one of the most successful programs in the public schools of the city of Rochester during the past ten years.

ACHIEVEMENT AND PUPIL TRANSFER

Although some of the children in the open-enrollment plan (Rochester, New York) are definitely not economically deprived, the target area of the program for improving educational opportunities for urban and suburban children assuredly embraces the economically deprived children. The study (Rentsch, 1966) is primarily an appraisal of shifts in children by race, but the family income of the black inner-city children is demonstrably below the poverty index. The initial open-enrollment program (1963–1964) involved 500 students in kindergarten through sixth grade. Transfers from six elementary schools with a mean enrollment of 90.3 percent nonwhite were made to eighteen receiving schools having a mean enrollment of 1.6 percent nonwhite. During 1967–1968, more than 2,000 children attended schools outside their regular attendance area. A unique part of the total program permitted 150 white children from the suburbs to voluntarily attend an all-black school in the inner city. Some of the noteworthy conclusions about achievement are reported below (Rentsch, 1966, pp. 238–245):

    1. Pupils who transferred from schools enrolling a high percentage of blacks to schools enrolling a high percentage of whites:
    a. Attained poorer report card marks than did pupils who did not transfer.
    b. Attended school more regularly than did pupils who did not transfer.
    c. Attended school on time more often than did pupils who did not transfer.
    d. Had a higher concept of self (California Test of Personality) than did pupils who did not transfer.
    e. Attained higher IQ scores than did pupils who did not transfer.
    2. The 150 white children who transferred to the inner city did not show any decrease in academic measures assessed by standardized tests.
    3. Teachers in the receiving schools did not deliberately provide intergroup experiences. Most teachers considered themselves prepared to participate in an open-enrollment program. There are many psychologists who would be severely critical of the teachers' belief that "no special preparation is or should be necessary in programs for the economically deprived."

ACHIEVEMENT IN FOLLOW THROUGH

Follow Through is a program funded by the Office of Economic Opportunity (OEO) but directed jointly by the Office of Education and OEO. During the 1968–1969 school year, the Stanford Research Institute (1967) began a very sophisticated evaluation of mental abilities and achievement of children in the $15 million experimental program aimed at facilitating and continuing any gains generated in the Head Start programs in the country. Although no data or analysis were publicly revealed in 1970 by the Stanford Research Institute, individual programs were reporting significant changes in children and in school systems. Teachers in the kindergarten and first-grade programs in Atlanta, Georgia (225 students), and in the first-grade program in Jasper, Georgia (200), emphatically reported that never before had the deprived children gained academically as rapidly as they did in Follow Through. First-grade teachers reported *total* classes (twenty to twenty-five children) reading in the fourth and fifth preprimers, in multiseries (four or five), during the month of November. Even the bottom five or six children in some classes who were still in readiness materials in November (1968) were far advanced over those in the conventional classes of previous years. One black child in the Atlanta city schools was reading at the third-grade level and using a typewriter after two months in the kindergarten program. Perhaps the most startling verbal feedback in these two Follow Through Programs was the statement by most of the teachers that there would be no failures in first-grade work. The success that has been observed in the academic achievement of these programs has been stimulated by many different instructional approaches, e.g., Lassar Gotkin's Interdependent Learning Model and the University of Georgia's Mathemagenic model.

When the broad range of programs for disadvantaged children is examined, the most powerful conclusion from research in the decade of the 1960s is an optimism about raising the achievement level of disadvantaged learners in a relatively short period of time. In 1960, Hansen, as well as Stallings, introduced hope for raising the educationally retarded levels of deprived learners by reporting academic gains on the Stanford Achievement Test after the children integrated into a white community. Even after five years of integrated classes with white students, black deprived students showed marked gains in achievement, especially in reading (Stallings, 1960). The lower socioeconomically classified child can and does succeed in many varied kinds of programs. The other chapters in this text deal with methods and procedures, teacher personality and skills, and programmatic ways of elevating the performance of deprived children. How much each of these contributes in general designs is not known, but the need for a reduction of teacher/pupil ratio, interaction techniques in the classroom, parent participation, and comprehensive services appears to be essential. Such a degree of confidence in working with the disadvantaged is being realized that it is common to hear teachers and administrators say, "Give me enough money and we'll change 'those kids,' too!" A confidence is spreading abroad in the North and South, East and West, that if teachers have aides and a reduced ratio of students, if they get the instructional materials they want, and if they obtain medical, dental, psychological, and sociological help for deprived children and parents, *all* children will learn. However, a great deal of jealousy and hostility is generated from some of the successful programs with the disadvantaged. A teacher who is not in an experimental program and who has thirty-five children and no aide is very frequently dissatisfied with her colleagues who conduct classes of twenty students with one or two aides and the "latest" classroom materials. Frequently, a Hawthorne effect is stimulated in control or comparison groups because some teachers are so disappointed in being left out of a program that they will "try to show them." The important thing is that a great many teachers feel confident about changing achievement levels of deprived children, whether in the inner city or in rural, isolated areas. The extremely high expenditures are always questionable. For example, a program in Rochester, New York, called the World of Inquiry School, spent over $750,000 during the first year for 120 children in grades 1 to 6. In 1968–1969, the program spent $250,000, or $2,400 per child. The pedagogy, the different kinds of adult stimulation, the reduced teacher/student ratio, the mixed type of student, and the excellent materials make the program an experimental masterpiece. In the late 1960s, however, many were questioning how much of the experimental design is really practical. No one is questioning that much more money is needed to do the kind of job with disadvantaged children that is necessary, but legislators, parents, and teachers are seeing the fallacy in purchasing a computer for each child. When can rural, isolated, or poverty-stricken school districts ever afford the huge amounts of money some programs are demanding in order to "be experimental"?

READING AND ORAL LANGUAGE BEHAVIOR

Anyone who is involved in work with children with limited experience recognizes the deficiency in reading, oral language, and writing that is generally applicable to all deprived groups. There are always exceptions. But whether in the ghetto of the urban-area schools or in rural, isolated communities, in classes in which there are a 35-to-1 teacher/pupil ratio and the old, established classroom instructional modes, an observer can expect the reading level of the class to be two or three years below actual grade level. Deutsch et al. (1964) examined the communication of information in the elementary-school class-room (grades 1 to 5) and found that there is a deficiency in language behavior according to social class and race and that this difference is also representative of IQ test scores. Similar retardation in reading ability was observed over a two-year period in Arkansas (Frost & King, 1964), with three elementary schools. The cumulative deficit that Deutsch speaks about in New York City is observable in Arkansas, Atlanta, Detroit, and Greenwood, South Carolina. It does not matter what geographic area is examined. The degree of retardation in classes of de-prived children becomes more severe with each passing year. When we consider the differences between advantaged and dis-advantaged language characteristics, it should be remembered that language is more than vocabulary. We use language to ex-press relationships among objects, actions, and conditions, as well as cause and effect and quantity and quality. A child's entire "feeling world" is subject to the medium of language. Deficiency in language behavior limits his ability to release his feelings as well as retards his readiness to read.

In a Midwestern metropolitan area, Thomas (1962) examined the verbal behavior of a lower socioeconomic kindergarten group.

The length of the children's responses, complexity of sentence structure, parts of speech used, and grammatical errors were recorded and cataloged. Thomas made a point of the fact that the standard word list for first grade was very different from the kinds of words used in the interview situation of the study. One of the principal contributions of the study to our knowledge of deprived children is that it affords an opportunity of noting the difference between conversing with adults and peer talk. When children converse with their peers, they are observed to use about 33 percent more words to the length of an average sentence than in conversation with adults. Too frequently, the oral language of deprived children is looked upon as an inferior type of speech behavior merely because it is different. Entwisle and Greenberger (1968) presented data on differences in semantic systems and linguistic development between black and white subcultural groups. One can imagine how much modern research would be limited if the differing semantic systems were not taken into account. From research of Entwisle and Greenberger and others, it appears that word meanings in kindergarten and first grade are vastly different for the black and the white child. Black college students have different associative patterns from those of white college students (Belcher & Campbell, 1968). Not all the advantages are in favor of white children. Entwisle (1968) surveyed word associations of black and white elementary-school children and found that inner-city children are apparently more advanced linguistically than suburban children at first grade in terms of paradigmatic responses (those with form class matching that of a stimulus). To the stimulus word *table*, for example, fifty-four white first-graders and fifty-two black first-graders responded with a noun, but the black children gave ten more different nouns (Entwisle & Greenberger, 1968). Blacks give more different responses than whites to the same stimulus. The variability of responses for blacks is most apparent at the first grade but decreases by the third grade.

We need more data on the semantic systems of deprived children, and furthermore, we have the responsibility of bringing the preprimers and primers in line with those semantic systems.

The disadvantaged child's vocabulary has been hypothesized to be about 50 percent of the average middle class child. Although two different languages are not necessarily predicated, some adjustment in the tactics of teaching reading and oral language should be envisioned. The Detroit city schools have been using their own reading series with the disadvantaged with a high degree of success. Lower class speech is used, at times, by all economic classes for a variety of purposes. Bernstein (1958) hypothesized that the differences in speech of upper and lower class youngsters are not an absolute language distinction but lie in the learning by the upper classes of standard English as well as the lower class forms. In all the instructional programs for the disadvantaged at early childhood, nothing is more needed than bringing reading techniques and content into line with the semantic systems of the children in each deprived area.

CREATIVITY

There are many programs for deprived children that aim at the development of creative productions and a nurturing of creative skills. The data about changes in the development of creative skills are hard to obtain. In many Head Start programs, an interested observer can examine some of the artwork done in the beginning of a year's program and compare it with that produced at the end of the school year. There are always questions about the source of creative expression. One of the most stimulating schools in which sculpturing, painting, and literary productions reach a high level of performance is the World of Inquiry School in Rochester, New York. Although the school's population includes children other than from poverty, the creative output appears to be as frequent and intense among deprived children as among advantaged children.

E. Paul Torrance (1968) described the *creative-aesthetic* approach to early-childhood development and pointed to the significant gains on all the verbal and all the originality measures except the Starkweather Originality Test (Table 1-3). The crea-

FIGURE 1-4 *The World of Inquiry School, Rochester, New York. Outstanding artists assist young learners in music and art.*

tive-aesthetic approach aims primarily at developing in pre-primary children the beginnings of intellectual skills, abilities, and attitudes which are able to transfer to later situations. In Chapter 2 of this text, the process variables in the creative-aesthetic approach are presented more fully and comparisons are made with more structured-cognitive approaches in early childhood. In describing the characteristics of the disadvantaged, data from the Torrance experiment support the contention that deprived children can develop creatively. Above all, must prepri-

TABLE 1-3 *Means, Standard Deviations, and Tests of Significance of the Differences between the Experimentals (Creative-aesthetic Approach) and Controls on the Creativity Measures in May, 1968*

Measure	Experimental		Control			
	Mean	Std. dev.	Mean	Std. dev.	t ratio	Level of significance
Verbal fluency (MGP)	10.17	4.19	4.28	1.47	6.652	0.01
Verbal flexibility (MGP)	7.92	2.53	4.25	1.46	4.706	0.01
Verbal originality (MGP)	15.92	6.42	4.43	2.40	8.420	0.01
Figural fluency (TTCT)	34.92	5.82	32.11	7.02	1.975	0.10
Figural flexibility (TTCT)	37.92	5.84	37.03	8.07	0.503	0.10
Figural originality (TTCT)	61.58	17.34	43.55	11.66	4.492	0.01
Figural elaboration (TTCT)	39.67	7.20	36.66	5.43	1.756	0.10
Originality (Starkweather)	36.67	15.24	16.89	16.06	4.900	0.01

mary educational stimulation be incompatible with creative development?

Starkweather (1968) reported that deprived children in an enrichment program (OEO) in a public school gained in originality and that children in a Montessori type of program gained in originality but lost in the freedom to use conforming and nonconforming behavior. It may or may not be that deprived children are more creative than advantaged children. The important thing is that some programs are teaching skills for developing creative expression. There are some data (Smith, 1965; Torrance, 1963) to indicate that children from disadvantaged groups compare quite favorably with those from advantaged groups on the figural tests of creative thinking but not on verbal tests. Perhaps the most difficult variable to discuss in assessing creative functioning of the deprived is their lack of "test know-how" and their deficits in coping with verbal directions.

AUDITORY DISCRIMINATION

In the few studies that have dealt with auditory discrimination, children with a limited variety of experience have not demonstrated the same level of ability to discriminate sounds that is manifested by more affluent subjects. The causes of the marked deficits in auditory discrimination among deprived groups are debatable, but the patterns of discrimination need to be examined. Dr. Norman Uhl of the Education Testing Service has developed a fascinating test for auditory discrimination. Validation for his test was directed toward deprived students in the Atlanta public schools. Diagnosing a deficit in auditory discrimination skills is only the beginning; the test of school competence and concern is to modify auditory deficits and to teach the skills of discrimination to deprived children very early in their development.

Social class differences are observed in auditory discrimination, especially when they are compared and analyzed with speech sounds: first-grade lower socioeconomic class children make significantly more mistakes on the Wepman auditory discrimination test than do advantaged youngsters. However, scores of older children on the Wepman test correlate only slightly with social class. Reading ability is also discriminable by the Wepman test among lower socioeconomic class children (Katz & Deutsch, 1963; John, 1965).

AFFECTIVE COMPONENTS IN THE DISADVANTAGED

Schoolteachers and administrators place greater emphasis on cognitive deficiencies in the disadvantaged, i.e., on deficiencies in vocabulary, reading, thinking, and scholastic achievement. Frequently, emotional variables are considered by teachers to be quite extreme and of interest only to psychologists and medical practitioners. The affect dimension of the learner relates to the total climate of the classroom, determines interpersonal relationships within the school, and controls the amount of psychic energy that an individual can put into learning tasks. When we focus on the emotional and attitudinal characteristics of the disadvantaged, it is necessary to observe the conflict that deprived children experience in resolving the behaviors of two cultures.

It is difficult for any person to span two cultures. If the discontinuities in the demands of the two contending cultures are mild, they may only dilute the socializing power of the school. If they are severe, such as is the case when the problems arising from social isolation, race, language, and differences in standards of conduct are combined with difficulties encountered in mastering alien content and new skills, they may lead to disorganization or neurotic behavior. [Allinsmith and Goethals, 1956.]

It would not be difficult to gather enough material about the affective world of deprived children to write a representative book. However, hard data resulting from experimentally controlled investigations are very limited. The emotions and attitudes of the learner are more important than his IQ or achievement scores, but the weight of importance is placed by school personnel upon the cognitive characteristics of schoolchildren. The deprived child has been restricted by his verbal deficit. His emotional life—his feelings about painting, people, and other concepts—are limited by inadequacies in verbal expression. Verbal ability is the end point of teacher instruction. This major point separates the effective teacher of deprived children from the effective teacher of middle class students. The expected behaviors that the teacher envisions for deprived children should deal primarily with the emotions, attitudes, and interests of the children with limited variation of experiences. The developing of a healthy self in any child is extremely important, but in the deprived child the "self" must first of all be detached from a crippling mode of life before it can gain the opportunity to "swing free" in its own individual way.

SELF-CONCEPT OF THE DEPRIVED

By the *concept of self* I mean the feeling one has about one's image with others. When that feeling refers to the present and immediate self it is called the *phenomenal self*. When it refers to what one hopes to become, it is called the *ideal self*. Children, or adults, who experience a large gap between their phenomenal self and their ideal self generate a high amount of anxiety about themselves. There is a significant relationship between the concept of self and personality (Rentz & White, 1967). In reading about a protagonist in a story, the self-concept as well as personality behavior of the reader is highly related to his perception of the main character (Kingston & White, 1967; White, Weaver, & Kingston, 1968). In deprived black youngsters, however, the negative self-image can be observed much more frequently (Powell & White, 1969; Richmond & White, in press) than among white advantaged children.

In reading books which emphasize wealth and comfort and success as ideals, deprived youngsters cannot help but perceive their "lower" self-image in society. Both the lack of black heroes or heroines in textbooks and the portrayal of the Negro as ignorant, weak, and lazy has its effect on the black child's concept of self. As White and Aaron (1969) found, it is not enough to merely place pictures of blacks in textbooks; verbal descriptions of the black as the strong, active hero are necessary to modify the feelings of black children about themselves. Beginning with Clark and Clark (1947), investigators have found that racial recognition appears about the third year of life and becomes more accurate year by year. Children learn very early to assign dark skin to inadequate housing and lower status roles.

Children who are consistently exposed to a social environment in which adult behaviors are most visible and where the social ills and depravities of a community dominate the culture are inclined to perceive their world as hostile and dangerous. The hostilities or the withdrawn behaviors of fourth-, fifth-, and sixth-grade students in ghetto schools are signs of the negative self-concept that has been learned from ages one to nine. There is no doubt that programs such as Head Start and Follow Through are attempts to prevent punishing effects on the concept of self. The prekindergarten, kindergarten, and primary grades present opportunities to utilize the readiness for positive learning about self and the world since the child appears to be less overwhelmed with the fear and hopelessness of living in a disadvantaged neighborhood.

Those men and women who have taught the disadvantaged child over a long period of time are aware of the punitive self-image that predominates in lower socioeconomic areas. Much of the lack of initiative in challenging tasks, however, is bound up with deficiencies in bodily health. The fatigue element that intrudes very quickly in testlike situations is just as much due to nutritional defects as to psychological inadequacies. Very deprived children do not display the intensive energy levels that are indications of young, healthy, advantaged children.

The feeling of self is less adequate among deprived children, no matter what the causes of this phenomenon. As teachers of poor children, we should be most conscious of the fact that children read the cues of our concern for them. If poor children perceive us as "feeling sorry" for them or "looking down upon them" to help them, they will learn the role of being pitied, of being second-class citizens. The emotional feeling that children obtain when they look into our eyes or when they join in the shared activity of the classroom is what determines their desire to learn (hope) or their withdrawal and failure to cope with their environment (fear).

The negative self-concept can be changed. Rentsch (1966) reported that most pupils who transferred from schools enrolling a high percentage of white pupils had a higher concept of self as measured by total scores on the California Test of Personality than did pupils who did not transfer. In kindergarten, there was no significant difference between transferred and nontransferred students. Again, the question is properly asked of teachers and administrators: Is the school contributing to the negative self-concept that is clearly observed among black children during the middle school years?

In his speech to the American Psychological Association meeting in 1968, McCandless describes his multivariate analysis of the affective components of deprived kindergarten children in the Atlanta school system. Four factors contributed about 70 percent of the variance of responses to eleven different measures: (1) adjusted middle-classness, (2) abiding by the rules of the game, (3) disillusionment, and (4) antialienation. These factors remained relatively stable throughout the kindergarten program. At first grade, preliminary data reveal that changes take place. The goal of McCandless and his colleagues is to find out which teachers in specified classroom environment contribute to positive, acceptable self-concepts and which teachers and climate determine the depressive, fearful concept of self.

FEAR

Deprived children in general appear to have a higher amount of fear and fear of a greater number of things than advantaged children. Even more in evidence is the continuous lack of hope which filters through any activity described as solving interpersonal conflicts and impulse control. One finds more fatalism and hopelessness among severely deprived children than among advantaged children. In school, deprived children fear tests and examinations to a greater degree than their peers in advantaged-area schools. The highly cognitive, heavily worded task arouses so much fear in the deprived child that he refuses to take tests or presents such incomplete responses that it is hardly discernible whether the student was sufficiently aroused to take the examination.

Some of the out-of-school fears were categorized by Taba and Elkins (1966, p. 29):

> . . . being attacked on the street, death, accidents (the number of these references is surprisingly high), rats, drunken people, incidents on the road when the family went down South to visit relatives, and punishment for their own misbehavior. Physical violence topped the list of reasons.

Fear of working alone   Fear of silence and fear of being alone are quite noticeable among disadvantaged children. Teachers of the disadvantaged realize the danger of asking children to work privately and alone on projects. Perhaps the insecurity of these children about problem-solving tasks arouses fear of coping and generates the anxiety. There are some who explain the fear of working alone as merely a high need for social approval. Apparently, the deprived children need the support of their peers more than middle class children. It may well be that the need for affiliation is able to be fulfilled only with peers since parental reinforcement is quite limited. Advantaged children receive a great deal of stimulation related to cognitive skills and frequent reinforcement of verbal skills and academic achievement.

ACHIEVEMENT ORIENTATION

Deprived children have a different kind of achievement striving. Apparently, children reared in poverty do not strive for cleanliness, punctuality, and orderliness to the same degree as children in the upper classes. Deprived children receive little reinforcement for school achievement from their peers. In fact, ridicule and punishment are frequently the expected peer reactions for excelling in school matters. It would be incorrect, however, to assume that children in poverty cannot be stimulated to excel in school objectives. The motivation for triggering classroom achievement must not be the total cognitive approach encountered in the traditional classroom, i.e., "You must study and work hard to go to college and to amount to something." To bring out achievement striving in deprived children, the emotion of fear must be reduced and the emotion of hope must be reinforced. Many deprived children find it difficult to defer gratification and can only "perceive" goals that are present and immediate. Economically deprived children have to have their rewards here and now. Their achievement striving is quite different from that of advantaged childdren. With comprehensive services and an upgrading of the living conditions in their homes, deprived children can learn to pursue more remote educational goals.

two

Teaching styles for the economically deprived

By the *teaching style* in a classroom, I mean the cluster of teacher behaviors that affect learning and development in relation to the clusters of the affective behavior of students. In brief, the observed interaction between teacher and students can properly be called the *style* of the teacher. The general aspects of a teacher's style will depend upon the teacher's age, sex, physical attributes, cognitive abilities, needs, values, and personality behavior and upon similar characteristics in his (her) students. In discussing teacher style for disadvantaged students, it must be understood that many of the essential components in being effective with deprived children and adults are entirely applicable in teaching the general population. The focus in teacher style is upon the process of what is going on in the classroom between the teacher and students. Measures of what is being processed in each classroom will help to determine when there is effective teaching. Even in affluent and academically motivating environments, however, the criteria of effective teaching are vigorously debated. To describe *the* "best" or most effective style in the teaching of deprived children is impossible at this time. Many contemporary styles of teaching disadvantaged learners can be classified and presented, however, permitting teachers of the disadvantaged, and those preparing to teach, to experiment and apply principles, procedures, and styles to bring creative approaches to the classroom.

ASSUMPTIONS IN TEACHER STYLE

Three assumptions should be considered in any discussion of pedagogical style and effective teaching (White, 1969):

1. Too many difficulties arise from the generalized use of the terms "good teacher" and "bad teacher." It would be much more meaningful to operationally define the "good" teacher as working in certain specific situations and with a certain kind of students, e.g., a teacher who is good (very effective) with mentally retarded students at ages six to nine years in a hospital situation. Just because a teacher is "poor" with primary school disadvantaged children does not necessarily mean he could not be good with high school seniors at a suburban school.

2. The task of teaching disadvantaged children is markedly different from that of teaching advantaged children. Many of the developmental stages may be the same, but the rate and style of passing through those stages are essentially different. An experienced teacher of advantaged children would have to shift his teaching style *significantly* in order to be effective with deprived children. The teacher may be successful, in time, *if* he is able to shift teaching style, i.e., to adjust in personality, knowledge, and attitudes to the behaviors of lower socioeconomic populations.

3. The teacher is *the* essential component in the learning process of children. A child's learning is a function of much more than the teacher, but the presence of a human model who directs the sequence of stimulus-response characteristics in the classroom and who is the primary identification figure in that room is the *sine qua non* in the total learning process.

Although William James in 1899 presented some excellent suggestions to teachers about instructional style that could have been applied in any decade over the past seventy years, two classical studies of teacher style (Anderson, 1937; Lewin, Lippitt, & White, 1939) laid the groundwork for classifying the process of what a teacher does in the classroom. Results of the Anderson study introduced the concepts of the *dominative* as opposed to the *integrative* style of teaching in elementary-school classrooms. The dominative teacher uses threats, shame, and a rigid demand for conformity, whereas the integrative teacher shows approval for students' interests and is supportive and understanding. Data were interpreted as meaning that integrative teachers bring about integrative behavior in their children; more spontaneity, initiative, and personal-social adjustment were observed among children in the integrative-style classroom. Dominative teachers produce dominative-type students, who show more resistance and engage in more incidental and distractive learning than do their peers in integrative classrooms. Children in classes with the dominative teacher are more inclined to look out the window, tease other students, and engage in daydreaming. More intentional learning takes place with the integrative teacher.

Lewin, Lippitt, and White (1939) are often quoted for their study of the "social climate" of a boys' club, in which ten-year-old boys had male leaders, or teachers, of small groups. Since the emphasis in the study was upon teaching style, the results have been generalized, in numerous texts, to elementary-school classrooms. This classic study used the semantically attractive classifications of *authoritarian, democratic,* and *laissez faire* styles of teaching as the bases for determining student productivity. The authoritarian male teacher states the objectives of the program and totally directs all the activities. Although personality is not mentioned in this classification, there are strong similarities with Anderson's dominative type of teacher behavior. When the group is classified as a democratic system, the leader participates as a member in the group, tries to be nondominative, and is willing to share his decision-making power with the students. Leadership in the democratic classroom possesses many indices that resemble the integrative-teacher definition. In the laissez faire group climate, no goals are established and no directions are given for individual or group behavior. This is probably as close to the definition of the ineffective teacher as anyone dares to state.

There were many complex results from the study. The children taught by the authoritarian-style teacher failed to initiate activity and became very dependent upon the leader. One of the authoritarian groups became very aggressive and rebellious toward its leader. The laissez faire style of leadership only generated confusion and minimal individual productivity. The teacher who was described as democratic found sociability, cooperation, and friendly interaction with his students. The quality and quantity of the student work output were highest in the democratic group. Above all, the democratic group initiated and carried through work projects even though the leader absented himself from the group for periods of time.

One should not draw the conclusion that the democratic style of teaching is, therefore, the best teaching style. It should be remembered that these were young white boys from middle class homes, self-motivated toward activity groups after school hours, e.g., making paper masks, building airplanes, and carving soap. And, although there are many elementary-school classrooms with excellent male teachers, no public school has an all-male faculty. There are as many dissimilarities as similarities between public school classrooms and the Lewin, Lippitt, and White research, but the design and the data can be used for building new hypotheses about social climates and, above all, for stimulating needful discussion about the process of interaction in the classroom.

CONTEMPORARY CLASSIFICATION OF TEACHER STYLE

During the 1960s, a large number of studies were reported which dealt with the observations of classroom behavior and which have given us various categories of teacher style. At great risk of misrepresenting some of the unique contributions to teacher education, four contributions can be used as a synthesis of all the information about teacher style during the 1960s.

Teacher-characteristics study   More than 6,000 teachers, representing 1,700 schools, cooperated in a comprehensive study (Ryans,

1960) over a six-year period which sought to identify the teacher characteristics that public school systems deem desirable. Based upon observations by trained personnel, written reports by the teachers, and ratings of teacher behavior, three common patterns appeared to be significant in the identification of teacher behavior (Ryans, 1960, p. 71):

Pattern X: warm, understanding, friendly versus aloof, egocentric, restricted teacher behavior

Pattern Y: responsible, businesslike, systematic versus evading, unplanned, slipshod teacher behavior

Pattern Z: stimulating, imaginative, surgent or enthusiastic versus dull, routine teacher behavior

When the data from Ryans' teacher characteristics study were examined for elementary and high school teacher comparisons, it was found that all three patterns (X, Y, and Z) consistently described elementary-school teachers but were not as consistent among secondary school teachers. Many interesting correlations were found. While female science teachers were relatively high on Pattern Z, male and female social studies and female English teachers were relatively high on Pattern X. It appeared to be logical that women mathematics teachers scored highest on responsible, businesslike, systematic behavior. Among both elementary and secondary school teachers, young teachers appeared to be warmer and more understanding. Over fifty-five years of age, teachers were observed to be more aloof and restricted in their teaching tactics. In general, warm, systematic, stimulating teachers reflect the style that is desired in public schools throughout the country. Ryans' study has contributed to our identification of various kinds of teacher behavior in various content areas. In the generality of classes, the most effective teacher style would be warm, systematic, and imaginative. It should be noted, however, that the teacher styles that are predicted in the teacher-characteristics study did not involve student perception. This appears to be a meaningful omission since White and Wash (1966) found that the perception of teacher effectiveness was a function of the student's need for social approval. Students are motivated by teachers in different ways, depending upon the kinds and intensity of need possessed by each student.

Teacher and pupil personality   In a New York City school, Heil, Powell, and Feifer (1960) reported that the teacher's behavior evoked different amounts of achievement among fifth- and sixth-grade pupils. Three teacher personality traits were identified and compared with the relationship of four pupil personality types to discover the effect on achievement scores. Elementary-school teachers were classified as either *fearful, self-controlling,* or *turbulent.* The students were defined by paper-and-pencil instruments as *conformers,* who incorporated adult standards, maintained a high social dependency, and emphasized mature conduct; *opposers,* who showed a disturbed relationship with authority and expressed opposition, pessimism, and disappointment over academic conflicts in the classroom; *strivers,* who showed a marked need for achievement and social approval; and *waverers,* who appeared to be anxious, fearful, and indecisive.

The major interest in the Heil, Powell, and Feifer study was directed toward the comparison of the achievement levels of different kinds of students when they interacted with three different teacher personality types. Teacher styles, therefore, depended upon the interaction of teacher and student personality behavior. As might be expected, the "strivers" and "conformers" achieved the highest grade levels, no matter what the teacher personality. was. When the achievement of "opposers" and "waverers" was examined, it was observed that teacher style did make a meaningful difference. The "self-controlling" teachers appeared to be the most effective with the "opposers" and "waverers." It would not take much experience in the classroom to recognize and predict that the "fearful" teacher would be consistently ineffective with all kinds of students except the "strivers," who seemed to achieve despite the teacher. The broad conclusion about teacher-pupil personality is supported by many who are convinced that if students are grouped for instructional purposes, the personality of the teacher must be considered.

Social-interaction teaching style *Interaction analysis* is generally considered to be a system for categorizing, observing, recording, and analyzing the classroom behaviors of teachers and students. Classroom behavior is defined and classified in a specific number of categories. Behavior has been majorly measured verbally, i.e., by the oral statement of the teacher and students. Recently, non-verbal behavior, i.e., gestures, facial expressions, and activities in the classroom, has been examined experimentally. In almost all of the more than eighty systems that have been reported in the literature, inferences can be made about the affective behavior of the classroom which give some description and index of teaching style. The important thing in interaction analysis is that a system is used to discover predictable variables in the teacher-learner process. Most category systems are one-factor systems in which each behavior is measured in terms of frequency (Rosenshine, 1970). Variables can be affective, cognitive, or both. The range of variables included in a one-factor system extends from six to thirty. Some are primarily affective (Flanders, 1965), others are primarily cognitive (Medley and Smith, 1968), and others emphasize teacher feedback (Zaharik, 1968). Every interaction analysis has been based upon or is highly similar to the Flanders model.

Flanders Model Amidon and Flanders (1963) pointed to the analysis of behavior in the classroom not only as a method for measuring teacher talk and student talk but also as an index of teacher style. Emphasis in the model is toward verbal interaction; i.e., the higher the verbal interaction between student and teacher, the higher the achievement level of the class as a whole. According to the Flanders model, the teacher is not merely stimulating the students but is also being stimulated by the students. Results from interaction-analysis studies indicate that teacher style plays an integral role among students striving for a high level of performance. Classroom dialogue can be categorized by having raters record verbal behavior every three to five seconds into the categories described by Table 2-1, e.g., 10-5-5-5-3-4-5-5-8-9-10.

TABLE 2-1 *Ten Categories of the Interaction-analysis Techniques*

TEACHER TALK	INDIRECT INFLUENCE	1. *Accepts feeling:* Accepts and clarifies the feeling tone of the students in a non-threatening manner. Feelings may be positive or negative. Predicting and recalling feelings are included.
		2. *Praises or encourages:* Praises or encourages student action or behavior. Jokes that release tension, not at the expense of another individual, and nodding head or saying "um-hm?" or "go on" are included.
		3. *Accepts or uses ideas of student:* Clarifies, builds, or develops ideas or suggestions by a student. (As teacher brings into play, shift to category 5.)
		4. *Asks questions:* Asks questions about content or procedure with the intent that a student answer.
	DIRECT INFLUENCE	5. *Lecturing:* Giving facts or opinions about content or procedure; expressing his own idea; asking rhetorical questions.
		6. *Giving directions:* Giving directions, commands, or orders with which a student is expected to comply.
		7. *Criticizing or justifying authority:* Using statements intended to change student behavior from nonacceptable to acceptable pattern; bawling someone out; stating why the teacher is doing what he is doing (extreme self-reference).
STUDENT TALK		8. *Student-talk response:* Talk by students in response to teacher. Teacher initiates the contact or solicits student statement.
		9. *Student-talk initiation:* Talk by students, which they initiate. If "calling on" student is only to indicate who may talk next, observer must decide whether student wanted to talk. If he did, use this category.
		10. *Silence or confusion:* Pauses, short periods of silence, and periods of confusion in which communication cannot be understood by the observer.

Permission by E. J. Amidon and N. A. Flanders, *The role of the teacher in the classroom: A manual for understanding and improving teachers' classroom behavior,* Paul S. Amidon, Minneapolis, 1963, p. 12.

Amidon, Amidon, and Rosenshine (1969) developed the *expanded interaction-analysis system* by adding from two to four subscripts to each of the ten categories developed by Flanders. The subscripts consisted of variables from such category systems as Gallagher and Aschner (1963), which focused on question asking. Instead of the original category of "teacher asks questions," four types of questions identified this important component in the teacher-pupil interaction process.

Using the recorded category numbers (e.g., 10-5-5-5-3-4-5-5-8-9-10), matrices are constructed by pairing up the numbers (e.g., 10-5, 5-5, 5-3, 4-5, 5-8, 9-10). The first number of each pair is placed along the row index, and the second number is used for the column index. Placing tallies in this fashion provides a heavy concentration of tallies in various parts of the matrix. When the matrix is examined, inferences can be drawn about the dialogue of the class being relatively more direct or more indirect. If there is a heavy recording of entries in those areas of the matrix that give evidence of intensive teacher-student talk, it is reasonable and valid to refer to the style of that teacher as more indirect, or student-oriented. Since 66 percent of elementary-school class time is generally consumed in teacher talk,

FIGURE 2-1 *Direct and indirect patterns observed in the interaction-analysis technique.*

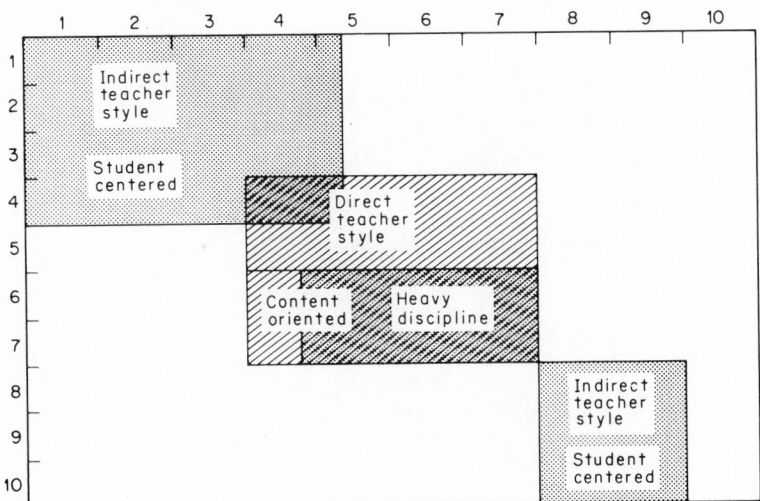

any class in which there is a high degree of interaction would make an excellent comparison. A great deal of research and development has modified the earlier Flanders model (Amidon & Hough, 1967). Different levels of thinking are applied to teacher talk and student talk. Thus, extension of verbal behavior in the classroom can be related to various kinds of concept formation. The modified system presented in Table 2-2 retains the ten basic categories but includes other discriminations of classroom verbal interaction that give more insight into teacher behavior. The style of the teacher can be described by a verbal-behavior model in which direct teacher talk can be discriminated by thinking processes.

TABLE.2-2 *Modified Categories of Interaction Analysis*

TEACHER TALK	1.	Accepts feeling		
	2.	(a)	Praises	
		(b)	Praises using public criteria	
		(c)	Praises using private criteria	
	3.	Accepts idea through:	(a)	Description
			(b)	Inference
			(c)	Generalization
	4.	Asks:	(a)	Cognitive memory question
			(b)	Convergent question
			(c)	Divergent question
			(d)	Evaluative question
	5.	Lectures		
	6.	Gives direction		
	7.	(a)	Criticizes	
		(b)	Criticizes using public criteria	
		(c)	Criticizes using private criteria	
STUDENT TALK	8.	Pupil response:	(a)	Description
			(b)	Inference
			(c)	Generalization
	9.	Pupil initiation:	(a)	Description
			(b)	Inference
			(c)	Generalization
	10.	(a)	Silence	
		(b)	Confusion	

Permission by E. Amidon and Elizabeth Hunter, *Interaction analysis: Recent developments,* paper presented at American Educational Research Association convention, February, 1966.

Reciprocal Category System   Interaction analysis developed by Flanders focuses a great amount of attention on teacher talk (seven of ten categories). Richard L. Ober (1966; 1967) strengthened the system by modifying the Flanders model, using nine common categories which can be used reciprocally for student-teacher talk. Data are recorded at three-second intervals and placed in category numbers on a matrix form for interpretation. The reciprocal category system (RCS) developed by Ober (1967) is briefly described in Table 2-3.

TABLE 2-3 *The Reciprocal Category System*

Category number assigned to teacher	Description of verbal behavior	Category number assigned to student
1	"WARMS (INFORMALIZES) THE CLIMATE: Tends to open up and/or eliminate the tension of the situation; praises or encourages the action, behavior, comments, ideas, and/or contributions of another; releases tension with jokes not at the expense of others; accepts and clarifies the feeling tone of another in a friendly manner. (Feelings may be positive or negative; predicting or recalling the feelings of another are included.)	11
2	ACCEPTS: Accepts the action, behavior, comments, ideas, and/or contributions of another; positively reinforces.	12
3	AMPLIFIES THE CONTRIBUTIONS OF ANOTHER: Asks for clarification of, builds on, and/or develops the action, behavior, comments, ideas, and/or contributions of another.	13
4	ELICITS: Asks a question or requests information about the content, subject, or procedure being considered with the intent that another should answer (respond).	14
5	RESPONDS: Gives direct answer or response to questions or requests for information that are initiated by another; includes answers to one's own questions.	15

Permission obtained from Dr. Richard L. Ober, University of Florida, 1969.

TABLE 2-3 *The Reciprocal Category System (cont.)*

Category number assigned to teacher	Description of verbal behavior	Category number assigned to student
6	INITIATES: Presents self-initiated facts, information, and/or opinion concerning the content, subject, or procedures being considered; expresses one's own ideas; lectures. (This category includes rhetorical questions not intended to be answered.)	16
7	DIRECTS: Gives directions, instructions, orders, and/or assignments with which another is expected to comply.	17
8	CORRECTS: Tells another that his answer or behavior is inappropriate or incorrect.	18
9	"COOLS" (FORMALIZES) THE CLIMATE: Makes statements intended to modify the behavior of another from an inappropriate to an appropriate pattern; may tend to create a certain amount of tension (i.e., bawling someone out, exercising authority in order to gain or maintain control of the situation, rejecting or criticizing the opinion or judgment of another).	19
10	SILENCE OR CONFUSION: Pauses, short periods of silence, and periods of confusion in which communication cannot be understood by the observer.	10

The script of the teacher-student talk in the classroom is recorded in small handwritten numbers. The numbers are converted from the script to the matrix for final analysis. Two fragments of teacher-pupil behavior are exemplified below. Corresponding numbers from the RCS are recorded.

		Data
Jim:	I have one more question. Can we work on these papers individually?	14
Teacher:	No.	5
Teacher:	You have the wrong idea. I wanted you in groups to work together on a project rather than each student working alone.	8
		6

Numbers are converted to a 19 × 19 matrix: Nine categories are assigned to student talk and nine categories to teacher talk. A single category is assigned to silence or confusion. The broad dimension of student verbal behavior appears to be treated more comprehensively. One of the unique features of the RCS system is that the 19 × 19 matrix can be divided into four submatrices: teacher-teacher talk, teacher-student talk, student-teacher talk, and student-student talk. Ober (1970) has attempted an excellent interpretation and application of his reciprocal category system. The RCS has been arranged in a systematic training program for teachers by Bentley and Miller (1969). As a training program for teachers in interaction analysis, the manual by Bentley and Miller has proved to be an expertly derived method for arousing teachers to examine their own pedagogical style and effectiveness in classroom communication.

Content-oriented style   There are many teachers whose style is determined by the logical operations of the classroom, with heavy attention to content and lessons. Teacher style which is determined by the course of instruction is best exemplified by B. O. Smith et al. (1963) and by the University of Georgia's *program development in early stimulation* (1968). Smith and his associates categorized thirteen "major acts" (i.e., defining, reporting, explaining, classifying, comparing, etc.) from electrically taped classroom verbal behavior. The frequency with which the verbal behavior of both teachers and pupils falls into one of the content areas determines the teacher's characteristic performance. The style of the teacher is classified by logical actions in the classroom.

The University of Georgia's *program in early stimulation* (Research and Development Center) is a complete curriculum concept emphasizing behavioral analysis and a programmed presentation of content for ages three to twelve years. Language arts, social sciences, science, mathematics, music, art, and physical education constitute the curriculum. The effective teacher in the Research and Development model (1969) is the one who can use the materials in such a way that students gain in academic performance. Apparently, neither the teacher's personality nor process variables enter into the model in any measurable way. Teacher-student behavior is determined by a direct teacher style, and the performance of students is measured on standardized tests.

Teacher style for tomorrow   During the 1970s, no single teacher style will be recognized as the most effective way to bring about student gains in classrooms. The effective teacher style in teaching deprived children will be a synthesis of many styles that have been labeled, during the past ten years, as experimental approaches. Teacher style will be viewed as a multivaried process in the life of the classroom, and measures of the effectiveness of teachers will depend upon many conditions.

No matter what type of classroom will be examined, future educators will be talking about (1) reduced teacher-pupil ratio, with the use of teacher aides, (2) small-group processes, in which the teacher will be viewed as a manager of small groups, (3) behavior analysis, and (4) teacher attitudes, personality, and expectations of students' behavior.

In tomorrow's classrooms, the conventional picture of one teacher and thirty to thirty-five youngsters sitting at desks, row by row, facing the teacher, following a lesson plan, will no longer be an acceptable criterion of effective teaching. Teacher training programs and the more progressive school districts will insist on teachers working in small groups. Assistant teachers will provide additional stimulus figures for instruction, as well as identification models. Assistant teachers will do more than clerical tasks, for they will teach and learn as well as free the teacher to do more insightful planning. Teacher preparation will involve the manipulation of groups and the analysis of each individual's abilities and history. More adults will be present in tomorrow's classroom, and continued attempts will be made to use programmed materials and computer facilities to obtain a proximity to the ideal—a 1-to-1 teacher/pupil ratio.

Schedules of reinforcement will be emphasized procedures in teacher training programs. External rewards for correct responses, which were so popular in the 1930s, will be frequently applied in order to obtain repetitive behavior. The professional teacher emerging from educational institutions will be informed of the manipulative quality of reinforcement and will have had laboratory training in modification of human behavior. Upon graduation, tomorrow's teacher will be well schooled in social learning. Intrinsic-motivation and creative-aesthetic systems will have some place in the training of teachers, but the heavy emphasis will be on contingencies of reinforcement. Whether it will be the M&Ms type candy or verbal praise, reinforcement will be tremendously popular as part of the style of teaching.

Just as Project Head Start was instrumental in generating the concept of kindergarten programs among various educators in all states, Project Follow Through will demonstrate the importance of reduced teacher/pupil ratio, comprehensive services, and the affect dimensions (personality, attitudes, etc.) of multi-teacher images. Teachers and psychologists will be engaged in many verbal- and social-interaction models in the classroom. Although both projects were funded for economically deprived children, benefits from experimentation will be generalized to the middle class environ and the total public school system.

TEACHING STYLES FOR THE DISADVANTAGED

To be successful in teaching disadvantaged children, *teacher characteristics* and teacher processes will play the determining roles. In discussing the teacher characteristics for the effective teaching role with deprived children, it must be emphasized that there is no one clearly defined constellation of personality traits or cookbook of tactical maneuvers. Teachers vary in their effectiveness depending upon the type of students, the organizational climate of the school, the subject-matter content, and the size of the class or group and the grade in school. However, there must be some relatively common factors which are shared by the many different kinds of teachers and different situations in which they find themselves. Teachers can be classified by the way in which they emphasize certain principles. Miriam Goldberg (1964, p. 161) succinctly described a hypothetical model of the successful teacher of the disadvantaged as "a mature, well integrated person who respects his difficult, unmotivated and apparently unteachable pupils." Trying to present at least one characterization of the "successful teacher" in a single phrase, Goldberg pointed to "ordered flexibility" as the best indication of successful teaching in the slums and in the suburbs.

The process by which economically deprived pupils achieve significantly better than their peers must also be discussed. Not only academic achievement should be considered the criterion of "effective teaching," the positive attitudes toward school, the teacher, the community, as well as self should also enter into a model of successful teaching. There are many and varied styles or processes which are being explored in helping deprived children to learn more effectively than they have been able to do in our public schools in the past. Some of these processes can be described and classified for those who are creatively seeking a solution to the question: How do you teach deprived children? For the most part, the styles, or strategies, for deprived children have been focused at the early-childhood level. It is relatively easy to understand why the weight of research interest is in preschool and the primary grades. We have known so very little about the developmental processes in early childhood that the thinking and feeling of young children is today an exciting and fascinating area of investigation. Even more important, the well-controlled research that has been accomplished with deprived children points to greater gains and more lasting changes when creative teaching has been applied to children who have not been conditioned to our conventional classrooms. With older children, changes are less frequent and attitudes and feelings are more firmly established. Some excellent research has been done, but the studies are generally small, emerging from many local interests and limited in their generalizations.

College for the disadvantaged   The general acceptance of the concept that education is the major vehicle for success in a democracy and that all citizens should have an equal opportunity to enter college has generated a few college programs for the disadvantaged. In response to a strong interest in assisting economically deprived students who are potentially able to complete college curricula, a very limited amount of federal and state money has been given to colleges to help economically deprived adolescents go to college. Gordon and Wilkerson (1966, p. 134) described the difference between compensatory practice and compensatory programs for the disadvantaged: "A continuing activity by an institution that helps disadvantaged students who could not otherwise do so to enroll and progress in college is . . . termed a *compensatory practice* . . . an organized group of related activities to the same end is . . . termed a compensatory program . . ." Financial aid, modified admission policies, and tutorial services are examples of compensatory practices, while special instructional programs would typify a compensatory program.

Common to compensatory college programs have been the remedial courses in English composition, remedial reading (included in a basic freshman English course or as a separate course), and mathematics courses. Students placed in these programs have been identified largely by use of standardized achievement and ability inventories, e.g., School and College Ability Test, the Iowa Silent Reading Test (Advanced Form), or the Nelson-Denny Reading Test. Diagnostic tests have been many and varied. Treatment in courses has been heavily weighted with programmed materials. Teaching styles continue to be curriculum-centered, using programmed materials, with some degree of counseling by volunteer or paid professionals.

To assist a number of students into the mainstream of preparation for higher education, at least five programs have received national recognition: Project Open Future (Hammond, 1968), A Better Chance (Kerr, 1967), College Readiness Workshop (Shepherd, 1967), Project Opportunity (Weber, 1967), and the College Discovery and Development Program (Tanner & Lachica, 1967). A high similarity can be recognized among the five programs. All had summer components programs, and all emphasized English and mathematics. Participants in Project Open Future attended Saturday morning classes for English and mathematics but in the afternoon chose courses that ranged from computers to Kiswahili, photography, and radio announcing. The teaching strategies seem to have been curriculum-centered but with a significant concern for individual motivation in a vocational way. Students were permitted some independent choice of academic interest without deemphasizing the strong need for remedial instruction in English and mathematics.

The kind of teacher for deprived children   The teacher who is causing meaningful changes among deprived students is well liked by his students and highly respected by his colleagues. Teachers who cannot identify with deprived children and who cannot become an adult figure whom the children would like to imitate ought to apply for a teaching position outside poverty areas. The effective teacher of deprived children is not the romanticist with missionary zeal. He is not filled with pious platitudes about searching for "beauty" and "goodness" among the dirty faces and torn clothes in an overcrowded area or among the black faces and body sores of those who live in shacks in the mud-red farmlands of Georgia. If a teacher has merely come to help, to contribute, or to bring the intellectual qualities of his affluent society to the poor, his degree of success among deprived children will continue to be quite minimal. In order for the teacher to be truly successful with disadvantaged children, he or she must view the limited world of the deprived as a place to learn and study. Teaching must be looked upon as a scientific enterprise. Set to learn more about the qualities in deprived children and how children with limited experience can learn more rapidly, the teacher becomes caught up in the psychosocial interaction in the classroom. Both teacher and student must change if effective teaching is to be realized in classrooms representing two or more cultures. The success, so far, has been in preschool classes.

For teacher and student to reach common academic goals and satisfy their personal social needs, they will have to share some common feelings—feelings about various events that bring happiness and feelings about certain experiences that stimulate sadness, disappointment, or even fears. Students must feel wanted; teachers need to feel important in assisting young people to mature and grow in knowledge and self-esteem.

Teacher and student will have to fulfill these needs, together. Affect is so very important in the classrooms of deprived children because of poor children's negative feelings about self, about verbal and intellectual tasks, and about the significance of others. The style of the effective teacher of the disadvantaged will be determined by the type of program, or process, that has been adopted by a particular school system. Deprived children must "learn" emotions as well as academic skills. The effective teacher is one who can help change the emotional lives of her children.

There is no known constellation of personality traits that permits us to say that "this kind" of teacher is the best for poor children. Evidence is just not available. One can only hypothesize, as others have done. The effective teacher of deprived children will most likely be warm, well ordered, and stimulating (Ryans, 1960). Above all, the teacher who works well with deprived children is not threatened by them or by the teaching task, is open to change, and continually searches for a better way of doing what he is doing in the classroom. It would be almost impossible for a teacher who has been described as warm, enthusiastic, and intelligent in the presence of poor children to fail in effecting positive and accelerating changes in the children. Reduced teacher—pupil ratio and acceptable classroom materials and facilities would have to be assumed.

Some thought must be given to a comment made to me by a well-known educator, E. Paul Torrance, "Any person who doesn't have any 'hang-ups' can be trained to teach poor children. If they love the children and don't have any 'personal blocks,' they can teach. Teaching isn't an oriental mysticism. Teaching deprived kids isn't a deep, dark secret; it is a science that can be learned, but the motive must be there."

The process of effecting change   The teacher's role in helping deprived students to learn the cognitive, affective, and physical skills required for a happy life depends heavily upon the style or strategies he (or she) uses to develop those skills. As we have noted in a previous section, the style or the pattern of strategies employed reflects the teacher's age, sex, type of training received in college, general intelligence level, creativity, and attitudes about student expectation and teachers' responsibility. The teacher is the primary motivator of change in the classroom, as well as the primary determiner of all the cognitive and affective dimensions of classroom behavior. The style, or cluster of strategies, used by one particular teacher would probably be ineffective with another teacher. Style fits the teacher and is inexorably bound up with the teacher's personality and intelligence. Style is personalized and should be examined as a multidimensional variable when classifying teacher behavior. In the process of effecting change, teachers emphasize certain principles of learning, and these become associated with a teacher's style. Distinct lines between styles are lacking, but broad guidelines can be identified. There is hardly a living psychologist who will deny that reinforcement works, but many question why it works. Some styles will place emphasis on external rewards as the determiner of the required behaviors of a child. Other styles will point to intrinsic motivation as the primary determiner of changes in the classroom. Figure 2-2 shows some broad, general categories of instructional styles that are found primarily in early-childhood programs with the disadvantaged.

Direct Style is recognized when the teacher gives more attention to structure, when the teacher does most of the talking (e.g., lecturing), and when the students' responses are the dominant

FIGURE 2-2 *Categories of teaching styles for the disadvantaged.*

Emphasis

Direct style	External reinforcement	
	Curriculum structured	Cognitive
	Association by contiguity	Affective
Indirect style	Social interaction—cognitive	
	Social interaction—affective	

objectives of learning, with little concern for the students' stimulation of the teacher. This is illustrated in Figure 2-3.

Indirect Style can be observed when the teacher asks more questions and has more student participation. Not only does the teacher praise, encourage, and reward correct responses of students, but also support is given for new, original concepts and skills which may not be part of the terminal objectives. When the style of a teacher includes the unplanned contributions of students, the teacher is stimulated beyond the lesson plan. Such substantive stimulation from both teacher and pupil is described in Figure 2-4. The students challenge, stimulate, and contribute to both the teacher and their peers. The teacher is not the only stimulating figure in the classroom.

In the many programs dealing with the direct style of teaching the disadvantaged, emphasis appears to be placed on one of three basic types of instructional styles (Figure 2-2). Each of these basic types is said to be the cause of the learning taking place in the child. *External reinforcement* refers to the learning principle that behavior will tend to be repeated when a person has been immediately reinforced (rewarded) for that behavior. Learning, or the change in human behavior, is said

FIGURE 2-3   *Communications in direct teacher style.*

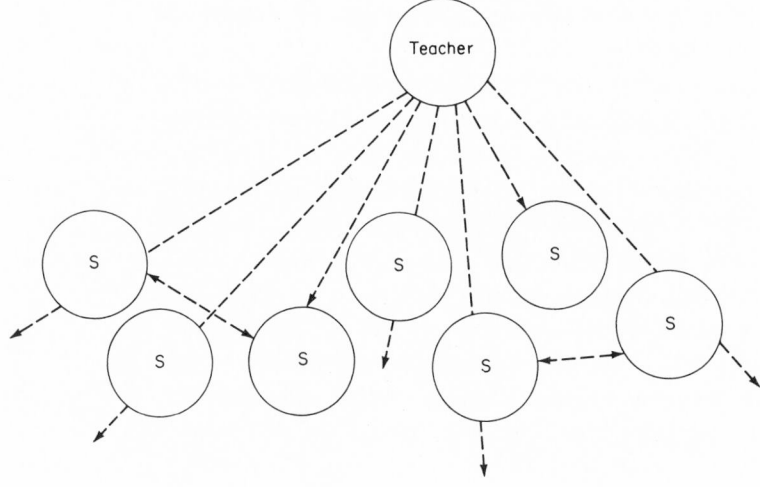

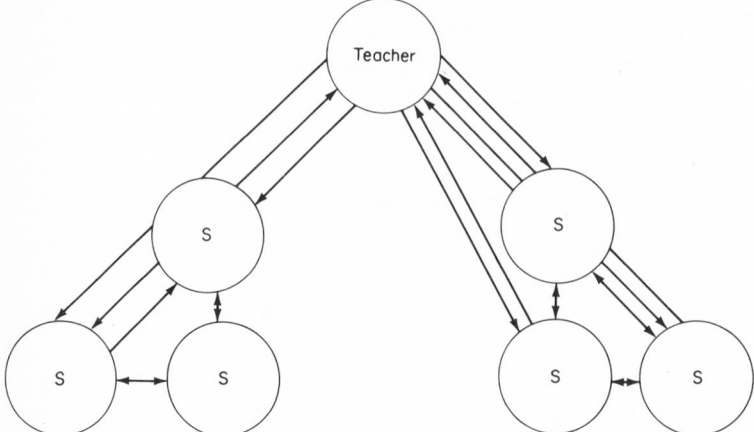

FIGURE 2-4 *Communication lines in indirect teacher style.*

to be caused by the reinforcement. Some external source (e.g., the teacher) is responsible for that reinforcement. In those programs in which the *curriculum* is the primary source of change, the teacher behavior and student behavior are determined by the structure of the lessons or units. If there is strict adherence to the format and sequencing of materials, the students are obliged to respond to the stimuli provided in the lesson plan. Responding correctly to the lesson content and its sequence, children will increase in vocabulary, concept formation, and other cognitive skills. Reinforcement is an integral part of the programmatic type of lessons, but the most important determiner (cause) of behavior is the structure of the curriculum.

There are programs which place their heaviest emphasis upon *environmental stimulation*. Rather than talking about reinforcement as the variable that triggers youngsters into learning, some programs emphasize a prepared environment which makes the expression of individual differences possible. For some, the environment is considered highly cognitive; for others, highly affective. In the Montessori method, the teacher teaches little but observes much. In fact, the Montessori teacher is referred to as the *directress of child development*. There is an insistence upon a limitation on teaching intervention. Children frequently work alone, developing as independent learners by solving the "problems" in the environment. Such an approach appears to be clearly distinct from the teacher influence in the behavior-modification models.

In the cognitive-interaction emphasis of the indirect teacher style, the teacher and students share in the contributions of the thoughts and words in the classroom. The sustained, self-directed inquiry by students in their classroom communication, which reflects their own strategies, requires a different supporting role on the part of the teacher. Students will be finding out what "they want to know," making "their own plans," and using "their own ideas" as part of the classroom structures. Students will be trained *to ask questions* as well as to respond to them.

In the affective-interaction model, emphasis is placed on the socioemotional welfare of the student. The interaction that is primarily advocated relates to attitudes toward self, to achievement orientation, to attitudes toward school, to teacher morale, and to the personal-social climate of the classroom. In models of this type, it is most difficult to discriminate a concern for emotion, attitude, or personality that does not include cognitive experiences. The learning environment, however, appears to be strongly stimulated by the psychosocial climate. The causes of the learning attitude are based upon stimulation from self and others.

Based on the guidelines of the teacher-style categories in Figure 2-2, attempts have been made to place certain programs in categories that seem to emphasize the highlights of the categories. Frequently, the programs mentioned here are very sophisticated and complicated, and perhaps they should not be relegated to the simple principle of emphasis that is being given them. In considering the teacher style of these programs, however, it seems that the emphasis of the program determines much of the kind of role the teacher will enact in his (or her) contact with disadvantaged children.

DIRECT STYLE—EXTERNAL REINFORCEMENT

University of Illinois Follow Through approach   The educational program at the University of Illinois (Becker & Engelmann, 1968) is an early-childhood focus upon modern behavior theory and upon a learning theory that is Thorndikian-Skinnerian in tradition. Central to this position is the principle that behavior is strengthened or weakened as a function of reinforcement. Behaviors are programmed from earlier learned behaviors, and thus sequencing of reinforced correct responses is essential. Objectives of the teaching program are specified in *terminal behaviors,* or operationally defined behavioral objectives. A terminal objective might be a quantity of responses on the Iowa Test of Basic Skills at a specified grade level. This general objective could be broken down into subsets of specified objectives within the skills of that test.

The teaching program begins with *entry* behaviors and concludes with *terminal behaviors.* Careful assessment of the verbal and intellectual functioning is made to determine an appropriate starting point for teachers to initiate their strategies. Building of more complex behaviors upon earlier, more simply learned behaviors is accomplished by the continuous analysis of task responses.

Children are motivated in a large number of responses, and reinforcers are applied to the desired behaviors (O'Leary & Becker, 1969). The goal is to establish praise, being right, etc., as effective reinforcers. The primary element for the teacher is to provide positive reinforcement when the child makes the correct response. The teacher appears to be more *directly* involved in the teaching strategy. This does not mean that students are not interacting. The method is identified, however, as a style in which the teacher manipulates the behavior of children by using *conditioned reinforcers.*

Two forms of instruction are being used by the Illinois-sponsored projects. All the schools using the approach begin their children on the Bereiter-Engelmann program in reading, language, and arithmetic (Figure 2-5). When children reach a 2- or 2.5-year reading level, commercial programs are employed.

A special group (four schools) has been using individually pre-scribed instruction (IPI), in which teachers prescribe special pro-grammed materials and tests for each individual child.

Bereiter-Engelmann program   The Bereiter-Engelmann program places emphasis on systematic reinforcement. Tasks are pre-sented in small study groups, but an attempt is made to indi-vidualize instruction by reinforcing each child in the group. The teacher's role is to require a greater number of responses from each child than could be accomplished in conventional classrooms. When a child responds, he is subject to intermittent or consistent reinforcement. The teacher programs the material so that primary skills are fully learned before proceeding to the next task. Some rather unique data have emerged from the

FIGURE 2-5   *A teacher in the Bereiter-Englemann program, P.S. 137 Annex, Brooklyn, N.Y. (Courtesy of* Grade Teacher Magazine. © *1969 CCM Professional Magazines, Inc.)*

Bereiter-Engelmann kindergarten programs in 1967. After two years of intensive training, an average gain of 24 IQ points was realized by the children. Range of the gains was from 10 to 42. The average IQ score upon graduation was 121. Range of the Stanford-Binet scores was 103 to 139. The average reading score of Bereiter-Englemann subjects upon kindergarten graduation was 2.6 on the Wide Range Achievement Test.

Behavioral analysis: A research approach to Follow Through   The approach toward early-childhood development by Don Bushell and his colleagues at the University of Kansas uses basic principles of learning which were promulgated in the 1930s to bring about new applications to the classroom. Behavior analysis has been developed in the University of Kansas program to the most advanced experimental application of reinforcement theory that we have in early-childhood programs. Motivation to study has been increased among preschool children (Bushell, Wrobel, & Michaelis, 1968) using careful management of behavioral consequences. The behavior-analysis approach defines in precise terms the exact behaviors which are to be modified. The capabilities of each child are observed and specified as well as the sequence of steps to the terminal objectives. A system of reinforcement of appropriate classroom behaviors becomes the key to the success of the program. Straightforward procedures are also available to deal with undesirable behaviors.

The teacher style of the University of Kansas approach is, therefore, classified as direct. No specific curriculum or materials are demanded in the program. Each teacher is free to choose those curriculum procedures and materials that best meet his (or her) needs and those of the children. The teacher style is determined by the role of the behavioral analyst. The emphasis upon reinforcement is well described in the token system:

Token systems allow the teacher to define a particular activity as being worth a given number of points or credits. Desired behavior may immediately produce a token, and each child can accumulate a number of tokens to be exchanged later for some preferred activity. For example, a recess might cost 20 tokens, and the correct solutions to math problems might earn one token each. Twenty correct math problems could then be exchanged for recess; or twenty-five problems could provide recess and five credits toward a story later on. [Bushell, 1968.]

Figure 2-6 shows a Hopi teacher conducting a reading lesson with a group of six children. Her hand is extended as she places a token in the cup of a child who is *in the process* of making a correct response. The materials in use are from the McGraw-Hill Programmed Reading Series by Sullivan and Buchanan. Because these books allow the children to progress individually, the teacher can move from child to child and give individual attention and reinforcement (praise and tokens) to those children who are "on task." All six children are on task, and none is engaged in so-called disruptive behavior. The tokens are later exchanged for child-selected reinforcers (activities such as recess, the opportunity to play with special materials, listen to a story, paint).

FIGURE 2-6 *Behavioral-analysis approach in a Follow Through program with Hopi Indian children.*

DIRECT STYLE—CURRICULUM-STRUCTURED

Conceptual-skills program The program at the Ontario Institute for Studies in Education (Bereiter, Case, & Anderson, 1968) attempts to work to higher-level skills by programmed steps. The skills program takes about a half hour of activities per day.

> The curriculum may be conceived of as progressing both horizontally and vertically. Horizontally, it moves from one to another attribute of things in the environment—color, size, shape, location, part-whole relation (what something is a part of or what its parts are), action, rise, and material. In dealing with each of these attributes, however (and combinations of them), there is a vertical progression from rudimentary to advanced levels of operation. [Bereiter, Case, & Anderson, 1968, p. 70.]

Emphasis in the conceptual-skills program appears to be on a sequential curriculum. Reinforcement is an important component in the program, but the materials carry the weight of the instructional process. The teacher's style is determined by the materials and high cognitive structure. The approach is very experimental, and conclusions about its effectiveness have not been reported to this date. It is hoped that spontaneity and genuine involvement on the part of the children will not be lost in the heavy emphasis on programmatic development.

Georgia intensive-learning model Developed by the Research and Development Center in Educational Stimulation at the University of Georgia, the Georgia model places heavy emphasis on the curriculum concept and the programmed presentation of content. The personality of the teacher or the affective development of the deprived student does not directly enter into the learning model. The style of the teacher is conditioned by the finely graded series of lessons in eight curriculum areas: reading, oral language, writing, social science, mathematics, music, art, and physical education.

Implementation of the teacher strategies focuses on responses defined as critical for children to master. Noteworthy is the earlier than usual presentation of certain curriculum materials,

e.g., reading at the kindergarten level. An introduction of curriculum terminology is considered difficult at first, but facility
is expected with familiarity. The reading program emphasizes
systematic visual-analysis training. Before a word is "learned,"
six behaviorally defined steps must be completed. The steps pinpoint the highly cognitive structure of the program and the
major concern for denotative meaning and the lexical interpretation of curriculum content.

Instructional materials appear to be most helpful with paraprofessionals, aides, and parent workers. In the Follow Through
program in Pickens County, Georgia, deprived children in the
first grade are achieving at higher levels than in any preceding
year (Figure 2-7). Although data have not been completely ana-

FIGURE 2-7 *Mathematics activity in a classroom in Pickens County, Georgia, where the Georgia Intensive Learning Model is being imple-mented. (Courtesy of the Pickens County school system.)*

lyzed, the effectiveness of the program is beyond all expectations. It will have to be determined, however, what contributions other components in Follow Through have made in the achievement gains of the disadvantaged children. Preliminary analysis shows the teacher variable to be the determining factor in all gains. The best materials will not accomplish the academic needs without competent teachers. Many of the programs in early childhood are demonstrating that the attitudes, personality, and skills of the teacher are the primary motivators of all gains in a classroom.

DIRECT STYLE—ASSOCIATION BY CONTIGUITY

The emphasis in this type of teacher style is upon competency in dealing with surroundings, i.e., upon finding development through mastering the environment. The association of one environmental stimulus with another stimulus determines the learning that takes place. The teacher does not interfere with each child's self-development but prepares, plans, and orders the classroom facilities and curriculum materials so that a systematic environment will consistently stimulate the learning process. The key is the highly structured learning environment.

Montessori for the disadvantaged   Principles of the Montessori method have been applied to educational challenges in the war on poverty (Orem, 1967). An example of Montessori educational principles for the disadvantaged can be found in the Day Care Department Association, Atlanta, Georgia. In a preschool class of thirty children, fifteen are economically deprived. Five major themes of the Montessori system (Pinko, 1967) characterize the type of program and help to describe the role of the teacher in such a method:

1.   *The Montessori methodology as freedom within a framework of preparation for individual full functioning (Figure 2-8).* The spontaneous, independent development of the child appears to be the basic principle in the Montessori programs. The teacher limits her interaction with the student. The atmosphere is quiet and hushed,

FIGURE 2-8 *Child works independently in a Montessori class at the Anderson School, Danbury, Connecticut. (Courtesy of* Grade Teacher Magazine. © 1969 *CCM Professional Magazines, Inc.)*

and children are surrounded by an environment that motivates them toward coping with the stimuli presented to them. The less the teacher teaches, the more the student will learn, for the school must permit free natural manifestations of the child.

The motives in the Montessori programs bear a marked resemblance to White's (1959) "concept of effectance" motivation. The intrinsic need of every child to deal with his environment was hypothesized by White to relate to each child's need to interact with his environment (competence) by exploring and manipulating the world about him.

2. *The Montessori method as activity and movement culminating in active "inner discipline."* In the prepared environment, the liberty of the child is paramount. The teaching material, the adaptable furniture, the exercises, and the nature activities reflect the movement opportunities which Montessori established as part of the prepared environment. The major pattern of behavior is that each child must act for himself.

3. *The Montessori methodology as sensory education and practiced observation.* The education of the senses appears to be of great importance. The touch of objects seems to be part of the beginning process in all learning. Letters of the alphabet and numerals are all coated with a rough substance to outline and discriminate the various symbols.

4. *The Montessori methodology as programmed autoeducation for intellectual competence.* The child is directed by the didactic material to help him reach success with a task and eliminate failure. The instructional materials control for every error since the aim is to achieve repeated success and few if any failures at tasks in the daily lives of the children.

5. *The Montessori teacher as a stimulator of life and directress of the child's development.* Since the child in the Montessori model educates himself using instructional materials structured to prevent failure, the teacher's role is primarily to observe. The teacher, however, is not passive and unknowledgeable but is a stimulus figure, mixing with the students in the classroom. The emphasis is to stimulate life, leaving it then free to develop and unfold.

These five major principles are applied in all programs harboring deprived children. The teacher in such a program plays a very different kind of role from that which has been described in other direct teacher styles. Since the emphasis is upon associations of stimuli in the environment which have been structured by the teacher, the model should be classified as a direct teacher style.

The autotelic-discovery approach   The procedure used by Dr. Glen Nimnicht in the *autotelic-discovery approach* (Figure 2-9) is much the same as that used in the program for three- and four-year-old children at the New Nursery School, Greeley, Colorado. The educational objectives are to help children develop a positive self-image as well as intellectual abilities. To achieve these objectives, procedures are based upon the following notions (Nimnicht, 1968):

1. The learning experiences should be intrinsically motivating and should not depend upon external rewards or punishments.
2. The child should be free to explore the learning environment.
3. The child should be self-pacing.
4. Whenever possible, the child should be immediately informed about the consequences of his acts.

FIGURE 2-9   *The autotelic-discovery (the Nimnicht approach) program at Mary B. Martin Elementary School, Cleveland, Ohio. (Courtesy of* Grade Teacher Magazine. © 1969 *CCM Professional Magazines, Inc.)*

5. The environment should be arranged so that the child is likely to make a series of interconnected discoveries about his physical and social world.

As in the Montessori approach, teachers in the autotelic-discovery model try to control what the student does by what is included or excluded in the learning environment. When the child enters the classroom, he is permitted to explore freely, spending as much time on an activity as he likes. The environment is planned to inform the learner immediately about the consequences of his actions. The behavior of the teacher and her assistants is determined by the kind of equipment that is used. The teacher's role is primarily to respond to the child. As in all other instructional models, there is need of a great deal of development in the system. The overall emphasis, however, appears to be on stimulation by a structured environment.

INDIRECT STYLE—SOCIAL INTERACTION, COGNITIVE FOCUS

Instructional games, independent-learner approach   Originally developed at the Institute for Developmental Studies, game formats are used by Dr. Lassar G. Gotkin of an early-childhood learning approach. The game process focuses on two dimensions: language and concept formation. As Dr. Gotkin describes it, "We play games, but we are not fooling around." The very word *game* implies some kind of interaction. The emphasis is upon interaction, upon the teacher-learner process. In the matrix games (Gotkin, 1967), children learn to (1) follow complex directions, (2) speak clearly, (3) solve problems, (4) be independent, and (5) develop new vocabulary and concepts. Children become "teachers" in the matrix games, as the leadership in the verbal dialogue shifts from person to person in small groups. Language behavior is developed in language lotto games (Gotkin, 1967), in puzzle games (1969), and in listening centers in which tapes and earphones assist the child in the verbal exercises.

The teacher in the *instructional-games approach* consistently interacts with small-group processes (Figure 2-10). Although the

FIGURE 2-10   *Kindergarten children at the English Avenue Primary School, Atlanta, Georgia, playing the matrix game.*

games provide cognitive structure in the early-childhood curriculum, it is expected that they will generate new and original behavior toward independence of the learner both in language behavior and in concept formation. The teacher plays the role of a manager of groups rather than using a direct teacher style, i.e., managing and directing one total group. The game format shifts the source of verbal expression to the students and places the teacher's responsibility more on groups of five or six children. The need for curriculum development is considerable, but as a process variable, the "games approach" is as socially interacting as any teaching model for the disadvantaged. Again, the instructional model has been focusing on kindergarten and the primary grades.

Creative-aesthetic approach   The *creative-aesthetic approach* (Fortson, 1969; Torrance & Fortson, 1968) aims primarily at developing in preprimary children the beginnings of intellectual skills, abilities, and attitudes important in school success. Activities are planned to elicit maximum amounts of creative thinking, problem solving, fluency of ideas, and fluency in verbal expression and to develop auditory and visual discrimination.

Creative ways of learning have a built-in motivation for educational achievement that makes unnecessary the application and re-application of rewards and punishment. Even when reward and punishment succeed temporarily in motivating learning, they do not supply the inner stimulation necessary for continued motivation and achievement. Such motivation is usually short-lived and requires continuous reapplication. The inner stimulation from creative ways of learning makes this unnecessary.

To learn creatively, a person first becomes aware of gaps in knowledge, disharmonies, or problems calling for new solutions. He then searches for information concerning the missing elements of difficulties, trying to identify the difficulty or gap in knowledge. Next he searches for solutions, making guesses, formulating hypotheses, and thinking of possibilities. Then comes the testing, modifying, re-testing and perfection of the hypotheses. Finally, there is the communication of the results. This process is a natural one. Strong motivations are at work at each stage. Once the process is set in motion, it is difficult to stop it. [Torrance, Fortson, & Diener, 1968.]

In a study of the creative-aesthetic approach in kindergarten (Fortson, 1969), children who experienced the creative-aesthetic program were significantly higher on all readiness tests and on all creativity measures than were controls. Continued gains in cognitive measures were observed one year later.

The teacher's role in the creative-aesthetic approach appears to be significantly different from that in behavioral-analysis models. Beyond expecting the correct responses from students, the teacher awaits the unexpected. Each child is expected to provide original contributions to the psychodynamics of the classroom (Figure 2-11). High social interaction is the key to developing the creative skills in the disadvantaged child. As in the instructional-games approach, the creative-aesthetic programs are concerned with process. The teacher plans for the intrinsic reinforcement that emerges when a child produces "something of his own." Learning, therefore, results from intrinsic as

FIGURE 2-11   *Each child will produce new combinations through manipulation of objects (creative-aesthetic approach).*

well as extrinsic types of reinforcement. The teacher assists the child in being successful in the direction in which the child chooses to spend his time. Engaged in role playing, children act out their inner feelings and express themselves in risk-taking behavior. Above all, children are trained to ask as many questions as they are expected to respond to.

INDIRECT STYLE—SOCIAL INTERACTION, AFFECTIVE TYPE

The Florida parent-education approach   Dr. Ira Gordon, director of the Institute for Development of Human Resources, is responsible for the Florida *parent-education approach,* which focuses on deprived children during their early development. Parental factors play an extremely important role in the Florida model. Although the Florida approach has been classified as a social-interaction affective type, this does not mean that in the structure of the model there is limited concern for cognitive processes. Since the focus is on parental emotional factors as well as on the self-concepts of children, major objectives seem to be in the direction of affect.

The emotional and attitudinal factors in parents include the consistency of management and disciplinary patterns, the parents' own emotional security and self-esteem, their belief in the internal as opposed to the external control of the environment, their own impulsivity, their attitudes toward school, their love of their children, and their work aspirations and patterns (Gordon, 1968). The Florida parent-education model intervenes directly in the home so that the home situation will lead to higher scholastic achievement levels in children as well as a healthier self-concept.

In the classroom, the Florida model presents ways of modifying classroom organization and teaching patterns as well as influencing the particular curriculum that a school district has adapted. Influence in the classroom appears to be through the use of paraprofessionals, systematic observation techniques, and curriculum development based upon Piagetian principles.

The key elements of the program are the training of the mother and the training of the classroom teacher to plan and implement the parent-education activities. The role of the teacher is more person-oriented than in most programs with disadvantaged children. Above all, the parent participation with the teacher is an outstanding characteristic of the program (Figure 2-12).

Bank Street approach to Follow Through   Bank Street College (Gilkeson, 1970) provides a program for the disadvantaged which requires each child to have a positive image of himself as a learner and as a person. Emphasis is upon personality development. One of the major objectives in the Bank Street program is the development of a supportive teacher-pupil interaction in which the teacher not only understands and accepts the child's

FIGURE 2-12　*Hillsborough County school system, Tampa, Florida, involved in the Florida parent-education approach in Follow Through.*

thinking and feeling but also responds and encourages the child's language and learning ability.

Four criteria seem to pinpoint the Bank Street approach to Follow Through (Figure 2-13):

1.　The establishment of a learning environment for children
2.　The development of a supportive teacher-child interaction
3.　The establishment of two-way communication with parents
4.　The development of a team with an organic life of its own (Gilkeson, 1970)

The strong interaction of teachers, parents, administrators, ancillary and auxiliary personnel, and pupils places the Bank Street approach in the indirect social-interaction style. The concern for personality, self-concept, and emotional security

FIGURE 2-13 *First-grade children in a Bank Street program in the Macon County Follow Through program, Tuskegee, Alabama. Permission of Follow Through personnel, Tuskegee, Alabama.*

directs the energies of the teacher toward the affect dimension. If the child is secure emotionally, he should be able to accomplish the academic standards in the classroom.

OTHER STRATEGIES AND PROGRAMS

There are many other attempts to do an effective teaching job with the disadvantaged. It is recognized rather generally that conventional instruction does not reach children with cultural and educational deficits who have already established a negative attitude toward themselves, school learning, authority figures, and the future. The varied approaches presented in this chapter are representative of institutional programs for the poor. There is not a sufficient amount of data about these programs to make scientific comparisons among programs or among teaching styles. There has been so much need for cooperation at the local level and with the federal government that it is only now becoming possible to draw up hypotheses about teaching the deprived. Follow Through will spend 30 million dollars in 1969–1970 and 70 million in 1970–1971 to conduct a scientific investigation of early stimulation of the deprived and a follow-up of gains made by a comprehensive program. The local school districts must bring their own resources to bear on the problems of the disadvantaged, using models developed in experimental programs similar to Follow Through, and must themselves provide better education.

The most radical departure in all the programs for deprived children lies in the fact that the teacher's role is different. Creative programs demand creative teachers and creative styles. The next chapter extends this innovative concept in teacher style by describing the teacher as an emotional conditioner in the classroom. The position is taken that the primary role of the teacher is to condition the emotions of children—that teachers of disadvantaged children should style their lessons upon modifying the emotions of children rather than upon communicating knowledge.

three

The teacher as a conditioner of emotions

There are many textbooks in educational psychology which remove the personalities of the teacher and students from the center of the stage. Some textbooks are explicit and state clearly that the personality of the teacher should be subordinated to the role of providing the conditions for learning cognitive tasks. Such textbooks present a large amount of well-ordered information and insist upon achievement scores as the major terminal objectives of classroom instruction. So emphatic are attitudes about knowledge, facts, cognitively styled teaching strategies, and curriculum content that the socioemotional climate of the classroom is comfortably bypassed. When the only function of the teacher is teaching children "to think," to return the correct answers, to maintain high achievement scores, and to excel in oral and written language, most of the deprived children are doomed to academic failure. The attitude and strategy of the teacher of the disadvantaged child have to be different from the attitudinal variables associated with the instruction of advantaged children. Strategies that teachers employ in the classrooms and their attitudes about learning processes reflect the type of instructors to whom they were exposed in college, as well as the textbooks used in courses with those instructors. Probably the most significant indictment of teacher training programs which place such a high premium on cognition, facts, and "brains" is their use of the single criterion of grades (GPA) as the measure of the successful teacher. For many schools, a student has only to demonstrate an acceptable grade of C+ in academic courses throughout the sophomore year to be admitted into a teacher education program. Graduation, certification, and placement are determined by the kind of grades that were maintained in the junior and senior years of college. It is a false assumption that a senior college student with an A+ average will be an effective teacher with the disadvantaged. The primary aim of teaching the disadvantaged is to modify and develop the skills and personalities of the students. Although the very bright college student may be an excellent teacher of advantaged children, special teaching skills and personality will determine his effectiveness in the classrooms of the poor. Breaking through the social class barrier to reduce anxiety and permit an identification with deprived children demands a special kind of teacher. Teachers currently responsible for the instruction of deprived children and those preparing to teach all kinds of children are looking for a modern theory of learning, or at least some principles of a theory, that may be more applicable in teaching children in metropolitan ghetto areas and rural, isolated communities. Four theories seem applicable for this purpose: conditioning, reinforcement, observational learning, and emotional learning.

CONDITIONING

Principles of conditioning are well established and continue to be utilized in the modern interpretation of human behavior. Conditioning can be described as an experimental development of a principle, anchored in philosophic thinking before the time of Christ, labeled *association*. When one thing occurs at the same time or place with another, an association or connection results.

In common parlance, individuals talk about the association of ideas—e.g., when we say *table,* we think also of chairs; when we speak of teachers, we think also of students. Psychologists talk about association, too, but they refer to the connection or association between a stimulus (in general, any energy change in the environment) and a response (a reaction to a stimulus). Learning in the classroom consists of connections made between various stimulus patterns and the responses that children make because of that stimulation. In many early-childhood programs and remedial reading programs, it is believed that the organized presentation of various stimuli will bring about the desired thinking, reading, and speaking responses that seem to be lacking among deprived children. One name is synonymous with the presentation of organized patterns of stimulation: Ivan Pavlov.

CLASSICAL CONDITIONING

Working with dogs, Pavlov made a contribution to learning theory that was as momentous as Freud's insights into personality. In classical conditioning models, one stimulus is associated with another stimulus in causing a response. Pavlov placed a hungry dog in a harness. The very smell or sight of food (unconditioned stimulus, or UCS) caused the dog to salivate (unconditioned response). The word *unconditioned* refers to that which is natural and is another way of saying that the stimulus is not dependent upon any conditions. It is natural and expected that a hungry dog, or human being, will salivate when he smells food or sees food. Salivation is said to be caused by the smell or sight of food (Figure 3-1).

Pavlov associated the UCS (sight of food) with the sound of a bell. Certainly, there seems to be little causality between a

UCS-------------------- UCR
(Smell or sight of food)   (Salivation)

FIGURE 3-1 *Unconditioned stimulus and response.*

bell sound and an animal's salivation. When a bell (conditioned stimulus, or CS) was presented a few seconds before, or simultaneously with, the smell of food (UCS) for a number of times (e.g., eight or nine), salivation began to occur. The animal was said to be conditioned to salivate to the sound of a bell (Figure 3-2). Thus we speak of learning having taken place.

From this basic principle, an entire theoretical system has been developed. The difference between this theory and other theories is not in the concept of stimulus and response. Classical conditioning places emphasis on the stimulus and states that learning takes place by substituting one stimulus (CS) for another (UCS). The model can be extended to higher-order conditioning. The sound of the bell which has become the conditioned stimulus evokes the same kind of response as the sight or smell of food. When a new neutral stimulus, a black square, is presented immediately preceding the sound of a bell, higher-order conditioning takes place and the sight of a black patch elicits the response of salivation. Classical conditioning principles were developed and refined in the animal laboratories. These principles are being extended to high-level cognitive processes, but the evidence is less well established than in psychomotor responses.

REINFORCEMENT THEORY

Perhaps the most famous interpretation of what takes place in learning was contributed by an American psychologist, Edward Lee Thorndike (1874–1949). The major conclusion which he handed down to posterity was that animals (and humans) tend to repeat what they have been doing if they are *rewarded*. Most

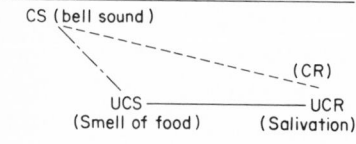

FIGURE 3-2 *Classical conditioning model.*

of the evidence for Thorndike's theory was obtained from animal studies, but the influence of the reward theory could be found among all the teachers who gave gold stars, made up honor rolls, or hung up the best papers for the class to see. All those who believe that the kind word or the verbal recognition of an accomplishment is essential for classroom success are supporting Thorndike's theory of the influence of reward.

Thorndike was caught up in the motives and beliefs of his own time. At the beginning of this century, hedonism, or the pleasure-pain principle, seemed to predominate in the culture of our large metropolitan areas of the country. The theory we know today as *reinforcement,* or reward theory, grew out of the thinking and attitudes of our Western philosophy. Thorndike crystallized the use of rewards to cause a repetition of responses in a statement which became known as the *law of effect:*

Of several responses made to the same situation, those which are accompanied or closely followed by satisfaction to the animal will, other things being equal, be more firmly connected to the situation, so that when it recurs, they will be more likely to recur; those which are accompanied or closely followed by discomfort to the animal will, other things being equal, have their connections weakened, so that, when it recurs, they will be less likely to recur. [Thorndike, 1911.]

According to Thorndikian theory, the individual who is going to "teach" another individual (or animal) will use *satisfiers* and *annoyers* to bring about desired responses. A satisfier is something we do nothing to avoid and frequently strive to attain, and annoyers are things we frequently strive to avoid. The use of satisfiers was best exemplified in Thorndike's teaching cats to unlock themselves from cagelike containers called *puzzle boxes.* A cat placed in one of the puzzle boxes could escape only by pulling a string hanging in the center of the box. The string was attached to the puzzle box via some pulleys. When the string was pulled, the door opened and the cat emerged to consume the reward in the form of raw fish. In a typical case, the hungry cat first encircled the cage many times, observing and smelling the fish. He generally pawed at everything in the box. When his paws caught in the "right" thing, the door opened. His reward

followed immediately upon the correct response. From the research of Thorndike, it took a cat about twenty-two trials to learn
his lesson perfectly. After that many trials, Thorndike would
place his cat in the box and the cat would respond immediately,
pulling the string like a professionally trained acrobat.

For a while Thorndike believed in annoyers and punishment, but in the 1930s he abrogated punishment, or negative reinforcement, as part of the learning process. Thorndike was
followed by an entire school of psychologists who did not believe
that one learns from punishment. The only thing that works,
according to this school, is reinforcement (Figure 3-3). In the
procedure of giving rewards, an individual is presented with a
particular stimulus—a reinforcer—immediately after he makes
a response. As demonstrated in numerous studies over time, the
individual will tend to repeat the behavior for which he is being
rewarded and to discontinue the responses if there is no reward.

If a teacher wanted to eliminate or extinguish certain behaviors in the classroom, she would merely fail to recognize or fail
to reinforce the student for those behaviors. Emphasis is always
upon the correct, appropriate responses made by the individual
learner. Those who adhere to some form of reinforcement theory
in handling classroom dynamics do not deny stimulus situations
but insist that change in behavior is due to reward which follows
the response. Stimuli merely set the stage for the reactions of an
individual.

Operant conditioning   The principles of operant conditioning are
attributed to Burrhus F. Skinner but emerge from the Thorndikian tradition of reward psychology. The term *operant conditioning* is opposed to the term *classical,* or respondent, *condi-*

FIGURE 3-3   *Reward following desired response.*

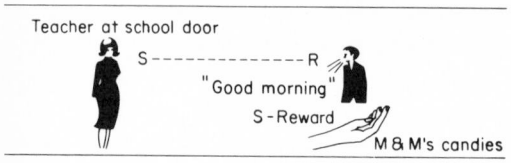

Teacher at school door

S -------------- R
"Good morning"
S - Reward
M & M's candies

tioning. In operant conditioning, the learner works upon the environment; in classical conditioning, the environment determines the learner.

The Skinnerian theory of learning employs the word *reinforcement* in place of the Thorndikian reference to reward. Skinner (1963) explained that he was attempting to remove the purposiveness from the concept of reward. Reinforcement does not contain the concept of "reward for something," but reinforcement does increase the probability that a particular type of behavior will occur again. When a child is reinforced by the teacher, many different kinds of behavior are subject to repetition. Focus is upon what the child does, i.e., upon the specific response of the child according to the reinforcement model. Learning has to be viewed as blind, dumb, and mechanical (Bugelski, 1964). Even superstition can be explained by reinforcement. Any kind of behavior can be strengthened by capricious reinforcement. For example, the teacher should be cautioned against approving a student's paper that has questionable authenticity. Many of us teachers believe in the warm, accepting way of acting in the classroom. There is a danger, however, in careless praising of students. Complimenting the entire class on a "job well done" or for "being courteous" or well-controlled is dangerous when a few members of the class have not been worthy of those compliments. The praise generalizes (Anderson, White, & Wash, 1966), and the deviant student is reinforced for being uncooperative, uncontrolled, and impolite.

Skinner and his followers continue to use reinforcers *to shape* the behavior of animals and human subjects through a series of successive approximations. If a particular terminal objective is desired, e.g., to score above the 90th percentile on the Metropolitan Achievement Test, reinforcements are presented step by step for each concept or item in the test package, gradually directed toward the ultimate performance that is required. Programmed texts are probably the best example of continuous reinforcement in the shaping of students' responses toward ultimate goals.

However, continuous reinforcement of the same response is not always necessary. When a student is learning material for the first time, it seems best to reinforce every time. Later on, after the student is responding beyond the operant rate, a reduction of the number of reinforcements has proved to be more effective. Reinforcing every so many times (for example, 5:1 or 10:1) has been called *fixed-ratio scheduling*, and reinforcing every so often (for example, every third, fifth, or tenth second) has been called *fixed-interval scheduling*. By scheduling reinforcements every so often or every so many times, experimenters can shape the behavior of animals, but teachers with twenty-five students in a class cannot display all the controls that are necessary. At best, a teacher can only hope to reinforce "frequently." The general recommendation of positively reinforcing whenever the teacher can do so is the best way to implement the theory of reinforcement in the classroom. It would be erroneous for teachers to "think" that they had to reinforce a child if he is going to learn any or all the correct behaviors. Children learn by intrinsic reinforcement as well as they learn by being rewarded externally. When a child brings closure to a task or makes "something on his own," he does not necessarily need external reinforcement. Building a soapbox racer or capturing certain feelings in a painting is in itself a powerful reinforcer for a child.

There are many psychologists and teachers who strongly assert that reinforcement is not everything. One of the theories which has added more to our knowledge of how children learn can be called a *modern learning theory*.

EMOTIONAL LEARNING

A learning theory that seems to integrate the Pavlovian and Thorndikian traditions was introduced by O. Hobart Mowrer (1960) and applied to classroom teaching by Richard Bugelski (1964). In Mowrer's theory, the major emphasis is upon the emotions and the autonomic nervous system.* Mowrer believes that Pavlov's model of how learning takes place is relatively

* The autonomic nervous system *is the nervous system that regulates our emergency and vegetative processes of the body. Called by many the physiological agent of emotion, it is located in the visceral and circulatory areas of the human body.*

accurate. But it was not the salivary reflexes of dogs that were being conditioned in Pavlov's laboratory. It was the emotions of the dogs which were being modified by associating one stimulus with another. When Pavlov's dogs were conditioned to the sound of a bell, the dog was "hoping" for food. That is why the dog salivated. When a dog was shocked a few times at the sound of a bell, it was the emotion of fear that was being learned. Upon hearing the bell, the dog feared (and then lifted his leg to avoid the shock). The important point, which has significance for classroom teachers, is that the only things we learn are to fear and to hope.

> We can only learn emotional responses to stimuli. All other "learned" behavior consists of performing certain responses we are already able to perform, voluntarily or otherwise. [Bugelski, 1964, p. 116.]

In teaching children to spell a word, e.g., *dog*, correctly, the modern learning theory of Mowrer suggests that the student is not learning merely to spell *dog*. The student already can spell *dog*. He is fully able to spell, or he could never pronounce the sounds in the word *dog*. The teacher does not have to teach the student. He knows how. The teacher is required to condition the emotions of the student. If the student responds "d–a–g," the teacher conditions him to "feel bad" (fear). The teacher's role, therefore, in teaching the correct spelling of *dog* is to make the child feel good when he responds with the correct letters and sounds and feel bad when he responds otherwise. Learning is a question of emotional conditioning (Figure 3-4).

How does the emotional-conditioning model differ from reinforcement theory in explaining how children learn? First of all, in the emotional-conditioning model, the emotions are modified; the books, the lessons, the performance on a violin, writing one's name for the first time are all conditioned to the individual's feelings of hope or feelings of fear. In reinforcement theory, it is the performance, the psychomotor response, e.g., saying "Good morning," which is rewarded. The same performance tends to be repeated because of a reward. Secondly, the reinforcement theory

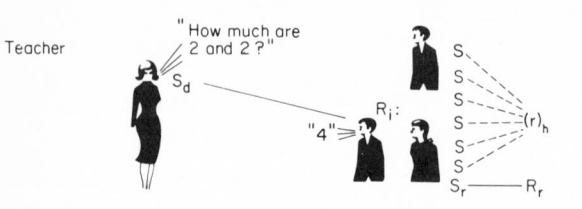

FIGURE 3-4 *Emotional conditioning.*

does not explain why reinforcement works. Reward causes the change in behavior. In the emotional-conditioning model, the emotions are affected. That is why a stimulus (e.g., a candy bar) may be a reward for one person but not for another (e.g., a diabetic). The same stimulus might be a stimulus for arousing fear as well as hope.

How does the teacher condition the emotions of children in her class? There are, of course, many ways to bring about emotional arousal in children. The important thing is that the teacher *perceives herself a*s the emotional conditioner of her students. It would be quite a shift in attitude for many teachers to firmly believe that their primary function is to change emotions—and not "communicate lessons, rules of grammar, or the truth." If teachers would focus on emotional change as well as have students repeat "over and over again" specific responses, much more effective learning would take place. Probably the most powerful stimulus for emotional arousal of students in any classroom is the *personality of the teacher.* The ability and sophistication of teachers to arouse emotions and control emotions are the tools for effective pedagogy. The teacher is the UCS for emotion. If he or she is cold, aloof, and dull, the classroom material, i.e., reading, chemistry, English grammar, will become the conditioned stimuli for dullness and apathy. The quick-tempered, defensive, verbally aggressive teacher arouses emotions characterized by fear and resentment. Children tend to "hate" the subject matter, the textbook, and the school, as well as the "mean" teacher. The effective teacher tries to arouse positive feelings of hope and love at the same time that he (or she) is presenting oral and written materials. Bugelski (1964) insists that if the teacher cannot make his student fall in love with the subject matter, he is not a teacher, no matter what his job is called.

The teacher's appearance, the sound of his voice, his semantic systems, the particular way in which he interacts with students, and his personality directly arouse the learned responses in the classroom. Our teacher training institutions should be aware that it is the personality of the teacher rather than his A+ average which determines effective learning in the classroom. Since the words the teacher uses, the concepts that are presented, and the information that is offered are all conditioned stimuli to hope or fear, the personality of the teacher must be recognized as the psychosocial determinant of academic achievement. Personality is not the only factor. Knowledge of the subject matter and skills of analyzing and synthesizing information, as well as creative concepts, are part of the makeup of the effective teacher. Without the warm, acceptable identification figure, however, the logical lesson plans, the "beautiful interpretations," and the superior scholastic ability will lose much of their effectiveness with deprived children.

Beyond the personality of the teacher, the two most successful tools in implementing change in the classroom are *dramatic presentation* and *role playing*. Both of these concepts have a great deal of common meaning, but there are important differences. In dramatic presentation, concrete-empirical props can be used to stimulate emotions as well as to describe and define difficult constructs at an abstract level. Children quickly get caught up in the living movement of dramatic episodes. There is the opportunity, at times, to identify with stimulus figures within the dramatic enactment. It can be an escape from the real world of poverty, neglect, and hopelessness. The cues of liveliness, enthusiasm, and hopeful expectancy are licensed at least temporarily in the dramatic presentation. The masterful teacher of advantaged or disadvantaged children knows how to use drama. Even the "good storyteller" uses the inflection of the voice, pauses, and facial expressions to dramatize an otherwise mere reporting of information in the words of a book. Dramatic presentation demands feelings, emotions, and personality.

Role playing offers an excellent opportunity to arouse emotions, for it allows an individual to live for a moment as if he were someone else in some other circumstance. In most cases with children, role playing is an unrehearsed dramatization pointed toward a specific behavioral objective. In classroom settings, children can role play and informally dramatize aggressiveness, politeness, dependence, independence, etc., as well as carry out roles of characters in stories, on television, and in purely imaginary situations. Emotions can shift with the change in character and setting. Focusing on feeling and emotion, children can extend their fantasies, their hopes, to levels never permitted in the dreariness and fear of their own real circumstances. Visiting kindergarten and primary classrooms, one can observe children going to the moon, flying the fastest airplane in the world, or being a famous baseball player.

EMOTIONAL CONDITIONING OF DISADVANTAGED CHILDREN

Children from deprived homes frequently give indications of fear and anxiety about learning cognitive tasks as well as a lack of hope in deferred-gratification goals. Threatened with an insecurity about tomorrow, next year, or when "they grow up," most economically deprived children search for immediate gratification, for the "here and now," for the tangible things they can see and put their hands on. Hope is not an easy emotion for deprived children to learn. Having so very little of essential needs and pleasures, children from disadvantaged homes find it difficult to rise above bodily needs and safety needs to acquire the self-fulfilling types of goals which are offered so profusely in our public schools as the real purpose of a good education. So frequently, failure to progress in economic standards and failure to obtain essential needs set the deprived child to failure in the classroom. Observing so much failure in their own parents and neighborhood just about stifles any hope in a child of being successful "by himself."

Teachers of disadvantaged children and adults have to be concerned about emotions. To put it epigrammatically, teachers must shift the students' feelings of fear and despair to those of hope and confidence. Children in deprived areas need hopeful adult models with whom they can identify. Teachers, therefore, who will be successful have to be hopeful, optimistic, and enthusiastic in expecting changes around disadvantaged youth. Deprived children observe enough hopelessness and defeat. The teacher who can cue off hope and success will provide the emotional conditioning necessary to accelerate scholastic achievement and a positive self-concept among deprived youth.

Taba and Elkins (1966), Torrance (1968), and a multitude of others have stressed the need for role playing and dramatization in teaching the disadvantaged. Since the limited experience of disadvantaged children has hindered flexibility and divergency in many of the children, it is important for those children to express their reactions to exciting stories in group diorama or in dramatic productions. Self-expression is developed, further, in the individual projections in painting and sculpting. The role playing in small-group procedures appears to be the most effective medium for discharging psychic energy and developing positive emotional strength.

Teachers can be trained to provide role playing in the classroom setting. Most colleges of education have relegated such training to mere "fun and games" without observing its powerful capabilities in the learning processes of children. Stimulating children to act like someone else permits them to have models which they can hope to be like. Torrance (1968), describing the creative-aesthetic approach (Fortson, 1968), places a "magic veil" over a child's head and encourages the child to go anyplace or even to be anybody (Figure 3-5). Within this dimension, emotional life can be explored and evaluated.

Another interesting way of teasing out varied affect in deprived youngsters (Torrance, 1968) is to consistently present the *incompleteness* of stories and of all types of information. There are many strategies that can be employed to stimulate children to ask as many questions as they possibly can, to look at the same thing from several different points of view, and to examine the anticipated and the unexpected. To make children believe that only the right answers should be sought stifles any concern for

FIGURE 3-5 *E. Paul Torrance helps children "become somebody else"
when they play under the magic veils.*

alternatives, for the unexpected, and for the creative solutions.
When children are able to risk taking the next step beyond what
is known, they grow in independence and deal with the possibles
instead of the here and now. The sociodrama, however, permits
the development of ego strength and the relationships with
others.

Teaching deprived youngsters will be much more fun and
much more effective if teachers are not so rigid about getting
answers to everything. This does not mean that the correct numerical solutions, the accepted grammatical constructions, and
logical thinking are not important. But they are not the only
things that are important. Unless deprived children can learn to
make attempts at solutions which are not under the threat of
failure, they will continue to show weaknesses in the scholastic
curriculum. Incomplete stories and information allow the child
to take a chance on an answer without being afraid of being
wrong.

CHANGING THE SELF-CONCEPT

Anyone who has worked with deprived children for any length of time gets caught up in the desire to do something about the inadequate feelings that these children have about themselves. It seems to be a unique phenomenon that the ghetto child is more likely to have a negative feeling of worth than the rural, isolated youngster. The economic factor is difficult to determine, but poor children in rural areas do not have as many mirrors of their deprivation. Ghetto children are constantly stimulated with the difference between the deprived and nondeprived. Many educators are quick to report the reading-level deficiency, the inability with signs and symbols, and the low achievement functioning of all deprived children. The disadvantaged are hampered by low IQs and almost nonexistent reading scores as well as "poor English" in oral language and "horrible" writing ability. A host of compensatory educational programs, together with an aroused citizenry, are focusing on how they can "raise the IQ," improve reading levels, and eliminate educational retardation. But very few programs teach the teacher to change the child's concept of self. It is assumed that if a child can score well on standardized achievement tests, show average reading ability, have an IQ of "over 100," and speak properly, his self-image will be adjusted. The emotional domain becomes a minor appendage to the cognitive demands. The alienation, self-rejection, and withdrawal behavior are left to psychologists. If the emotional domain is considered in any educational program, it is given little connection, or no connection, to learning processes. The disappointing factor in teacher training programs is that no structure or procedures are established for changing affect.

Teachers of the disadvantaged cannot be ignorant of base-line attempts to measure emotional needs as well as the tactics for changing affect, especially the concept of self.

The best tool for assessing the concept of self in the classroom is teacher observation. The self is an inference made from observable activity.

The best direction for teachers to take in changing the concept of self among deprived children is toward creating an atmosphere in which the strongest needs of the self are fulfilled. Certainly, needs vary from individual to individual. The different kinds of deprivation and the various levels of intensity of the deprivation contribute heavily to presence of those needs. There are basic needs, however, which are present in all humans. Maslow (1953) refers to the needs listed below as representative in human motivation, but he insists that motives have to be considered in a hierarchical order. Unless lower needs are met, the upper needs cannot be fulfilled.

6. Need for knowledge
5. Need for self-fulfillment
4. Need for self-esteem
3. Need for love and belongingness
2. Safety needs
1. Physiological needs

Followers of Maslow's theory about needs assert that in the education of the disadvantaged child, we must be careful lest we place upon children demands to achieve intellectually in school before their hunger for food has been satisfied. Consistently hungry children find it very difficult to focus on intellectually challenging tasks. If teachers and administrators desire to change the self-feelings of disadvantaged children, they will have to be very alert to basic needs and actually work at the task of fulfilling them in each child.

The *physical need* for an adequate diet is discussed in the next chapter, which deals with comprehensive services. At this point, emphasis is placed on the primary need of deprived children for physiological satisfaction before the teaching of signs, symbols, and relationships makes any sense.

The *need for security* seems to be powerfully incorporated in the *need for love*. For this reason, I want to point out to teachers just what is meant by the need for love. Very few teachers lack a strong love for their students, but teachers of deprived children must know how to react to the obvious psychosocial needs of most of their students. Each individual must learn *to give* and *to receive love*. Many teachers respond to their students with some manifestation of love, but the majority of teachers do not teach students to give love to their parents, teachers, and peers. Falsely, it is assumed that the question of love belongs in the home. If teachers assume that learning how to give and receive love is the responsibility of the parents and the home and if there is very little love in the home, sooner or later the child will have serious problems of adjustment and most likely will need special help because of such problems. Within school situations, love can best be thought of as a social responsibility (Glasser, 1969). Children must learn to help one another with a great many educational problems. Every child comes to school wanting to love someone and, at the same time, searching for someone who will love him. He will search until he finds peers who will accept him. Frequently, he will go outside the law, if necessary, to find someone who cares. Teachers should not expect children to love one another in the classroom as brothers and sisters in a family love one another. Nor will it help much if the love for others is merely "the polite thing to do." Children must be taught the value of social identity. There are many patients in mental hospitals who are there because they rejected dependency on any other person.

Schoolteachers probably understand more easily the basic need children have for self-esteem, i.e., to feel worthwhile. Self-worth appears to be highly related to the need for love and belongingness. In the need for self-worth, however, knowledge and the ability to think are essential components (Glasser, 1969). Success in school is required of all who will have an adequate concept of self. Teachers can improve the self-concept by presenting each student's new learning task as a small step from prior successful past events. Step by step, each child should be guided in his basic learning, being prevented from failure because of careless and illogical procedures. The important cue for teachers in changing the low self-concept of deprived children to more healthy feelings of self-worth is to help children understand that they are responsible for fulfilling their own needs. No teacher should assume that responsibility. Children must learn to take risks in the search for knowledge and to be responsible for their failures. Deprived children are fearful of taking academic risks.

Students from povertous areas must learn to deal with failure. Teachers can observe and discriminate the responses children make to classroom stimulation. Discussing with students the consequences of their responses in a nonthreatening way is the best vehicle for effecting positive change in the concept of self.

Glasser (1969) presented valuable descriptions of classroom meetings in which the teacher leads the entire class in a nonjudgmental discussion about what is relevant to their daily lives. The meetings are suggested as parts of the regular school curriculum. There are three directions in which these classroom meetings can take place: (1) social-problem-solving, (2) open-ended questions, and (3) educational-diagnostic concepts. Basic to all the meetings is the teacher's ability to deal with group processes. The feelings of others become a fundamental learning principle in the social interaction.

Although Glasser's (1969) meetings provide an excellent vehicle for therapy with the children, other models could be used to diagnose and modify the self-concept. The teacher can effect change in the self-feelings of her students with the same skills with which she changes her own feelings about herself.

OBSERVATIONAL LEARNING

Teachers should be informed about the many different ways in which children learn. It is as important to recognize the processes (styles, interaction, etc.) in learning as to know the content (English, mathematics, etc.) of subject matter. Identification is a concept that has been used increasingly during the last decade to interpret how one person learns from another. It refers to the "process that leads the child to think, feel, and behave as though the characteristics of another person or group of people belonged to him." (Mussen, Conger, & Kagen, 1969, pp. 356–357.) In teaching severely deprived children, teachers should be aware of the need for children to "incorporate" the behaviors of a model into their own lives. A great deal of the learning that goes on in the classroom can be explained by the exposure to the *stimulation of a model* and different *patterns of reinforcement*.

Stimulation by a model   A large amount of research supports the belief that children and adults learn much more easily by observing various types of models (White, 1969). Models who have prestige or competence and who have power over rewarding resources provide greater stimulation than those who do not have status or power. An interesting research example that explains the power of the model to determine the behavior of students is found in Grusec and Mischel (1966). Two different kinds of teachers were presented as models to nursery school children: (1) a highly rewarding adult model who had control over the "future resources" of the children, (2) a nonrewarding model who did not have control of "their future." The same woman served as the model for both experimental treatments. The model presented herself to the students as a new nursery school teacher (future control) or as a visiting teacher for one day (no future control). The measure of imitation, or identification, was how much each child remembered and imitated the female model when the model was absent.

Students in classes in which the model played the role of the new teacher (future control) were found to be more imitative and were able to reproduce significantly more of the teacher's behaviors than students in those classes in which the teacher was merely a *visitor* for the day. The "future control" or future power in the model appeared to be a powerful determiner of the social behavior in the classroom. There are many of us teachers who have been faced with the trials and tribulations of substituting in a classroom for one day. Not being familiar with the students and cognizant of only the general concepts in the prescribed lesson plans, a substitute teacher has to be dependent upon the students for a great deal of the cues in that particular classroom. Students are quick to note that the teacher is there "only for a day," and gauge their behavior on the transitory quality of her remarks. The stability of the image of the substitute teacher is so minimal that many students conceive it a holiday when there is a substitute in the classroom. The characteristics of the teacher as a model will determine much of the kind and number of responses that students make in the classroom and elsewhere.

Probably the "warm sociableness" of the teacher is the most important characteristic in bringing about strong identification with the teacher. The warmth that Mussen (1961), Ryans (1958; 1960), Sears (1954; 1963), and others have pointed up in their research is the major affective type of variable used in measuring the effectiveness of a teacher. It should be noted that children and adults perceive a particular teacher differently (White & Wash, 1966). Students who have a high need for social approval are likely to feel that warmth is the primary variable in a "good" teacher, while students with low affectional needs perceive the interesting, stimulating qualities of a teacher as more important. Warmth, however, seems to be the most consistent motivator of children in the general population. Warm, affectionate teachers tend to have pupils who not only like the teacher but have a very high regard for one another (Sears, 1963). The teacher is a high-status person and, like a parent, has a strong influence on the imitative behavior of children exposed to him. How many of us have regretted the uncontrolled expression, the derogatory statement, or the vulgar label in the presence of small children? The influence of the teacher in the imitative behavior of deprived children is heightened because of the frequent absence of one or more parents in the home, the probable large number of children in the home, and the discouragement and despair that prevail in economic deprivation.

The absence of the father from the home has been a critical variable in research with boys for many years (White, 1969). The personality of boys up to five years of age appears to be affected by the absence of the father from the home. Boys seem to need their fathers in order to imitate the masculine aggression trait so frequently attributed to males in our Western culture. Since primary-school and elementary-school boys are almost totally exposed to female models, one has to ask if the conflicts with boys in elementary classrooms is not generated by the lack of male identification figures.

Consequences to the model   What happens to the model has a powerful effect on what the learner does. It could be an effect that has been built up over a long period of time, e.g., great wealth, academic titles, or athletic prowess. A number of experiments have pointed to the influence of a prestigious model upon the learning of young children (Bandura & Walters, 1963).

The effect of consequences to the model can be exemplified in an experiment by Bandura and Kupers (1964) in which young children participated in a bowling game. An adult teacher (experimenter) rewarded himself by praising his own performance and taking candy when he exceeded a particular score in the game (20 points). If he failed to score the 20 points, he reprimanded himself. In another testing group, the teacher directed the same game but reinforced himself with candy and praise when he merely obtained a score of 10. Children in both groups watched the experimenter play the game and then participated in the bowling game. When the scores of the boys and girls were examined, it was easy to see that the children's pattern of reward matched extremely well with the way in which the experimenter had rewarded himself. The question of reinforcement is very strong in the Bandura and Kupers study, but there is sufficient demonstration that the consequences to the model affect those who are observing. If a teacher is rewarded by the principal, or if the teacher is successful in completing science experiments in the classroom laboratories, or if teachers are successful in putting on school plays, or in publishing the school newspaper, students who observe will be influenced by what happens to the model.

Characteristics of the learner   No one has to tell teachers that dependent children are more likely to imitate the teacher and do what they are told than children who are notably independent. There are many other characteristics of the student (observer) which have been reported to be associated with identifying with a teacher, e.g., the need for praise, incompetence, and the emotional condition of the learner, but the variable of dependency-independency has been more researched than any other. Especially with deprived children, the teacher needs to know a great deal about dependency and its impact on learning. Although his study did not involve disadvantaged youngsters, Ross (1966) investigated dependency behavior among fifty-two preschool children. Dependency was identified as behavior "seeking approval, attention, help, physical contact, and proximity." Two different kinds of learning were examined in the teaching situation: (1) intentional learning, which resulted from planned lessons that were stimulated by specific instructions, and (2) incidental

ch resulted from no specific training. An adult
ʌt twenty-six high-dependent and twenty-six low-
αϵᵨ   independent) children specific behaviors in the role
of a post office clerk (intentional learning) and yet carried on
other behavior that was not part of the instructions (incidental
learning) for the post office job. In the practice part of the study,
each child played the role of the post office clerk. Observers
recorded what each child actually did during his portrayal of the
post office official. Low-dependent (i.e., more independent) children showed a higher percentage of intentional learning and yet
very little incidental learning, while the highly dependent children imitated the teacher in both intentional and incidental behaviors.

When speaking about observational learning among pre-
schoolers, we must bear in mind that dependent children differ
from more independent children in what they learn. In general,
boys will be more independent than girls, but it will be the way
the children have learned to be independent in their homes
that will make the difference in the classroom. Deprived children have been recognized by every teacher as having a high
need for approval, attention, help, and physical contact. Perhaps
it is because they are frequently deprived of these psychological
supports in their homes. No matter how complicated it appears
to be, economically deprived children will be more dependent on
teacher models. There will be a much higher frequency of atten-
tion-getting tactics, desire to have physical contact, and need
for consistent reinforcement of intellectual activity among deprived populations. The teacher in classrooms of disadvantaged
groups is needed much more as a figure for identification than in
classrooms of more advantaged children. If disadvantaged students are more sensitive to the influence of their teachers,
greater responsibility is placed on teachers in classrooms of the
poor to provide better models for learning. When teachers of the
disadvantaged are ineffective, their impact is more threatening
to the deprived student than to the advantaged pupil. The unique
characteristic of higher dependency among deprived children
warns all of us to be better prepared in our attempts at teaching
the disadvantaged.

four

Elimination of deprivation effects only through comprehensive services

By *comprehensive services* is meant the nutritional, medical, dental, psychological, and social components of programs for deprived children. The basis for the comprehensive services is the fact that physical and psychological health is a determiner of learning processes just as much as classroom instruction and materials. School administrators, local school boards, teachers, and parents recognize that emotionally disturbed boys and girls cannot achieve in the classroom in the same way or at the same pace as well-adjusted youngsters. The serious problem exists formidably in helping poor children. There are many who serve in administrative positions or on school boards who are not committed to doing *more* for poor children than for the "regular" (advantaged) children in the school district. School systems are so frequently structured toward the taxpayers' sons and daughters that they lose sight of the needs of the poor. In many schools, the poor occupy such a large percentage of the population that revolutionary tactics are prohibited by the strain on the budget and the attitude in the community toward classroom teaching (of the "normal population").

It is a pitiful experience to enter some school districts and observe those classrooms in which severely deprived children have poorer equipment and fewer books and materials than regular classrooms, with a higher teacher/pupil ratio, e.g., 35 to 1. The striking impression on any fair-minded observer is that much more is needed than mere classroom instruction, e.g., reading series, audio-visual materials, and programmed materials. This does not mean that instructional materials and processes are not excellent approaches to learning, but there is much more to educating the poor than "good instruction."

Generally, when school officials are questioned about medical, dental, and nutritional services foor poor children, the response is that there is no money for those things. Why? The answer is quite obvious. Individuals responsible for the education of children in the community must have vision and attitudes that are broad enough to include all the essential needs in learning. Tax levies and budgets reflect the philosophy and attitudes of those individuals with respect to the various needs of children. When the economic deprivation and slum conditions of the youngster are said to be caused by the "bad" home or by the fact of being on welfare, it demonstrates that education merely means putting a teacher in front of a class with books and a chalkboard. Scientifically oriented individuals know that learning goes beyond that concept.

Teachers, parents, and administrators who believe that the teacher learning process with deprived children demands more services than it does with advantaged children must consistently work toward the enlightenment of the community about what really determines learning in a child. B. F. Skinner (1969, p. 23) stated it very well: "Teachers do not change minds, or therapists personalities: they change the worlds in which students and patients live."

NUTRITION

In order to provide the necessary physical resources for the learning process, an adequate food program must be developed. Inadequate diets are responsible for the large number of colds and diseases that are prevalent in the rural, isolated and urban ghetto communities. High absenteeism among deprived children is a complex variable, but it is indisputable that poor dietary conditions have a major part in their frequent absences from school. More noticeable than the high rate of absenteeism is the low vitality index, or fatigue level, that appears consistently among deprived children. Many teachers of the disadvantaged have been heard to say, "Those children just don't have the energy to do a full day's work in school." Lacking the proper diet, deprived children are not ready for the learning that teachers demand for school performance.

Many programs, e.g., Title I, Follow Through, Head Start, insist on a hot lunch each school day of the program and, generally, a morning and afternoon snack. There are many programs which serve breakfast to all children who want it. Indeed, a few inventive programs begin their school day with "breakfast with the teacher." Conversation with teachers and teacher aides is considered as essential as stimulation with books, language masters, and pencils. Since the children are starved for conversation, the need for interacting verbally with an adult model can be fulfilled in the lunchroom and the classroom. Advantaged children have more family conversation at mealtime than do children from deprived areas. However, the language and social skills of deprived children can be facilitated by interaction at breakfast and lunchtime.

Teachers trained in traditional modes might shudder at the thought of arriving at school to have breakfast with children who have yet to learn table manners, appreciation of various foods, and social relationships. A substantial number of teachers might be heard to say, "I was trained to teach children, not to waste time eating with them." It reflects an attitude that must be modified before any large-scale effectiveness among disadvantaged children can be accomplished.

Extensive research demonstrates the positive relationship between malnourished children and classroom underachievement. A teacher of deprived youngsters related a fascinating story about the sacrifices of a little girl who scraped all the food off her plate every day but did not drink her carton of milk at noon. She would hide it or desperately cling to it in order to bring it home to her sister, who did not come to school. The sacrifice for her sister was heroic. Observing or teaching youngsters with such love for one another and with such a dire need for food, one can have no doubt about the value of a nutritional and food program for the disadvantaged. It is always evident in deprived areas that many children on Monday mornings have not had a "good" meal since the Friday free lunch at school. Teachers and administrators who have taken time to observe one free lunch program for poor children have no difficulty in understanding the need. School attendance is immeasurably aided by a free lunch program. In Randolph County, Georgia, attendance in one school jumped from 600 to 800 when free lunches were offered. Another school, which had 75 absences a day on the average, showed a decrease to about 30 a day after a free lunch program was introduced.

Many schools have a minimum reduced-price lunch for about 15 cents. Others permit a child to pay even a penny for his lunch (Atlanta, Georgia). One of the reasons for this is to protect the self-image of the children. Being provided food "like other children" protects the self-worth of the disadvantaged child. Although the issue of nutrition is more important, the concern for self-concept of the disadvantaged youth is evinced in free lunch and snack programs. No child should have to come to school hungry. The starved, deprived youngster cannot feel safe and secure. His feeling of self-worth can never be adequate. Children who are deprived of food and water can never make choices about the highly cognitive responses in the classroom. They are too busy worrying about satisfying their hunger. No discussion of teaching the disadvantaged child should be made until the problem of nutritional deprivation has been resolved. Food first, and then what to teach can be argued and tested.

Learning in the cafeteria   Children who have a well-planned nutritional component in their school lives will learn about a variety of new foods and their labels, colors, and characteristics. Some programs use the cafeteria as a "classroom" for learning acceptable eating habits and also learning about other cultures and their eating customs. The gradual introduction of new textures, smells, and tastes can be associated with various types of people and locales in our own country as well as foreign countries. Consideration should be given to the cultural backgrounds of the children to maintain familiarity and attachment to their customary foods at home. At the same time, a broadening of concrete experiences of other cultures can be accomplished.

With disadvantaged children, teachers do not assume that facility with eating utensils has been learned at home. Frequently, children have developed minimal or no skills in table manners. More important than learning the proper use of the knife and fork, the conversation skills and attitudes at table provide the child with a vehicle for emotional outlet and cognitive stimulation. Children should be happy when they are eating. This attitude should generalize to the psychosocial concepts that become part of the discussion at meals. Teaching culinary as well as social skills should not be relegated to early-childhood programs. Eating habits become more complex as children get older. In a strong nutritional program, children can learn to prepare tables so that eating will be an inviting experience. Cleaning up after meals provides an opportunity for the development of social responsibility. Programs for older disadvantaged children can focus on the nutritional composition of food as well as on the various ways to prepare food.

PSYCHOLOGICAL SERVICES

The need for psychological services in the education of the disadvantaged is just as great for teachers as it is for the children. In one of the elementary schools in the Atlanta public school system, the student population of 85 percent white children shifted to 90 percent black children in one year's time. The black children in this instance represented the lower socioeconomic class in the Atlanta area. The teachers became frustrated because they just did not know how to handle the rapid change in class values and achievement. Such schools need a school psychologist to help teachers understand their children as well as help children understand themselves. It was interesting to note at that particular school how much better the teachers felt about their problems after an announcement that an intern in school psychology would be placed there in a matter of three weeks. Just as patients are known to feel better when they have been told "the doctor is on his way," these teachers felt much more hopeful when they learned that someone would share the burden of resolving behavioral problems.

In deprived or target-area schools, psychologists are primarily needed for two basic functions: (1) identification of learning abilities and disabilities, and (2) consultation with team members (parent workers, social workers, teachers, health workers, and administration) in resolving problems of the teacher learning process and of the individual student. Identification of the mental ability and achievement level in each child is extremely important, especially in early childhood. A frequently observed characteristic of deprived children is best described as "tremendous variance" of perceptual and cognitive skills. The range of convergent and divergent thinking skills is so great that teachers feel unable to cope with so many different levels of ability. Since there are so many deficits in language development, teachers are frustrated in knowing where to begin with each child. Teachers need feedback on each child, at the beginning of the school year and regularly throughout the entire scholastic period, to be able to cope with the erratic learning patterns of the disadvantaged learner.

The psychologist can assist in suggesting and administering standardized and teacher-made tests to assess the complex abilities of the deprived youngster. In many schools within advantaged areas, the Metropolitan Readiness Test is used as an index for discriminating various verbal and reasoning skills at the first-grade level. With deprived children, many more indices must be used to assess the same abilities. Frequently, in deprived classes all the children score below the raw score of 24 or the D range of the Metropolitan Readiness Test. Further discriminations are then required to note what specific abilities the deprived children do have. Merely to state that students failed the test is not stating very much. Tests which assess children's discriminations about shape, color, and form at lower levels would seem to be indicated. So few tests have been prepared for disadvantaged groups that special training in tests, measurement, and statistics is required. The interpretation of various abilities and levels can and should be provided to the teacher by the psychologist. Oftentimes teachers with a great deal of experience are very capable in the identification of cognitive skills in youngsters. Psychological service is needed, however, to support teachers in their appraisals and to extend base-line knowledge about each child.

Identification of emotional needs is perhaps even more important. Psychological service would be most helpful in the appraisal of each child's concept of self and his attitudes toward school, teachers, parents, and the home. Youngsters with disciplinary problems are not "bad kids," but are expressing symptoms of unmet needs. Teachers in disadvantaged areas desire and deserve the help of a psychologist in handling the emotionally disturbed student. Neurotic children need to substitute nonneurotic responses for neurotic responses to the stimuli that are causing them to display deviant behavior in class. The psychologist can assist in pinpointing the various stimuli which are causing the unacceptable behavior. Working with children in relearning their responses to life's experiences, psychological service personnel contribute to the real growth and development of deprived children.

The multidiscipline approach to each child's problem is the only sure way to help deprived children. Teachers should recognize that they cannot do it alone; psychologists know this, and sociologists are quick to recognize the need for other resources in effecting change. Therefore, validation of assessment from various sources in case studies protects the child from unitary theories and directions and provides a more confident approach to suggested plans for dealing with the children.

Continuous feedback on information to the teacher (information-systems approach) is the best guarantee of effective teaching with any child. Through an information-systems approach in education, an exchange of information about persons, situations, and materials is provided to various people in a school program.

The system has two or more parts, which are placed in a single interacting relationship. An analysis of information provides an interpretation of what is operating within the system. The purpose of a systems analysis is to reduce the many complex relationships of a program to a simple, logical classification of information.

Presently, very few schools have staffs adequate for systems planning and procedure. If they do, the information about the various aspects of the program is channeled back to an administrator or research department and stays there. One of the major advantages of the systems approach is that teachers and other instructional personnel are given information feedback in a meaningful way and rapidly. Many schools collect large amounts of data and publish something at the end of the school year or put the data in the school file for the coming year. If teachers can receive back quickly valid and reliable information from other professionals, in a language that can be understood by the teacher, instruction stands an excellent chance of being effective. A systems approach demands that teachers, psychologists, and administrators talk a common behavioral language. When a system is inaugurated, a particular mode of thinking is adopted and a common language is applied. Information about student performance and classroom activity is brought into an orderly, classified scheme, where it can be stored for future use but also can be retrieved rapidly at any given moment. Psychological services can provide an information-systems approach to the entire school and improve the ability of the teacher to change situations and materials for child growth. An information-retrieval system with a meaningful data bank that is periodically presented to the teacher will provide the scientific materials to close the gap between advantaged and disadvantaged children. When a continuous data system is generated by psychological services, evaluation of the program is much improved. Comparisons of information over time provide the indices of growth and development and the knowledge of whether there is success or failure in a program.

The psychologist's role, therefore, of defining criteria, building measures of expected behaviors with teachers, collecting information, analyzing the data, and interpreting the analysis to teachers and staff can be regarded as essential only to the education of deprived children.

SOCIAL SERVICES

Since the achievement level of children is so heavily dependent upon the conditions in the home, the education of deprived youngsters is most dependent upon improving the social situation at home. Most school systems which have a large percentage of deprived children under instruction have a difficult time raising the tax levy for a budget which merely puts a teacher in the classroom. Very few rural communities or smaller communities have been able to obtain a qualified social worker. They neither have the money nor could persuade such a professional person to risk financial security in coming to their communities. Since the demand for trained personnel far exceeds the present supply, some communities have been employing personnel who have some level of equivalency, e.g., a degree in sociology or experience in community action agencies. There must be some vehicle to close the gap between the home and school. The social situation, i.e., the home, community, and federal and state agencies, can no longer remain outside the goals, procedures, and funding of the education of our children. The autonomous, isolated school community, with its tunnel-visioned view of each child's welfare, is archaic and predictive of failure among disadvantaged groups.

The role of the social-work personnel in a school setting varies by reason of local resources and available funds, yet some functions seem fundamental. The social worker would:

1. Work as a team member in the identification of children who have social needs that interfere with classroom performance.
2. Maintain contact with social agencies, i.e., public health, family, and children's services, probation departments, and philanthropic agencies.
3. Continue follow-up on referrals to the social agencies, providing an information resource to all agents willing to help with the needs of the disadvantaged children and their families.

4. Initiate and support social services in the neighborhoods. One of the notable deficiencies among disadvantaged people is the lack of organizations with which the poor can identify, discuss their problems, and move the citizenry to action. Among advantaged (or more middle class groups), there are more agencies and services available because money can frequently call upon private and state-sponsored agencies to procure assistance for solving family problems and economic issues. Advantaged children have parents who will be involved in various community activities through club membership and political meetings. Advantaged parents know whom to ask and where to go for help with family problems. Middle-income families have more firmly established agencies with whom they can relate and to whom they can express their feelings about education, finance, jobs, and justice. Poor people, for the most part, lack these vehicles of public expression. Perhaps this is one of the best reasons why the poor resort to strikes and marches to gain public attention. Social-work personnel can assist in creating the organized and acceptable modes for meeting community needs.

5. Train and supervise paraprofessionals who can visit homes and help organize individuals in the community to do something for themselves. Although welfare and federal assistance are essential for deprived populations, individuals tend to become dependent upon the welfare allotment. Independence can best be learned through self-improvement efforts. Neighborhood organizations linked with the school can offer the encouragement to improve self, family, and community as well as reward those who demonstate such improvement.

Paraprofessional social workers can generate the enthusiasm and knowledge to upgrade the community. The Atlanta public schools system has developed a far-reaching program for paraprofessionals in the classroom and for parent workers (social service personnel). For the first sixty to ninety days of their training period, parent workers spend most of their time in the classroom learning about the curriculum and various teaching strategies. At the terminus of the training period, the parent workers begin working more fully with the home, yet maintaining a strong contact with the child and the classroom.

6. Promote maximum parental participation in the education of the children.

There are many individuals who insist on parents having a voice in decision-making processes of school matters. Many parents are demanding a greater say in school matters than merely voting for the members of a school board. The social worker can assist parents in developing a variety of ways of sharing in the changing behaviors of the children and of obtaining more parental decisions about life in a school. Numerous early-childhood programs have promoted a heavy parent-participation component; e.g., a pupil-parent-teacher Follow Through model has been advanced by the Southern Central Regional Educational Laboratory. Dr. Ira Gordon and his colleagues at the University of Florida have developed the Florida parent-education approach, in which two parent educators in the classroom try to bring about the powerful involvement of parents in the matters of school.

MEDICAL-DENTAL CARE

Wherever the value of Head Start is debated, no honest investigator denies the tremendous value of the medical and dental screening and treatment of poverty children that has been a criterion since the initiation of the Head Start program (1965). In general, it can be said that poor children do not have adequate health care unless some agency supplies the required medical-dental facilities.

Children must be big enough, strong enough, and in the proper physical and mental health for any significant learning to take place. There is only one way to identify healthy and sick children, namely to have qualified practitioners examine them. The form shown in Figure 4-1 is a model used by many Head Start and Follow Through personnel to identify specific medical variables. Treatment would follow from the diagnosis of the various indices represented. If a child receives the immunizations outlined in the form and the remainder of the examination, there is every confidence that the health of the child will be identified. Schools have firmly demanded immunizations prior to enrollment in school. If poor children do not have the financial means to obtain the immunizations from a private physician, most county public health agencies would supply the necessary medical treatment.

In children deprived of nutritional foods and teeth care for long periods of time, there is a phenomenally high incidence of caries and gum disease. Those teachers who work in rural, iso-

Budget Bureau No. 116-6605; Approval Expires August 31, 1967

CAP-HS Form 31
(6-1-67)

OFFICE OF ECONOMIC OPPORTUNITY
PROJECT HEAD START

MEDICAL/DENTAL INFORMATION
SUMMER

IDENTIFICATION

Grant No.	Center No.	Class No.	Child No.	OFFICE USE ONLY			
				a	b	c	d

1. Child's name	Last, first, middle initial, Jr., Sr., etc.

2. Child's address	Number and street or RFD

	City	County	State	ZIP code

	Month		Day		Year
3. Date of birth					

4. Sex of child	1 ☐ Male 2 ☐ Female

5. Is this child? *(Check one box on each line)*	**5a.** 1 ☐ White 2 ☐ Negro 3 ☐ Oriental 4 ☐ Other
	5b. 1 ☐ American Indian 2 ☐ Mexican American 3 ☐ Puerto Rican 4 ☐ Eskimo 5 ☐ Other

	Month		Day		Year
6. Date of this report					

MEDICAL/DENTAL HISTORY

7. How long since child visited a Doctor?	1 ☐ In the past 12 months 3 ☐ 2 or more years
	2 ☐ More than 1 year but less than 2 years 4 ☐ Never

8. How long since child visited a Dentist?	1 ☐ In the past 12 months 3 ☐ 2 or more years
	2 ☐ More than 1 year but less than 2 years 4 ☐ Never

IMMUNIZATION HISTORY

VACCINES	Received	Series status
9. DPT	**9a.** 1 ☐ Yes 2 ☐ No 3 ☐ Don't know	**9b.** 1 ☐ Complete 2 ☐ Incomplete 3 ☐ Uncertain
10. Polio	**10a.** 1 ☐ Yes 2 ☐ No 3 ☐ Don't know	**10b.** 1 ☐ Complete 2 ☐ Incomplete 3 ☐ Uncertain
11. Measles	**11a.** 1 ☐ Yes 2 ☐ No 3 ☐ Don't know	**11b.** 1 ☐ Complete 2 ☐ Incomplete 3 ☐ Uncertain
12. Previous smallpox vaccination received	1 ☐ Yes 2 ☐ No 3 ☐ Don't know	
13. Previous tuberculin test	**13a. Received** 1 ☐ Yes 2 ☐ No 3 ☐ Don't know	**13b. Results** 1 ☐ Positive 2 ☐ Negative 3 ☐ Don't know

FIGURE 4-1. *Medical-dental form used by Head Start during 1966–1967.*

lated communities or ghetto schools know very well that deprived children have poor teeth. The physical pain and the self-concept deterioration emerging from such poor dental health seriously impair classroom learning. An interesting letter from a dentist in South Carolina emphasizes the need for early dental treatment as well as the need for a dental health program for deprived children:

Donald C. Corbitt, D.D.S.
Gold Street
McCormick, S.C.   29835

February 17, 1969

G. M. A. Community Action
Box 707
Greenwood, South Carolina

Dear Mr. Pruitt:

I would like to call to your attention the following findings concerning this dental health program for these kindergarten Head Start children from the Plum Branch and McCormick area.

After comparing our dental records following completion of these fifty-three children I feel without a doubt this dental program has been extremely more beneficial than last year's regular Head Start dental work. This is why: practically all of these children were one year younger in age than the regular Head Start child. As a result these primary teeth we were able to restore. If we had not seen these children in this office at this age at this time, without a doubt I would have had to extract these teeth within six months to one year. Our records indicate that the ratio was five restorations to one extraction for these kindergarten children.

In comparison to last summer's Head Start program, the ratio was between five and six extractions to one filling. This is hard to believe, but this is what can be done if we can see these kiddies one year sooner. Extensive silver fillings in conjunction with primary steel crowns were used in restoring a lot of these badly decayed primary molar teeth that these children should retain until the age of ten to twelve. As a result, when these children reach the age for the regular Head Start program, it is going to be very interesting to find out that we will have very little dental work to do for them.

I sincerely hope you will mention our findings to the co-ordinated three county Head Start program.

Respectfully yours,

Dr. Donald C. Corbitt

DCC:ap

Enclosure

Teachers of disadvantaged children are always concerned about medical and dental care, but the question is: How can we do anything about it? There is no pat answer to this question, but two solutions are within reach: (1) Teachers can collaborate on writing for experimental program grants, e.g., Head Start and Follow Through. Most often, teachers think they are not qualified to write applications for special assistance from federal or state resources. The techniques and procedures can be learned. It is the motivation to help students that cannot be turned down. The persistent demand for deprived students will be rewarded. A visit to the state or federal Office of Education will supply information about what kind of grants have been given and what kinds of grants are available. Within this range, some assistance for deprived children can be found. (2) Medical assistance funds are often available through Title XIX, Medicaid, or through public welfare programs. Services are often supplied through public or private clinics, programs for crippled children, and school health programs.

Health education and counseling for children, parents, and teachers should be a necessary part of every curriculum. Teachers can bring about advances in health education by comparing what is being done in their school system with what could be done if professional effort were brought to bear on the problems of the disadvantaged.

five

Reduction of class size
and small-group processes

If any teacher in the primary or elementary grades is asked about the "best" number of students to teach, he (or she) will admit that he cannot do as good a job with thirty students as he can with twenty. No one knows the "best" teacher/pupil ratio, for what is most comfortable and efficient for one teacher is "just too many" for another. There are many educational psychologists who insist that the best teacher/pupil ratio is a 1 to 1 relationship. There does not seem to be much of an argument against the view of "one teacher for each pupil" except that it is economically impossible in the public school environment. The closest any school has come to implementing a 1-to-1 relationship is through programmed instruction and individual prescribed instruction. Through the utilization of programmed materials with behaviorally defined goals and procedures for each child, a few experimental programs in compensatory education have shown some gains for children. The closer we come to the private-tutor concept in our classroom dynamics, the more power we can provide in the instructional component of education. There is more to education, however, than instruction. The

teacher and peers are also the stimulus figures for imitative behavior. The teacher affects the students, and the students affect
the teacher. Teachers and peers become powerful models for all
kinds of behaviors. Above all, the teacher, or teachers, becomes
the emotional conditioner in the classroom. The effectiveness
with which the teacher can condition students to be hopeful,
joyful, and in love with school subjects is dependent upon the
size of the class.

The complexity of teacher-pupil relationships brings about
many influences upon the size of public school classrooms. In a
review of numerous studies of class size, McKeachie (1962)
found that statements about the benefits of large and small
classes were inconclusive. Basically, the number of variables
and the differences in criteria for judging effective learning make
comparisons very limited and discouraging. Four major factors
that determine the differences in class size are (1) purposes of
the class membership, (2) subject-matter content, (3) group
processes, and (4) money. The evidence is that if any school
district could pass a tax levy that would permit a reduction of
the teacher/pupil ratio, they would certainly do it. No matter
what section of the country one cares to examine, teachers and
administrators are displeased with their roles if they have thirty-
five or forty children in their classes. Usually, the primary
reason given for such a large teacher/pupil ratio is a lack of
funds, but it goes deeper than that. Lack of classroom space,
poor planning for future enrollments, and "yesterday's attitudes"
in the present-day board members and parents are also important
variables. Schools which have only one teacher for forty children
are just not in touch with modern pedagogy. When the public
does not want to put enough money into education to do an effective job, the teacher-pupil ratio is bound to be high. There are
other factors, however, which determine class size.

PURPOSE OF THE CLASS

The purpose for which a class has been assembled determines
what kind of a contact and how much contact there will be
between teacher and student and among students. The class can

have as many members as spectators in a football stadium, or it can be a simple, tutorial, 1-to-1 relationship. If the purpose of some group's gathering is merely to state facts or disseminate information, the size of the group can be relevant to being heard or, perhaps, even extended through the use of radio and television. Since many students are "taking courses" via television and teachers are receiving in-service training by television, the size of the class must include the numbers who learn by these means. As long as the students can hear the teacher (better still, if they can also see him), the teacher can "teach" facts, i.e., she can present an array of stimuli and test for proper responses to those stimuli. There are many skills—reading, oral language, writing, and listening—which cannot be taught in the same way one lectures to college students about scientific facts. Science laboratory exercises in junior and senior high school demand individual student attention. The teacher must be able to reach each child and, as often as necessary, meet the goals of each particular child. When the purpose of the class is to train young children in basic skills, a high-level type of interaction between teacher and student is required. At the same time, when information is presented via films and records or through drama in the school's auditorium, the lessons to be learned can be witnessed by a very large group. A varied experience in functioning in many different-size groups for different purposes should be an essential part of a child's preparation for life, but what kind of experiences are being taught will probably play an even greater role in determining the size of the class.

SUBECT-MATTER CONTENT

There is bound to be a great deal of overlap between the purposes of class membership and the subject matter of the class. Some kinds of subject matter appear to be more amenable to teacher-pupil interaction. There are many scholars who believe that all classroom subject matter has to be reassessed and taught with a high level of teacher-pupil interaction and adhere to the principle that the learner must be active. The learner who asks more questions and gives more answers should gain the most in the classroom. The student who gets more involved with the curriculum should learn much more. The content, or the curriculum, will determine how involved a student can become.

Reading demands a great deal of teacher-pupil and pupil-pupil interaction. Holmes and Singer (1964) identified 64 percent of the specific abilities that result in competent *reading* performance: knowledge of vocabulary in context, ability to understand verbal analogues, auding, and knowledge of vocabulary, in general. The common factor in all these specific abilities appears to be the use of language as a symbolic system. Verbal experience demands listeners and speakers, as well as readers. The content area of reading demands a high level of person-to-person contact, which can be accomplished effectively only by speaking and listening in relatively small groups.

The *social studies* curriculum area is too broad to be adequately covered by all students, so that a definitive verbal model is presented to the entire student body. There are, of course, many educators who would relegate social studies to a "sequence of facts" type of course and who estimate that a teacher could present those facts to a very large class. Other social studies subject matter would demand a small-group process with a high verbal interaction.

Social studies should emphasize important qualities of good leadership, intelligent selection of leaders and the choice of courses of action based on probable effects rather than an emotional appeal. To a tendency to be prejudiced toward people who are different or who may hold other points of view, the social studies should stress common characteristics of mankind, helping the pupil to understand why racial, cultural, and political differences exist. Feelings of inadequacy and exposure to peer rejection may be diminished in classrooms where the value and understanding of human dignity is developed by respecting the ability of all groups to contribute to society. [Strom, 1969, p. 51.]

SMALL-GROUP PROCESSES

It is very difficult to say whether teachers are working toward a group participation or toward a group cohesiveness when they direct their questions to a few members of the class. Frequently, teachers will ask the "class" for responses, but it is merely a procedure in which a small number of the "better" students respond. This does not mean necessarily that the teacher has her favorites and is carrying on a comfortable conversation with students she likes, but the question is always there. Unless there is an active participation by all members in the group, there is only a surface type of interaction. One of the serious drawbacks in using a modified Flanders interaction scale (White, 1969) for describing verbal interaction in a classroom is that a high-level interaction analysis of the class could mean merely that the teacher and a few students were doing all the interacting. Students who merely sit, look, and listen can learn, but student participation is the best evidence that a student is awake, aroused, and attentive to the learning situation. Students who are actively communicating by asking questions, commenting, responding correctly to the teacher's questions, and evaluating the dialogue in the classroom will stimulate a high level of achievement for the entire class.

The communication structure of the group determines how much learning is taking place. If disadvantaged children cannot communicate easily and frequently, they will never approach the gains of children who speak and are heard, nor will they have an adequate self-image in society. The major emphasis in teaching deprived children is on increasing the *communication index.* Miller (1957), speaking about the size of groups, insisted that as the number of members in a group increases, the number of interpersonal relations that must be maintained also increases. However, the opportunity that each has for keeping up with these relationships becomes correspondingly less. This is what happens in large classes. The teacher does not have the time to verbally interact with each child. But how large is too large? Certainly, the personality of a teacher and her enthusiastic energy must have a great deal to do with how much a teacher can verbally interact with her students. There must be some number, however, at which the majority of teachers would fail in the quantity and quality of verbal communication required for successful learning of skills. Is there a group size at which the frequency and kind of questions change significantly?

71113

ASKING QUESTIONS

Experimenting with a creative-aesthetic approach to readiness
levels in five-year-old children, Torrance (1969) investigated the
effect of group size on the quantity and quality of questions of
five-year-old children during a specified period of time. The mean
verbal-ability score, as measured by the Peabody Picture Vocabulary Test, was 102. Each of the test situations was preceded by a
warm-up exercise, and then the children were instructed in the
following way:

One way of finding out things is to ask questions. I am going to
show you a picture and I want you to think up all of the questions you
can about what is going on in the picture.

Your questions should be about things that you can't tell for sure
by looking at the picture. They should be about the things in the
picture, the people, and the things they are doing. I'll try to write
down your questions as fast as I can. [Torrance & Freeman, 1969,
p. 3.]

The stimulus pictures were colored by 12- by 14-inch prints of
Mother Goose rhymes. Ten minutes were allotted in each of four
periods, conducted over a four-week study. Children were assigned randomly to groups involving twenty-four, twelve, six,
and four members. The significant differences among the four
types of questions for each size of group are reported in Table 5-1.

Although the sample was small and there is difficulty in generalizing to varied kinds of populations, a very clear hypothesis

TABLE 5-1 *Number and Kinds of Questions in Different-size Groups*

Size of groups	Number of groups	Total quest.	Non-why quest.	Discrep. quest.	No. repeated
24	4	15.25	0.75	2.25	14.00
12	4	19.75	1.50	3.75	4.50
6	7	21.28	0.83	6.57	1.14
4	12	28.58	4.25	6.17	1.75
F-ratio		5.077	4.129	5.312	36.068
Level of significance		<0.01	<0.05	<0.01	<0.001

emerged from the Torrance and Freeman study: Group size has a significant effect on the number of different questions asked, the number of non-why questions, the number of discrepant-event questions, and the number of repeated questions. Four-member groups were observed to ask almost two times as many questions as twenty-four-member groups. As the group size diminished, children began to ask more questions. When examining Table 5-1, it should be noted that the number of repetitious questions declined significantly with the size of the group. About 48 percent of the verbal performance of the largest group (twenty-four members) consisted of questions that had already been asked. Only 5 percent of the questions were repeated in the six- and four-member groups. Torrance and Freeman indicated that the problems of inattention and short attention span among young children may be overcome by adopting small-group instruction. The regressive behavior which has been identified so frequently in large kindergarten and first-grade classrooms may be eliminated by reducing the class size, by working with teacher aides, and by using small-group strategies.

Since preprimary children are learning basic skills and beginning to achieve control over attention and delaying responses while another is talking, small-group instruction is of much more value in early-childhood programs than later on, in the upper grades of school. Especially with disadvantaged children who have greater need for learning verbal skills, the small-group processes seem to be extremely necessary. The small-group techniques are more applicable not only in comparison with larger groups but also in comparison with individual prescribed instruction. Torrance makes an interesting point when he says that the average number of questions asked by individuals from first to fifth grades during a ten-minute period is about ten. The mean for six- and four-member groups in the Torrance-Freeman study was between twenty-one and twenty-eight.

SPAN OF CONTROL IN THE CLASSROOM

In discussing what size groups work best in the classroom, it should be remembered that Bales (1950) reported that the optimum group size, for discussion purposes, seemed to be five members. In both two-man and four-man discussion groups, there is the difficulty that a deadlock in the solution of a problem might merely mean that the group would terminate all its activity and become ineffective. In a three-member group, there is the threat of two members "lining up" against a single individual. The fearful position of being alone "against the world" is certainly not very desirable. As many other investigators have recommended since the early days of Bales, the optimum number for a group membership for discussion seems to be about five. Above that number, the complexity of the group structure begins to restrict the participation of the members. When the group number is thirty or more, as in many of our public school classrooms, the group (above thirty) demands that the leader have great skills and a universal personality. In classrooms filled with economically deprived children, we have to ask a question about how large a subgroup a teacher can control physically and mentally. Deprived children are significantly different from advantaged children, and the span of control that the teacher maintains will be closely related to the characteristics of deprivation.

For a teacher, recording and keeping in mind which members have special skills, which students have specific linguistic deficits, or which students have emotional assets and which have emotional deficits becomes a formidable task. The span of control is extremely difficult for the teacher of any small group to maintain, but it is even more difficult among the disadvantaged. There are many teachers, parents, and politicians who have been reinforced so strongly in middle class values that they "think" that deprived children are a homogeneous group. In fact, we frequently hear the statement, "If you've seen one ghetto kid, you've seen 'em all." The debilitating characteristics of deprived children are so numerous that there is a tendency to classify and stereotype poor children into one kind of deprivation. Teachers who have taught the disadvantaged, and have not turned sour, know that the variance of skills, information, and emotional life in poor children is overwhelming. There are so many things in each individual deprived child that deserve special attention—varied health factors, varied linguistic measures, cognitive styles, and conceptual levels—that the mental book-keeping of deprived children is phenomenal.

Even if the complexity of the disadvantaged children were not enough, the limits of our perceptual abilities control the span of our thinking about people. Three perceptual limits which determine our cognitive span over groups has been well described by Miller (1956): span of attention, recognition, and memory.

Span of attention   Research has told us that it is very difficult for individuals to keep in mind seven or eight objects at a time. If seven or eight marbles are randomly placed on the floor, a quick glance will not provide enough attention to determine the exact number of marbles. As early as 1859, Sir William Hamilton claimed that an individual would find it difficult to view more than six or seven marbles at a single glance. Since that time we have found that the span of attention will vary with many aspects of the situation, e.g., the *duration* of glance, the *grouping* of items that are observed, the *familiarity* of the objects to the observer, and the *set* with which the observer comes to the task. If items are grouped, they can be recognized more easily and quickly than if the items are presented singularly and in isolation. The dots displayed in Figure 5-1 demonstrate the case in which twelve dots can be recognized as quickly as four dots since the dots are presented in groups of three.

There are some psychologists, however, who believe that we really cannot attend to more than one thing at the same time. Most of their opinions are based on experimental demonstrations similar to the following (Kimble & Garmezy, 1963): A light pressure is applied separately to one of the fingers of each hand. Simultaneously, a number of graphed lines are presented to the subject by means of a tachistoscope.* The subject is asked to report the number of lines and, at the same time, to indicate which pressure on his fingers was strongest. The interesting result of such testing is that when the trials are presented separately to the subject, the subject always discriminates correctly. When the tasks are presented together, subjects can do no

---

* *A device, somewhat like a projector, which presents stimuli for very quick, controllable periods of time.*

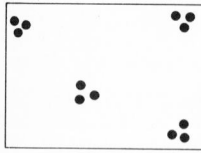

FIGURE 5-1 *An observer could recognize these twelve dots as quickly as he would be able to recognize four dots.*

better than respond correctly 12 percent of the time. The apparent conclusion is that we cannot attend to two different things simultaneously.

Span of absolute recognition   One of the interesting characteristics in all of us is that we can recognize only five or six values of a particular stimulus object, e.g., intensity of light, the noise the object makes, when a number of values are presented at the same time. Subjects will fail to recognize seven, eight, or nine values shown at the same time. Beyond the small number of recognized values in our perceptual systems, our cognitive span would limit our work with group formation and processes.

Span of immediate memory   Our memories have limitations which determine our control over auditory type of information in groups. When an adult is asked to repeat orally numbers in a sequence which have been verbally presented by an examiner, he will be able to recall about seven digits in the order given. The remembering of the sequence of a number of digits both forward and backward is widely used as a component on intelligence tests. Recently, we have learned more about the limits of the average man in handling different kinds of materials, but the span of memory remains about seven.

Immediate memory is limited by the number of items, not information; a word carries more information than a single letter but about seven of *either* can be learned simultaneously. . . . I have, therefore, distinguished between a *bit* (unit of information) and chunk (conjoined collection of bits). The span of immediate memory seems to be dependent on the number of chunks and almost independent of the number of bits in each chunk. [Milller, 1956.]

Selected strategies in learning or processing information in groups appear to be limited by our cognitive span. When we are confronted with large amounts of data or large groups, we try to organize the information in a way that "breaks it down" into small groups. Grouping, categorizing, synthesizing leave their special mark on our social behavior. It is natural for us to operate psychologically in small-group patterns.

ACHIEVEMENT OF SMALL VERSUS LARGER CLASSES

There are hundreds of school districts which have specially funded programs in which the teacher pupil ratio is reduced and small-group processes are implemented. Project Follow Through 1970–1971, for example, has 150 programs in the fifty United States. Almost every program has maintained less than twenty-five children in a class with teacher aides and curriculum specialists. Small-group procedures can be observed in every program which is adopting the Follow Through guidelines. Achievement gains are being reported in a host of early-childhood and elementary-school programs using small-group approaches, but many other variables share with small groups in determining those academic gains. It is very difficult to isolate the effect of small groups upon classroom achievement since teacher aides and special curriculum materials and reading specialists are also contributing to the success of the children in the classroom. Experimentally, a number of changes are being made in the traditional classroom, in an attempt to make an impact on the performance of deprived children. The research design of the programs has not been sufficient to sort out the separate influences of the many factors that are essential components in the program.

In Rochester, New York, the city school district adopted (1963) a policy statement committing its future actions to the reduction of racial imbalance in their schools. By 1967, a fifteen-point plan was implemented in the schools which had as its goal the reduction of racial isolation and the provision of quality integrated education for all children. At Nathaniel Rochester School No. 3, class size was reduced sharply to fifteen children. In addition, a teacher aide, living in the immediate area, was employed for each classroom. A full-time specialist in reading instruction was added to the staff at No. 3. The Rochester school system compared the achievement of children from kindergarten to the third grade in school No. 3 with the achievement of students at the same levels in schools No. 2 and No. 4, which maintained a class size of twenty-five. School No. 2 did not have teacher aides or curriculum specialists; the teacher/pupil ratio was, therefore, 25 to 1. Results of the analysis (Rock et al., 1968, pp. 21–22) are summarized below:

Kindergarten　　The two groups did not differ significantly on any of the three measures (Peabody Picture Vocabulary Test, Perceptual Copy Form Test, and Goodenough Draw-A-Man Test) used at this level.

Grade one　　School No. 3 pupils were compared, first, with school No. 2 pupils and, second, with school No. 4 pupils on the four tests in the Metropolitan Primary I battery. For the first comparison, school No. 2 pupils did significantly better in reading while school No. 3 pupils did significantly better in arithmetic. When school No. 3 pupils scored higher on word knowledge, word discrimination, and arithmetic, school No. 4 did better in reading.

Grade two　　At this level, the difference between the two groups was significant for three of the comparisons involving the five Metropolitan Primary II tests. The differences in word discrimination and reading favored the school No. 3 pupils, while school No. 2 pupils scored higher in arithmetic.

Grade three　　The achievement of the school No. 2 and school No. 3 pupils on the two New York State tests (reading and arithmetic) was not significantly different. When school No. 3 pupils were compared with school No. 4 pupils, the school No. 3 pupils had a significantly higher mean score in reading.

Of a total of twenty cognitive-type comparisons between students in school No. 3 and students at schools No. 2 and No. 4, ten cognitive variables were found to be significantly different. Seven of those differences were in the direction of the students at No.

TABLE 5-2 *Summary of Differences between Schools No. 3 and No. 4*

		Group	
Name of test	Test date	School No. 3 mean raw score (87 pupils)	School No. 4 mean raw score (75 pupils)
Metropolitan			
Word knowl.	May 1968*	18.3	15.9
Word discrim.	May 1968†	19.5	17.1
Reading	May 1968†	16.4	18.6
Arith.	May 1968*	37.5	32.8
New York State			
Readiness	Oct. 1967	40.2	45.8

* Difference significant at 0.01.
† Difference significant at 0.05.

3 school. The most striking changes seemed to be at the first-grade level. Table 5-2 summarizes the differences between school Nos. 3 and 4 on the Metropolitan Achievement Test (Primary I) and the New York State Readiness Test. Information described in Table 5-2 does not "prove" the case that small-group processes are more effective in establishing achievement levels than larger groups. The small numbers in the study ($N = 162$) do not permit generalizing to large populations and to other geographic areas. Studies of this kind, however, support the hypothesis that small class sizes and small-group processes are bringing about changes in teaching strategies that are causing better performances on standardized achievement tests.

SMALL-GROUP PROCESSES AND THINKING CHANGES

There appear to be a large number of early-childhood attempts to creatively group children for the high teacher-pupil interaction that brings about changes in concept formation and cognitive styles of the children. Studies of the language development of disadvantaged children consistently show that deprived children are verbally underdeveloped. Even though the deprived child comprehends more than he communicates, it is a universal characteristic that he is verbally deficient. The use of language is basic to the development of thought. The cognitive development of a deprived child is slowed down by his difficulty in attaching labels to objects and people and by his difficulty with the grammatical structure of the language taught in the school. The early experience of children in disadvantaged areas shows a lack of word-object reinforcement and a failure to develop a stable learning style, or set. Overcoming the deficit of disadvantaged children involves establishing a system by which those children can quickly gain word-object stability and a pattern of solving problems. One of the recent attempts to improve the thinking and verbalization of young children is by Dr. Lassar Gotkin, senior research associate at the Institute for Developmental Studies, New York University, who has been changing the thinking patterns of deprived children through the use of games. Gotkin insists, however, "We play games, but we don't fool around." The format of games provides the motivational force as well as a system of reinforcement for learned behavior in the classroom. The format of games also lends itself extremely well to small-group interactions. The development of matrix games, language lotto, card games, puzzle games, and Listen-Mark-and-Say has provided the major impetus for using the kinds of games and the modality in which learning is emphasized (Figure 5-2). The matrix games are carefully sequenced sets of pictures and instructions to be used with small groups of young children in order to give them systematic practice in language concepts and oral expression. The lessons range from ten to thirty-minute periods, depending on the content of the matrices and the length of the span of attention of children on a particular day.

Imagine five or six children sitting on the floor with a teacher, teacher aide, or parent. There are other children in the classroom; they are grouped but are busy with other activities. In the small group, a child is talking while the teacher and the remaining members of the group are raising their hands to answer a question or are just sitting, looking and listening. It is very likely that you would hear the question, "What's the same in all the pictures in this column?" or, "What can you tell me about these pictures?" Some child will be heard to say, "They are all walking a dog" or "They are all riding a horse." The child who is playing

FIGURE 5-2 *Principals and teachers in the Atlanta school system play the matrix game.*

a teacher's role may say, "Who's riding on a horse?" The child who is responding will say, "A man, a boy, a girl, a woman; they are all riding on a horse." The child playing the teacher role might say, "That's right; very good. Now I want to ask another question." The children are generalizing and dealing with abstractions. Thinking patterns are shifting from the simple to the complex, from the concrete to the abstract, from singular to multiple directions, and games involving absurdities are introducing complicated learning problems. Children are giving directions, correcting errors, and solving problems at a much higher level of mental processing. All the while, there is an intensive interaction of language. As the development of the language increases, conceptual formation is strengthened. Children are freed from simple sets in responding to reflective types of problem solving and in questioning. The search for alternatives broadens the scope of the possible solutions and brings about divergent types of behavior.

In the Atlanta public schools, kindergarten and first-grade

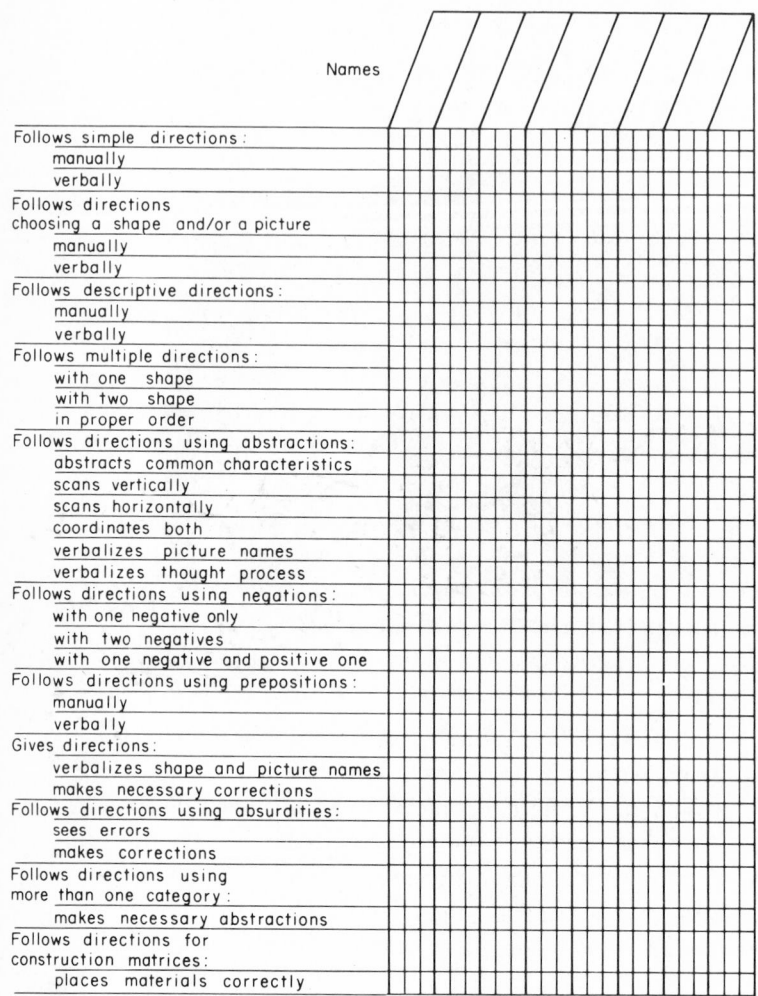

FIGURE 5-3 *Checklist of components in the Matrix Games published by Appleton-Century-Crofts for Dr. Lassar Gotkin.*

children who are economically deprived are playing games using abstractions. The majority of kindergarten children complete the concept attainment described in Figure 5-3 by eight weeks of school. All 225 children in the Follow Through program fulfilled the criteria of the matrix games at the end of the school year. Other games (e.g., card games) build on the verbal and conceptual processes obtained in the matrix games. The high verbal interaction is the secret to the matrix games played in small groups of young children (about five or six). Thinking patterns are derived and reinforced. The verbal communication among members of the small group controls attention, reduces anxiety, and provides participation of *every* learner. Thinking patterns are controlled somewhat by the sequence of the various skills suggested in the game checklist. Individual differences can be observed in the speed with which criteria are fulfilled and also in the steps taken toward building matrices and becoming an independent learner. The end result of the games is to make a learner independent in the use of words and the ability to think.

One of the most fascinating approaches to small-group processes has been defined by Gotkin's games. If teachers of the disadvantaged are willing to become childlike and play games with children, thinking patterns and verbal skills can be mastered by those deprived children. So frequently, teachers establish all the rules, all the concepts, and all the words. When everything is established, there is no freedom for anything but the dependent behavior prescribed by the teacher's values. When teachers sit on the floor and play games (in small groups), they cross the chasm into the child's world and observe each child's use of words and his strategy of solving problems. Shifting from the teacher-stimulus to the peer-stimulus type of instruction, children will be free to be independent and yet play according to the rules of the game. As can be quickly observed in matrix games, children interact more frequently and use a greater number of words and more varied kinds of words when playing games. The school world of the child becomes happy and easier to comprehend when he attends to programmed materials in a game circumstance. If the teacher is willing to play the role of a child for thirty minutes a day and is willing to share in the child's world through games, deprived children will find easier the transition to the adult world, with its demand of verbal and thinking skills.

six
Measurement of social behavior

In most preservice training courses for teachers, serious attention is given to the measurement of social interaction in the classroom. General knowledge about the sociogram (Moreno, 1934) is just as familiar to teachers who received their certificates in the late 1960s as it was to those who have been teaching for a number of years. There is a recent trend, however, in colleges of education to focus not only on sociograms but also upon relatively recent measures of social life in the classroom, such as interaction analysis, syntality, and multidimensional scaling techniques (White, 1969). It has been sufficiently established in preceding chapters that teachers of disadvantaged children must become more concerned with emotional, attitudinal, and interest dimensions of those children than in classrooms of advantaged children. The heavy emphasis upon cognitive factors observed in schools for deprived children continues to bring about failure and despair in the children and disappointment with teachers. The self-concept of each child and his perception of his teacher and peers ought to be the primary objects of teaching plans in classes where the children are severely deprived of early stimulation.

This does not mean that scholastic achievement levels and the acquisition of verbal skills are not important, but they should consume the teacher with such dedicated zeal that grades, achievement scores, and reading levels are the only things that matter. Teachers of deprived children must recognize that their primary function is to condition the emotions of each child so that a positive self-image emerges and develops. Conditioning the socioemotional lives of children toward positive, healthy goals demands that the climate of the classroom reflect social adjustment.

Teachers in ghetto areas and rural, isolated communities want to know how to identify and modify person-to-person relationships in the classroom. Above all, teachers are continually presenting some kind of simple applied social psychology to their students so that children in their classrooms will have a working knowledge of their social growth. The information and the attitude that are emphasized in this chapter is that student behavior rarely proceeds without a reference to other persons, i.e., to parents, teachers, and peers. It is difficult to think of any individual student's activity that does not have some social impact and that, at the same time, does not cause feedback from the group to the individual's behavior. Teachers must know about the psychology of group dynamics and must work with the personal-social characteristics of groups. To teach effectively in small-group processes, teachers must be familiar with the measurement of social behavior.

Psychologists and teachers are convinced that positive classroom social climate facilitates the mental health of students and their classroom learning. When pupils show high respect for one another, they provide the best chance of helping each other with intellectual tasks.

INFORMAL SOCIAL STRUCTURE AND THE SOCIOGRAM

Informal social structure involves the ways in which each member relates to others. An informal characteristic of classroom groups is the pattern of students' preferences for one another. The sociogram, which was devised by Moreno in 1934, has become the most popular method for teachers in measuring the interpersonal dynamics of a classroom. The sociogram is not so much a test as it is a method by which each member of a group selects the names of other members of the group based on a criterion requested by the teacher or by a social scientist. The criterion is usually stated in a format such as the following:

Name three persons you would like to have work with you on a science project.
Name the three persons who would be the most fun to play with after school.
List the three boys (or girls) whom you consider to be your best friends.

When the teacher has collected all the responses, he begins an analysis by constructing a diagram in which the subjects are designated by numbers and figures and the choices by lines with arrows. The clearest and simplest way is to have triangles represent boys and squares represent girls. As presented in Figure 6-1, a relatively small class of fifteen students can be identified by numbered circles and triangles. The elements of group cohesiveness can be graphically observed. The popularity or intensivity of friendship is represented by the shading of light to dark. Sociograms such as that in Figure 6-1 allow teachers to analyze the patterns of group organization, to identify isolates, cliques, and cleavages. The informal patterns of social acceptance are graphically described, and patterns of rejections are suggested by a lack of selection by students. In studies of classroom structure, Schmuck (1966) found that peer groups with a wide sociometric dispersion, compared with groups with concentration of choices, had more cohesiveness and supportive norms concerning educational goals. Moreno (1934) used a formula of isolates, mutuals, and unreciprocated choices as the measure of group cohesion. Every experienced teacher recognizes the need for a class to function as a cohesive unit, i.e., to work together as a unit. Various measures of cohesiveness have been reported for more than two decades. Some investigators have tried to measure the desire of classroom members to "stick together" as the criterion of cohesiveness. Others have referred to the number of

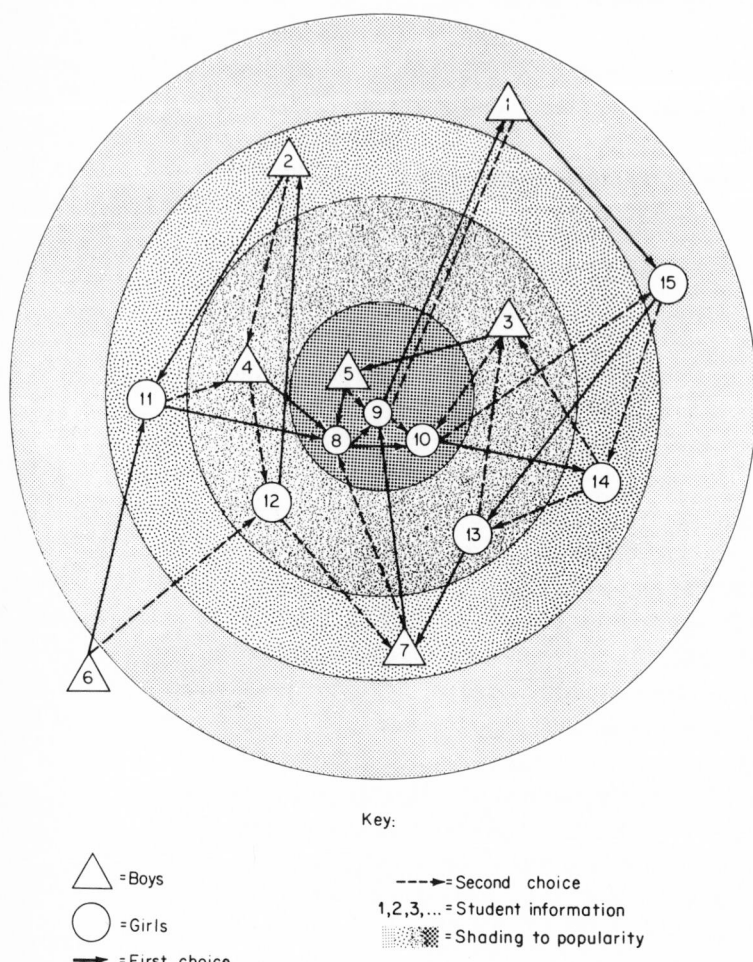

Key:

△ = Boys   ---►= Second choice

◯ = Girls   1,2,3,... = Student information

──► = First choice   ▓ = Shading to popularity

FIGURE 6-1   *Sociogram of first and second choices for a class of fifteen children.*

"we" remarks used in interview situations compared with the frequency with which the pronoun "I" was heard in the dialogue with examiners. Sometimes group productivity has been used as an index of "working together," especially by those who want to infer a high degree of friendship as a prerequisite for group productivity. Just as many psychologists have been interested in the cohesiveness of groups, numerous teachers have been interested in defining the elusive variable called the *cooperative classroom*. A recent advancement in the measurement of meaning has opened the door to the measurement of the affective (feeling) component of dimensions of classrooms.

AFFECTIVE-MEANING SYSTEM

Osgood (1952) and Osgood, Suci, and Tannenbaum stimulated an avalanche of studies (Snider & Osgood, 1969) dealing with the connotative aspect of meaning, i.e., with the meaning of words that arouse feeling rather than merely presenting abstract symbols. Osgood and many others have used the semantic differential as a way of measuring aspects of meaning attributed to person or thing concepts. The semantic differential is essentially a simple method of presenting a number of associations together with a scaling procedure for measuring certain concepts. Each subject is given a concept to differentiate, e.g., *car, money,* or *mother,* and a set of bipolar adjectives with which to do it. The only task is to indicate the direction of his associations (feelings) and their intensity about that concept on a five- or seven-point scale. Figure 6-2 represents the concept *my teacher* with scales to help the student rate his feelings about his teacher. The real value of the scale is to differentiate the feelings (direction and

FIGURE 6-2 *A semantic differential scale of the concept of "my teacher" with twelve bipolar adjectives.*

(My teacher)

LARGE	___:___:___:___:___:___:___:	SMALL
UNPLEASANT	___:___:___:___:___:___:___:	PLEASANT
FAST	___:___:___:___:___:___:___:	SLOW
DULL	___:___:___:___:___:___:___:	SHARP
THIN	___:___:___:___:___:___:___:	THICK
HAPPY	___:___:___:___:___:___:___:	SAD
WEAK	___:___:___:___:___:___:___:	STRONG
GOOD	___:___:___:___:___:___:___:	BAD
MOVING	___:___:___:___:___:___:___:	STILL
UNFAIR	___:___:___:___:___:___:___:	FAIR
NOT ACTIVE	___:___:___:___:___:___:___:	ACTIVE
HEAVY	___:___:___:___:___:___:___:	LIGHT

intensity) about the particular concept. Starting from the center of each scale (meaningless) and moving in both directions, the subject quantifies his judgment by "slightly," "quite," and "extremely" points on the scale. If the student places an X in the center of each scale, the response pattern of the student does not indicate very much. Thus, the objective is to obtain a free and open response along the continuum of each scale in judging each concept. Adjectives are descriptive terms by definition and tease out the semantic difference by which we place limits around, or define, any concept. A real problem has occurred over the past twelve years (Snider & Osgood, 1969) in selecting the appropriate adjectives to use with specific populations for measuring more common concepts. Are the same adjectives applicable for eight- and nine-year-old children as for college students (Di Vesta, 1966)? Are the semantic systems of young deprived black children the same as those found among more advantaged white children (Entwisle & Greenberger, 1968)?

It appears that the connotative meaning systems of children and adults are significantly different, no matter what the race, but can be explained in terms of three major factors: *evaluation, potency,* and *activity* (Table 6-1). No matter how many bipolar adjectives are used to describe a single concept, a factor analysis

TABLE 6-1 *Factor Loadings in the Concept of the "Disadvantaged Child" from Semantic Differential Ratings of 1,200 Teachers*

	Factor loadings*			
Items	*Evaluation*	*Potency*	*Activity*	h^2
Large–small		0.77		0.60
Unpleasant–pleasant	0.79			0.67
Fast–slow			−0.69	0.55
Dull–sharp	0.63		0.39	0.56
Thin–thick		−0.81		0.66
Happy–sad	−0.67			0.52
Weak–thin		−0.44	0.60	0.59
Good–bad	−0.81			0.67
Moving–still			0.66	0.44
Unfair–fair	0.75			0.57
Not active–active			0.71	0.56
Heavy–light		0.85		0.73

* Only loadings above 0.30 or −0.30 are included.

of the responses will reveal that more than 50 percent of the variance will be attributed to the evaluation, potency, and activity factors. Of course, this means that 35, 40, or 45 percent of the total variance remains accounted for. Since the individual contribution of each of the factors other than evaluation, potency, and activity is extremely small (2 or 3 percent), the number of the remaining factors is probably very large but the influence of each factor is minimal. For our purposes in this chapter, it is sufficient to emphasize the relative stability of three general factors of semantic meaning. These three general semantic dimensions provide us with a means of describing the sociometry of the classroom.

SOCIAL CLIMATE OR THE CLUSTERING OF CONCEPTS IN THE CLASSROOM

It can be verified by more than 1,600 studies (Snider & Osgood, 1969) that the semantic differential is a reliable instrument for measuring a very limited aspect of affective meaning about person or thing concepts. Suppose we are interested, now, in measuring the feeling components that twenty members of a class have for one another. Student names of the entire class are placed in three columns on the blackboard, in a random order. Each student finds his name and rates on the semantic differential the six or seven names of peer concepts found in the column with his name. When the student comes to his own name, he writes *self* and rates the self-concept. All responses are factor-analyzed by the principal-components solution, and the rotated factor scores are used for an analysis. If we can picture a general semantic space, a region of some unknown dimensionality and euclidean in character, let us place those twenty person concepts in semantic space by taking the midpoint of the three factor scores on the evaluation, potency, and activity dimensions for each concept (Rentz and Olson, 1968). The plots in semantic space will have a graphic representation similar to the design in Figure 6-3. The distance between each concept can be measured in a number of ways. When these distances have been determined, the relative location of each group member can be described and the relational structure of the particular group can

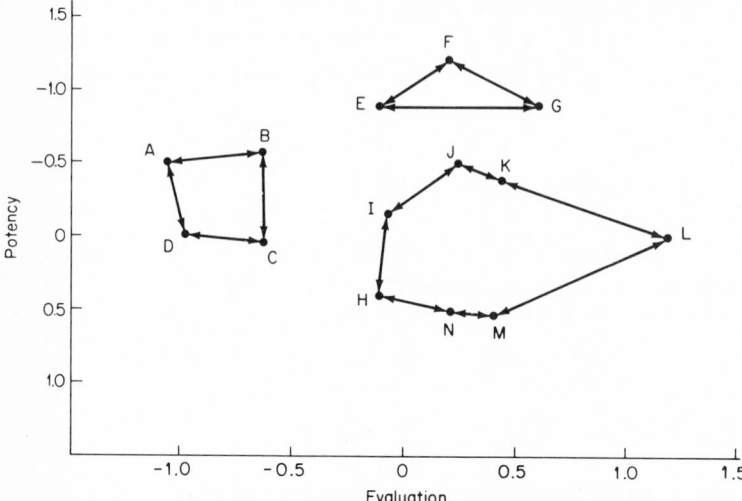

FIGURE 6-3 *Spatial plots and social distance markers for members of a twelve-man group.*

be graphically presented. The geometric distance between student A and student B or between student A and student N can be called the *social distance* between and among students. Clusters of person-concept groups, i.e., the size of the group and its cohesive strength, have been described recently (Rentz, 1969). Such a technique, as presented in the *multidimensional interrelational affective model,* offers us the means for assessing the cliques, the groups, and the social relationships in the classroom.

Not all questions about classroom groups are answered by the multidimensional interrelational affective model, but it lays the foundation for measuring the feelings that group members perceive in one another. Once the connotative meaning that members perceive in the name of a peer member is defined, teachers and psychologists can begin to investigate why certain members cluster more closely to some members than to others. The affective map of a group's feelings about its members can be drawn more logically and validly than ever before in sociometrics.

Rentz's model of affective relationships (Figure 6-4) cannot be applied very easily by the average teacher of disadvantaged

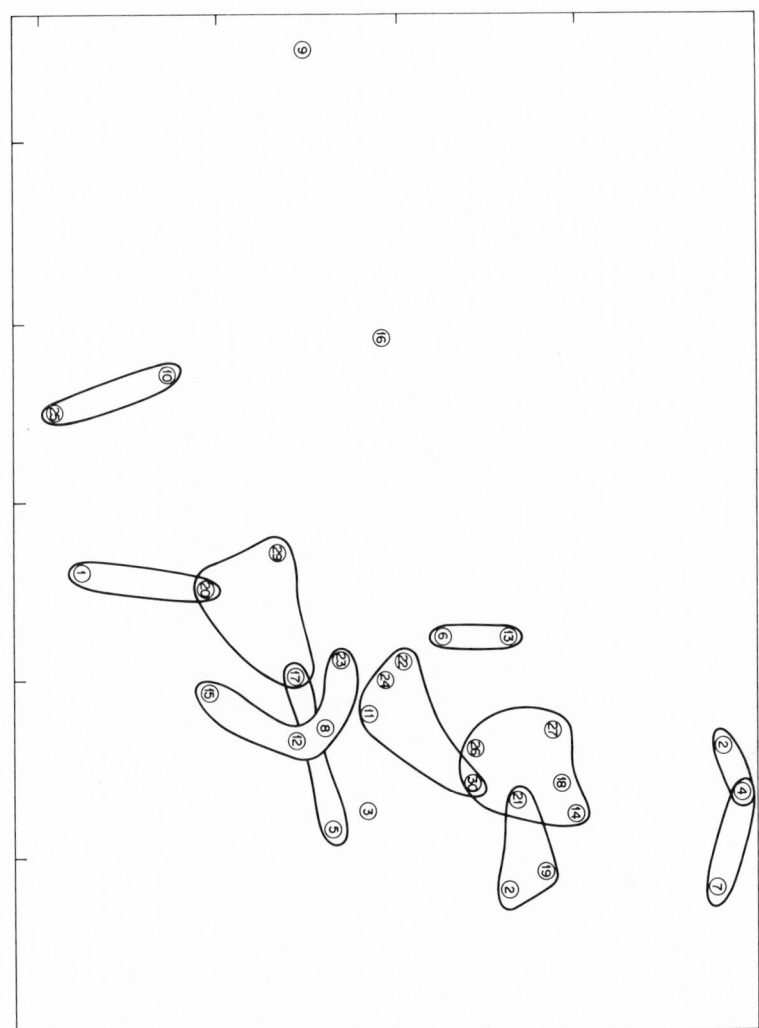

FIGURE 6-4   *A two-dimensional projection of a reading institute group structure based on the multidimensional interrelational affective model. (Permission by R. R. Rentz, Multidimensional interrelational affective model, unpublished doctoral dissertation, University of Georgia, 1969, p. 75.)*

students. First, a knowledge about factor analysis is fundamental in obtaining the three semantic factors of evaluation, potency, and activity. Secondly, access to computer facilities is almost essential in handling the quantity of data and the higher level of statistics. The clustering of the person concepts in Figure 6-4 is quite abstract at this time. The numbers represent the thirty persons who are grouped by reason of the feelings each member has for another. Subjects 9 and 18 are isolates, who are quite distant from the social acceptance of the thirty-man classroom group. The most powerful group of students by reason of cohesive strength seems to be the unit with members 26, 30, 21, 14, 18, and 27. It should be noted that student 30 and student 21 are also "locked into" other groups, which communicate with some attitudinal similarity.

At the present level of development, the multidimensional interrelational affective model offers a better way of dealing with emotional identification than do the older sociometric devices. The teacher who is advanced in measurement techniques and the school psychologist can begin examining why certain groups and subgroups cluster in semantic meaning. The practical, everyday use of Rentz's model is not immediately perceptible, but the way is cleared to do something worthwhile with the difficult dimension of affect in classrooms of advantaged and disadvantaged children.

Not only will the next five years reveal the clustering of groups of disadvantaged as well as advantaged children, but the motives and patterns of disadvantaged subgroups will be hypothesized and tested. The defensiveness and the striving for security will clearly be examined during the next decade when small-group processes in the classroom will be the primary focus and responsibility of teachers.

TEACHER PERCEPTION OF STUDENTS' BEHAVIOR

The teacher's information and feelings about the personal social behavior of students in his classes are indispensable in any attempt to describe the sociometry of classrooms. Teachers spend so much time in the classroom, observing, judging, and reporting the specific abilities of children, that their judgment is accurate and most valuable. The problem in talking with teachers about critical behaviors of students is one of semantics, i.e., the vocabulary used to describe behavior. Standardized tests that have built some substantial norms and have shown some relatively high reliability coefficients assist greatly in communicating with teachers about the methods and words used in describing classroom behavior. There are a few scales which have been used in measuring social relationships in the classrooms of disadvantaged learners, even though these scales were not built merely to define limits among deprived children.

The *Vineland Social Maturity Scale* (VSMS) was devised in 1935 by E. A. Doll but was revised in 1953. It is generally described as a developmental individual scale concerned with measuring an examinee's ability to accept responsibility and look after his practical needs. The test may be used in assessing infants and adults, but the instrument seems to be more successful for younger children. Since the child being rated does not have to be present or respond verbally, the scale seems appropriate for measuring deprived children at the convenience of the teacher. There are 117 items in the test, grouped to reflect progressive maturation and adjustment to the child's environment. All items can be grouped into eight basic categories: general self-help, self-help in eating, self-help in dressing, self-directions, occupation, communication, locomotion, and socialization.

The social behavior scores for the subjects measured by the VSMS can be correlated with intelligence test scores and are generally quite impressive ($r = 0.80$). The Vineland scale yields a *social age,* which is divided by the chronological age to give a *social quotient.* Since the test has been used with many different populations over many years, teachers of disadvantaged children should find this one of the more valid ways of getting a total social competence of their students.

Kim, Anderson, and Bashaw (1968) developed a *Child Behavior Scale* (CBS) based mainly on sixty-six items from the Vineland Social Maturity Scale and Pechstein and Munn's Rating Scale of Social Maturity. The CBS appeared to be quite applicable in the study of social maturity among white and black second-graders. Three fairly independent factors identified the dimensions of social maturity in a particular study of second graders: (1) academic behavior, (2) interpersonal behavior, and (3) emotional behavior. Table 6-2 shows the factor structure of social

TABLE 6-2 *The Factor Structure of Social Maturity for Academic, Interpersonal, and Emotional Behavior of Negro Children**

	Factors†			
Items	*Academic*	*Interpersonal*	*Emotional*	*Communalities*
1. He can work alone for a period of time.	751	375	265	775
2. He returns to a task unfinished from the previous day and develops it.	923	141	149	871
3. He carries his activities to completion.	879	323	145	898
4. He carries out brief individual assignments in school without supervision.	886	275	184	894
5. He reads on own initiative.	885	267	045	856
6. He enjoys books, newspapers, and magazines.	868	347	069	878
7. He enjoys team games, group games.	222	814	233	766
8. He makes friends quickly and easily.	319	576	507	691
9. He takes part in competitive games.	340	827	160	826
10. He takes initiative at play or in classroom.	271	788	210	739
11. He is friendly toward other people.	326	681	396	727
12. He assumes group leadership for a given activity.	405	740	−096	722
13. His remarks about others are kind; that is, he does not say things to hurt others' feelings.	315	−058	790	727
14. He reacts properly to teacher's approval or disapproval.	−184	338	716	661

TABLE 6-2 *The Factor Structure of Social Maturity for Academic, Interpersonal, and Emotional Behavior of Negro Children* (cont.)*

	Factors†			
Items	Ac-ademic	Inter-personal	Emo-tional	Commu-nalities
15. He is inclined to sympa-thize rather than laugh at those in difficulty.	112	−044	823	692
16. He remains calm when he cannot get what he wants.	−070	184	759	615
17. He can lose with grace (fair play).	141	282	792	727
18. He knows how to take turns at games, talking, and in the use of facili-ties.	237	267	791	753

* Permission by Y. Kim, H. E. Anderson, and W. L. Bashaw, *Educational and psychological measurement*, vol. 28, p. 151, 1968.

† All decimals omitted.

maturity for sixty Negro boys and girls (thirty each). Samples of white children revealed essentially the same kind of factor structure. The scale is also being used as an inventory of pre-school behavior. Continuous studies with the eighteen-item scale, which has proven to be most stable, should indicate whether the three social factors from the scale are identifiable across age, sex, and culture. The Child Behavior Scale is relatively easy to administer since only eighteen questions are presented about each child. Probably its most serious difficulty is in the inner-judgmental reliability of teachers regarding the concept of social maturity. One wonders whether the personality of the teacher would enter into the perceptions of student behavior and cause a great deal of difference in what behaviors are measured. As a measure of the perception that teachers have of the social matu-rity of students in class, the CBS certainly should be considered, but concern should be given to teacher differences. Interesting hypotheses about social interaction of students can be examined by the CBS. For example, deprived children are said to dislike working alone, and yet the ability to work alone (independently) seems to be a basic goal of achievement in school. The CBS can assist in the comparison of deprived and nondeprived groups on the academic factor of social maturity. In Table 6-2, deprived black children were perceived as very independent academically. Perhaps deprived children can be taught to work alone. Social measures provide a teacher with an essential component in the total learning of each child and the emotional adjustment of the group.

SCREENING EMOTIONALLY DISTURBED CHILDREN

Screening for emotionally disturbed children generally begins in the classroom by the observations teachers make regarding their students. Teacher ratings of student behavior have been recognized as a highly valid technique for measuring poorly adjusted children in the classroom (Bower, 1960). There are many teacher scales with various strengths and weaknesses in screening for emotional disturbance or for inadequate personal-social behavior. Three teacher scales that have been used with some success with disadvantaged populations are the Bristol Social Adjustment Guides (Stott & Sykes, 1967), the Classroom Behavior Inventory (Schaeffer & Aaronson, 1966), and the Devereaux Elementary School Behavior Scale (Spivack & Swift, 1968).

The *Bristol Social Adjustment Guides* (BSAG) are able to detect behavior disturbances and to give some diagnosis about the type and degree of social relationships. The contribution which the BSAG makes in social measures is that it deals with behavior that is observed by the teacher rather than based on inferences coming from projective techniques. The social adjustment of children from five to sixteen is systematically recorded by the teacher, giving a large number of "bits of behavior," which are classified in a way to bring about freedom from personal judgment. The BSAG does not claim to measure personality, but it tries to quantify tendencies of children who fail to come up to the social expectations of the cultural group. The major areas (Stott & Sykes, 1967) along which children are classified are:

Inhibition: lack of confidence, assertiveness, and curiosity
Withdrawal: defenses set up against human contact and against being loved
Depression: irritability, ups and downs of energy
Anxiety concerning interpersonal relations with adults
Hostility toward adults
Lack of concern for adult approval
Anxiety concerning peer acceptance
Hostility toward peers
Restlessness: inability to concentrate and persevere

The BSAG provides a vehicle for screening a child's contemporary adjustment with his social environment. Teachers of disadvantaged children would have an excellent opportunity over six months or a year to observe the extent to which more acceptable social attitudes are replacing maladjusted ones. The "social health" of a classroom can also be examined over time to quantify group changes due to teaching style. Teachers have little difficulty in completing the forms for the BSAG, but the scoring is complicated and demands a good deal of time and interpretation.

The *Classroom Behavior Inventory* is a teacher rating checklist of twelve behavioral traits and appears to be most valuable at preschool and primary grade levels. Traits measured include verbal expressiveness, hyperactivity, kindness, social withdrawal, perseverance, irritability, gregariousness, distractibility, considerateness, self-consciousness, concentration, and resentfulness. Based on the traits and scales ranging from *well adjusted* to *clinically disturbed,* the overall assessment can provide a general screening device for discriminating emotional disturbances from patterns and characteristics of economically deprived children.

Another acceptable teacher rating inventory for measuring problem behavior that might be related to academic difficulties of children from kindergarten through twelfth grade is the *Devereaux Elementary School Behavior Scale.* Although the scale has had limited use thus far, there is no reason why this teacher rating technique, measuring eight traits, should not be used in longitudinal studies dealing with problem behavior in the classroom.

SYNTALITY: GROUP PERSONALITY CHARACTERISTICS

Methods of assessing the personality of groups of young children and adolescents have been along a continuum going from high structure to a level of low structure. At one end of the continuum are the paper-and-pencil inventories, such as the Guilford-Zimmerman Temperament Survey (Guilford & Zimmerman, 1949), the Early School Personality Questionnaire (Coan & Cattell, 1961), the California Test of Personality (Thorpe, Clark, & Trigs, 1953), the Children's Personality Questionnaire (Porter & Cattell, 1959). These tests consist of a large number of multiple-choice questions seeking the students' responses to attitudes, interests, and past experiences. Major focus in the inventories is upon interpersonal relationships and how they affect the mental health of individuals. The interpersonal psychological health of groups can be inferred from the mean scores of the class members. At the other end of the continuum are word-association tests, picture-association techniques in groups, story completions, and those tests which ask for drawings on various topics.

On the basis of the individual scores of the children obtained in a group testing situation, the "personality" of the group can be inferred. Cattell (1948) used the label *syntality* to refer to the "togetherness" or personality of a group. Probably no living psychologist has done more in the measurement of personality variables than Raymond B. Cattell. Any effective research on the behavior of groups, Cattell believes, must be prefaced by adequate syntality measure. When teachers are concerned with the person-to-person relationships in classrooms, it seems disappointing to fail to measure the behavior of the group as a group. One of the unique contributions of Cattell and his colleagues to the measurement of personality has been the continuity of the same systematic way in assessing children from five years of age until they reach adulthood. There are many instruments for measuring the traits at various age levels, but the theory and the system are the same. In trying to assess the personality of disadvantaged children, there is always the concern for the reading level of the students, which, in turn, influences the validity of the test responses. Before any personality test is given to children, the reading level should be identified by an informal reading inventory, a Cloze test (Bormuth, 1968), or some standardized reading test.

The *Children's Personality Questionnaire* (CPQ) is designed to give the maximum information in the shortest time about the greatest number of dimensions of personality (fourteen factors) for children ranged in age from eight to twelve years. The CPQ, like most personality questionnaires, is clinically oriented and can be used with other information to screen individuals with emotional conflicts. The instrument can also be used to compare group characteristics as well as social interaction. A hypothetical question about the personality behavior of students who were integrated compared with those who were left in segregated classes could be answered from responses on the CPQ. The group personality characteristics of the integrated black students and the segregated black students could be identified and compared. If the CPQ were used, fourteen comparisons could be made on the primary factors given in Table 6-3. Those boys and girls who volunteered to transfer to the integrated school might be expected to show more mature, sociable, controlled behavior and to be

TABLE 6-3 *Titles and Descriptions of Personality Dimensions of CPQ*

Trait designation	Trait description
A	Stiff, aloof vs. warm, sociable
B	Dull vs. bright
C	Emotional, immature vs. mature, calm
D	Phlegmatic vs. unrestrained
E	Mild vs. aggressive
F	Sober, serious vs. enthusiastic
G	Casual, undependable vs. conscientious, persistent
H	Shy, sensitive vs. adventurous
I	Tough, realistic vs. esthetically sensitive
J	Liking group action vs. individualistic
N	Simple, awkward vs. sophisticated, polished
O	Confident vs. insecure
Q_3	Uncontrolled, lax vs. controlled
Q_4	Low ergic tension vs. high ergic tension

Adapted from R. B. Porter and R. B. Cattell, *Handbook for the IPAT Children's Personality Questionnaire*, Institute for Personality and Ability Testing, Champaign, Ill., 1959, pp. 6–7.

somewhat higher on the scale (factor B) indicating intellectual ability. Perhaps students remaining in the ghetto might maintain higher aggression, have more realistic characteristics, and be quite high in ergic tension. Discussion of the social characteristics of groups permits an investigation into personal-social relationships within each group and between groups.

Other instruments for measuring patterns of personality behavior can provide insights into the general social behavior of groups, e.g., introversion-extroversion, anxiety, and independence. If a group of disadvantaged students is found to be academically superior to another group, there will be the concern that the children's intellectual gains may be accruing at the expense of their social and emotional development. The group's "affect system" can be measured by various personality inventories, and syntality can be evaluated.

Rentz, Fears, and White (1968) found that the personality traits of high school students in three remedial English classes were highly related to the perceptions that group members had about themselves. Personalities of group members, therefore, were related to group structure. It is possible, with future research, to map the clusters of groups in semantic space and identify these clusters by specific personality characteristics. The social behavior of various groups of disadvantaged children can be compared within a deprived population or with the social structure of more advantaged populations. There are many questions yet to be answered by research regarding the classrooms of deprived children: Do disadvantaged children have the same social group structure as their more affluent peers? Do deprived children perceive their social lives in a manner similar to that of children who are not deprived? What personal-social characteristics identify groupings of deprived children? Are there different traits in the classroom grouping of advantaged children that accelerate achievement levels above those of disadvantaged children? The measurement of social behavior will play a significant role in understanding the deprived child and the social dynamics of the classroom.

seven

Reconciliation of race
and power

Tactics for teaching the disadvantaged will always depend upon the attitudes that teachers maintain toward political and social concepts. It is almost impossible to think about teachers of the disadvantaged today without talking about integration, neighborhood schools, freedom of choice, separatism, civil rights issues, the "white noose" around the inner city, the educational park, racial balance, and quality education. Our educational institutions have experienced the thrust of a social revolution since the Supreme Court decision of 1954, which stated:

In the field of public education the doctrine of "separate but equal" has no place. Separate educational facilities are inherently unequal. [*Brown v. Board of Education of Topeka,* 347 U.S. 483 (1954), p. 881.]

There are some school districts in which a very large segment of the population is economically deprived and which yet do not have a racial factor to resolve in school programming. However, school districts in every large metropolitan area throughout the country and in most of the rural Southern areas are faced with the effects of racial differences in the classrooms. The Supreme Court decision made it clear that a dual system of education, motivated by racial discrimination, would violate the rights of citizens guaranteed by the United States Constitution. As long as a school is labeled a *black school* and other schools are labeled *white schools* (even if a token number of blacks are registered in the white school), the black school will be judged inferior. In any school system in which two types of racial schools can be described, the school represented by the minority race brings about a lower self-concept among children in the "minority type" school. In turn, minority-group children with an inferiority concept will lower their motivation to learn as well as lower their scholastic achievement.

Regardless of a beautiful building, an excellent black teaching staff (with some white teachers), and reduced teacher/pupil ratio, a school in a black community with 75 percent black children and 25 percent white children is viewed by parents of both races as inferior to one in which the racial proportions are reversed. Although scholastic achievement data may someday demonstrate that the black schools are not academically inferior, present attitudes about such schools are prevalent and firm: black schools are intellectually inferior to white schools. Another attitude that has developed since 1954 and needs serious attention is the belief that no black school can be acceptable under the terms of the Constitution unless white students take classes there. White children and parents are led to believe that they belong to a super race, and black children and parents feel that regardless of personal attainments, blacks are less able and can expect only a second-rate type of "pursuit of happiness" without the assistance of white children and teachers. The complexity of the effects of the Supreme Court's decision (1954) becomes the concern of teachers and administrators. No matter how motivated a teacher happens to be, the suit of Oliver Brown, seeking admission of his eight-year-old daughter Linda to a white school in Topeka, Kansas, has shaken the role of all the teachers in the United States. The direction of the integration movement during the past fifteen years has been toward some form of integrated education. School systems, however, seem to have received the major impact of the movement toward integration, and the concern for civil rights has been almost entirely directed toward schoolchildren and teachers. The effects of the integration movement have been largely evinced in school programs for the disadvantaged, particularly in Title I and Title III under the Elementary and Secondary School Act (1965) and in Projects Head Start and Follow Through. Although the movement has been centered in schools and the burden of integration has been carried by public school personnel, the vision of the Supreme Court went beyond classroom walls:

Segregation of white and colored children in public schools has a detrimental effect upon the colored children. The impact is greater when it has the sanction of law; for the policy of separating the races is usually interpreted as denoting the inferiority of the Negro group. A sense of inferiority affects the motivation of a child to learn. Segregation with the sanction of law, therefore, has a tendency to retard the educational and mental development of Negro children and to deprive them of some of the benefits they would receive in a racially integrated school system. [*Brown v. Board of Education of Topeka*, 347 U.S. 483 (1954), p. 881.]

THE TEACHER ROLE IN THE RACE ISSUE

Stereotypes are handed down in classrooms by teachers, students, and curriculum materials. Stereotypes are images of certain groups of people who are said to possess common characteristics. In the attitudes of many American public school students, Mexicans are "dirty," Germans are "hardheaded," Italians are "greasy," and Jews are "conniving, conscienceless" individuals. Negroes are "lazy and comedylike" in character. Strong reinforcement of ethnic stereotypes is found in the communications media, especially the movies. Although there has been a decided shift in the black image in the movies and on television, the history of derogatory views of minority groups is strongly rooted in our white, Anglo-Saxon, Protestant culture, and these views are very difficult to change. In the classroom, the racial attitude of the teachers and the attitudes which children bring from home determine most of the stereotyping. Elementary-school textbooks have continued to support stereotypes by pictures and words (Klineberg, 1963). In general, Klineberg found that over 80 percent of the American characters in stories are blonde and fair-skinned. Dark-skinned people either are servants to wealthy white protagonists or are pictured with loincloths in Africa or with turbans in India.

We have been finding more faces of black individuals in textbooks since the time of Klineberg's review (1963), but a situation exists today that is very similar to the presence of black faces on our television programs. Until black people are described with adjectives such as *good* and *valuable, strong* and *tall, active* and *moving, intelligent* and *verbally competent,* the presence of black faces on film and in textbooks will do little to change the stereotypes in the minds of viewers and readers (White & Aaron, 1969). Pictures of black faces alone will not determine changes in the stereotypes. The semantic description that has negatively identified minority groups for so many years will dominate all verbal and written communication. Perhaps the greatest harm from the stereotyping of ethnic origins is that a student from a racial minority group can be ignored, baited, and maligned by members of his peer group. Frequently, those hostile invectives —"Dago," "Chink," and "Nigger"—will only be introduction for physical abuse by frustrated white adolescents. Looking for innocent targets upon whom they can vent their anger about parents, schools, and their own self-image, students who are meeting classroom goals very poorly strike out at individuals and minority groups in order to release their disorganized emotions. The hallways, playgrounds, and classrooms are likely to become battlefields for waging wars of personal-social adjustment concealed under the color of ethnic banners. Race frequently becomes the scapegoat of many problems children have with badly managed classrooms and poorly administrated school systems. On the surface, there is the appearance of a racial conflict, when the real causes are defined by poor teaching, poor facilities, and a low behavioral expectancy.

Racial prejudice is harmful not only to the minority student but also to the teacher and to the students who initiate the racial aggression. Students who are bottled up with hatred and fear of minority students and who strike out with derogatory invectives or physical abuse lack flexibility in dealing with social and educational problems. As teachers, we frequently observe the narrow, bigoted, highly prejudiced youngster, who is not able to learn from others the varied thinking patterns and solutions that are well known to other cultural groups. So much tension is created by racial prejudice that psychic energy is withdrawn from the worthwhile goals of education and transferred to defense mechanisms that merely distort reality. Teachers in biracial classrooms have at least three serious responsibilities in the teacher-learner process:

1. *Teachers must consistently look for the causes of human failure in an inadequate learning history.* With disadvantaged children, deprivation of verbal and auditory reinforcement will determine much of the failure of the student in the classroom. When a teacher recognizes the emotional deprivation of a particular child, he will be much more adequate in diagnosing why a child is not performing at an acceptable level. Causes of academic and personal-social problems will be found in deprivation, poor reinforcement histories, and the lack of adequate models for identification. The color of the skin will not add much to the information about cause and effect.

2. *Teachers must recognize and put into practice the principle of individual differences.* Instructors who maintain that there is only one type of acceptable classroom behavior are doomed to fail in working with the disadvantaged. There is a normal distribution of talents, skills, and intelligence among disadvantaged children, just as there is among more advantaged populations. Those teachers who believe that black children are all the same or who expect them to act in a particular way are so racially prejudiced that they are actually harmful in the classroom. The scatter or dispersion of abilities among deprived children, both black and white, makes it even more difficult to teach them than to teach a middle class white group of children with varied intelligence levels.

If teachers assume that black students are poor intellectually, or even poorer than white children, failure of the black child is inevitable. If teachers assume that Japanese or Jewish children are all very bright, many of the minority students will suffer, as well as other students in the classroom. The minority child will "learn" that he is more capable than he is. Race does not make one superior, but experience does. Children with limited experience will not perform as well as those with more organized patterns of stimulation. Perhaps teachers ought to keep in mind that we teachers tend to "bunch up" or group students too quickly. Because of our many responsibilities, we frequently classify students for "mental economy" into bright, dull, aggressive, monsters, "EMRs," and other categories. Ethnic groups make us especially vulnerable. Our responsibility in teaching should be to discover how children differ from one another as well as how similar they are. I have always felt that the cognitive abilities of deprived children (and, frequently, this would mean the black student) can be described by a comparison (Figure 7-1) with children who have had much more stimulation. There are large differences among individuals in each type of population; there is a wide range of cognitive ability scores in each group. The overlap of scores is quite noticeable. It would not be surprising to find a number of deprived children scoring well above the mean IQ or the mean achievement level of advantaged children. The extreme high scores of advantaged children are not expected among deprived students. The difference in scores results from exposure to early patterns of organized experiences. The reason

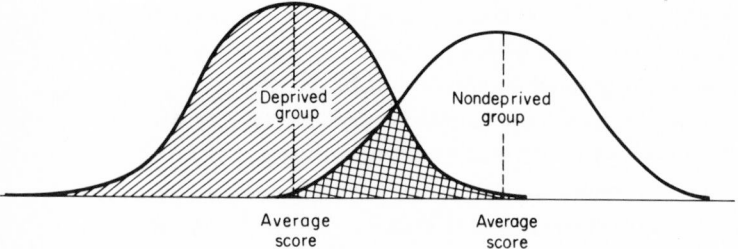

FIGURE 7-1 *Distribution of skills and competencies of deprived and nondeprived students.*

for two kinds of distribution (which overlap to a great degree) is "limited learning," not merely genetics.

3.   *Teachers have to expend the energy to identify each child's present level of verbal and performance skills.* Knowledge about mental ability, achievement levels, and psychosocial variables is essential in teaching any person who has limited experience. Standardized tests are not the best method or the only way to identify the different kinds of functioning of deprived children. Teachers, however, cannot assume that economically deprived children "don't know anything." At least some positive skills must be found. Base-line data on each child should assist the honest scholar and the effective teacher to know just where to begin in developing the learning potential of each child. Providing equal opportunity means identifying a starting point in learning and providing the necessary models and reinforcement to direct a child toward the development of skills and attitudes to cope with living today and tomorrow.

Standardized tests are frequently biased for the disadvantaged learner. The culture-free and culture-fair tests are not able to "rid us of our culturalities," but they are less bound to cultural structure than other scales. The teacher's difficult role in identifying the specific abilities and disabilities of disadvantaged children is compounded by the lack of valid and reliable equipment presented by educational psychologists.

THE SCHOOL INTEGRATION MOVEMENT

There seem to be two major issues in the integration movement that are not entirely independent but permit more clarity in discussing the problem and what has been accomplished. The two issues can be presented in two questions: (1) Are public school children intellectually better and happier when they are racially separate or racially mixed? (2) What school integration plan has worked best in the North and South? Almost all the problems of integrated education can be classified under those two questions.

RACIAL SEPARATION AND INTEGRATION IN PUBLIC SCHOOLS

Pettigrew, one of the leading scholars on racial issues (1964; 1968; 1969), projected the "newest new Negro" image as "relatively released from principal social controls, from the restraints of an extended kinship system, a conservative religion, and an acceptance of the inevitability of white supremacy" (Pettigrew, 1969, p. 36). Although the gain in Negro status and privileges has been phenomenal over the past decade, the dream of equality for the black is seriously questioned by young blacks, and many have rejected integration for separatist goals. Perhaps one of the strongest reasons for pessimism about the future of blacks in public school integration is that the life style of the dominant group (white middle class) has advanced more rapidly and farther in the past fifteen years than the minority group of "Black America." In discussing separatism versus integration in the schools, care should be taken to discriminate "black power" from racial separatism. Pettigrew insists that there are numerous variants in black separatism. Only a limited number of black separatists seek to overthrow the existing government and dominate the white establishment. The majority of black separatists want merely to separate and "go it on their own." The spirit is one of racial pride and local control. On the other hand, there are black militants who want to destroy the white power which has determined black patterns of behavior for more than a century.

Will separation be successful? Separatism seems to draw both blacks and whites into the acceptable resolution of permitting each racial membership to carry out its own school program. There are theories to which whites and blacks adhere in their attempts to maintain a racial isolation in solving social problems. White supremacists as well as black separatists believe in the "like by like" principle, i.e., that members of a particular race are happiest and most comfortable with their own kind. There are many white segregationists who sincerely believe that black people feel more confident and secure when they are associating with members of their own race. Black separatists, on the other hand, fear that "whitey" will gather them up and dominate them with a white value system. For both groups to accept one another, some attraction must be found in each race. According to many scholars, there must be contact between the races in order that members of one race can perceive any attractiveness in members of the other race.

Belief similarity and race   One of the interesting directions of research in the last few years has been to examine the concept that attitudinal differences are more important than racial differences in determining dislike or prejudice in members of another race (Rokeach & Rothman, 1965). The evaluation of a stranger (or person of a different race) depends upon agreement with him about attitude objects. The white American who rejects the black American is motivated much more by the *belief* that there are value differences than by a racial difference. The problem of separatism is more affected by belief dissimilarity than by the color of the skin. The importance of belief similarity or dissimilarity has been reported in numerous studies across cultures and types of subjects: Stein (1966) studied gentile, black, and Jewish students; Smith, Williams, and Willis (1967) examined white and black subjects in several areas of the United States; Triandis and Davis (1965) reported belief similarity among college students; and Insko and Robinson (1967) assessed belief congruence among Southern white children.

The meaningfulness of the belief-similarity principle in interracial situations is somewhat limited, however, by evidence that while belief similarity is more important in simple matters of interpersonal attraction, race is still more important in the more intimate forms of personal contact, e.g., in marriage and in holding public office. Smith, Williams, and Willis (1967) critically suggest that the phenomenon of belief similarity is much more of a problem in desegregated schools than in segregated schools. Apparently, contact between the races is not the only variable in bringing about a belief in similar values.

There are many blacks who do not wish to integrate, just as there are many whites who refuse to integrate. Frequently, black high school students will defer biracial education, especially if they have experienced only a segregated school situation throughout their elementary-school years. Pettigrew (1964) commented on a serious problem in Louisville, Kentucky. Black high school students who had been attending an all-black junior high school elected to attend an all-black high school, while the majority of the black students in each of the nine biracial junior high schools chose to attend the biracial senior high school.

THE NEIGHBORHOOD SCHOOL

Housing patterns and neighborhood school policies have been the determining causes for schools in a community having almost all (if not all) black students while others have almost all white. Many Northern educators would like to have us believe that the historical basis for assigning pupils to schools has been the locus of residence. School zones are usually established from such basic factors as distance from school, automobile traffic patterns, bus routes, size of school buildings, and "unknown variables." As a result of all the rules and reasons, both in the North and in the South, as well as in the West, there has been an almost mystical dedication to keeping schools "culture-bound." Zones have almost always locked in the poor, the black, and the Puerto Rican. Zones are changed, now and then, as enrollments change, but somehow the system of keeping school populations homogeneous has been ingeniously successful. The deprived black student and his family are not fooled a bit by the distinction a Southern board of education uses in legislating a dual system or by a Northern board which mandates, through zoning, that blacks go to one school while whites attend another. The results are the same. De facto segregation is not very hard to find. Surface reasons are different, but somehow school zoning always reverts to racial power.

Every community has its "good" schools and its "difficult" schools. Parents frequently move into areas where their children can attend a "good" school. Generally, these schools are found on the periphery or in the suburbs of larger metropolitan areas. Difficult schools are found in the inner-city areas or in the ghettos. The "good school" is characterized by a stable faculty who have more advanced degrees and are research-oriented, higher achievement levels of students, a low dropout rate, newer buildings and equipment, college-bound seniors, and the strong interest of parents in their children's scholastic achievement. In the month of August, 1969, parents in a suburban community outside of Athens, Georgia, petitioned the courts for an injunction against the Clark County school system in the busing of white students to a school which served all black children in an economically depressed area. The school system had a plan for resolving the problem of segregated schools, which was approved by HEW three weeks before school began. Parents in the suburban community argued for the *neighborhood-school concept.* Their petition stated that they had moved into the area to be proximate to a fine school, with new buildings and a very selective staff, within walking distance from their homes, and reflecting the development of the suburban homes. The Clarke County school system's plan called for the busing of students 4 miles into an all-black school, which had poor facilities and was totally staffed by black teachers. The parents argued, further, that their children were the only ones who were being forced to integrate in the system and that this action was discriminatory.

The school system revised its plan to include a black-white student ratio of 67 to 33 in every elementary-school building in the county. Teachers were assigned in a similar manner. Two very noticeable effects took place: (1) Many parents with strong leadership qualities joined the PTA and exerted a positive, promising effect on the school. (2) School buildings were repaired and made very attractive.

During 1970, the neighborhood-school concept appeared to be passing out of the legal concept of modern education, and parents were accepting a wider range of clustering of students. There are many economically deprived blacks, as well as disadvantaged whites, who want to keep their neighborhood school, but recent legal interpretation indicates that such a concept will not take precedence over the segregated-school hypothesis. The federal courts, rather than HEW, are deciding the issue of integration. The legal federal authority in each specific area is making judgments about all proposed plans for eliminating the dual system of education. The action in the 1970s appears to be the responsibility of the Justice Department rather than Health, Education, and Welfare. Many are looking upon the new direction as one of the significant forward steps in the integration problem, yet the black white ratio (67 to 33 or 53 to 47) does not seem to be an education decision. Only time will tell if it will provide educational gains as well as politico-social advantages.

Two New York City communities, Ocean Hill-Brownsville and Bedford-Stuyvesant, have become leaders in protecting the advantages of the neighborhood-school concept. As in areas of Boston and Washington, they have extended the neighborhood school to what is now being labeled the *community school*. Proponents of the community school raise the question: Can black schools run by black communities stimulate the black deprived child and upgrade his lower achievement level to equal that of his white counterpart? The issue of the community school is not merely one of a movement against segregation or the dual system or the cumulative-deficit effect. The stimulus is found in big cities such as New York and in rural counties which are majority black districts. "The establishment tends to call it decentralization, or parent participation; the black communities—Brooklyn's Ocean Hill-Brownsville and Harlem, call it Community Control." (Calhoun, 1969, p. 11.) In October, 1968, in a special report of the Civil Liberties Union in New York City, it was stated that:

The demand for community control of the schools began with the failure of the central board to effectively implement integration. . . . The growing sense of betrayal among ghetto leaders who had been repeatedly promised integrated schools came to a head during the P.S. 201 (Harlem) controversy. . . . Disenchanted black parents decided that since they were once again stuck with a segregated school, they might at least run it themselves. Thus was born the movement for community control of black schools. It is crucial to remember that integration was not abandoned by black parents but by the Board of Education, which consistently failed to deliver on the promise of integrated schools. . . ." [Calhoun, 1969, p. 13.]

The historical events of the Ocean Hill-Brownsville and Bedford-Stuyvesant affairs are complicated and very detailed. A brief history and a fair appraisal appeared in the *Integrated Education* journal, entitled "New York: Schools and Power—Whose?" (Calhoun, 1969). Among the many educational and political leaders quoted by Calhoun, John Doar seems to reflect the feeling of the progressive educators determined to do something better than has been done. Doar adopted the phrase *local responsibility,* which seems to be synonymous with the terms *decentralization, community control,* and *parent participation.* Smaller systems, which exercise better control over day-to-day problems, would be more effective in those deprived black areas of Bedford-Stuyvesant and Ocean Hill-Brownsville. Asked about the demands of the community for fiscal control in the hands of the local people, Doar stated that you cannot give administration without at the same time giving fiscal control. Above all, Doar and others like him are not pessimistic about decentralization and community control. (There are many others who insist that the community school is the route by which some middle class black educators are searching for self-aggrandizement rather than for the common good.) There seems to be hostility on each side. Somewhere along the line, an exemplary community model that is reaching some success must be opened to public assessment. The strange part about the concept is that it must be given the opportunity to be successful. As H. I. Kalodner, New York University law professor, stated: "Everybody else had tried and failed. We want our chance to fail and it may very well be that we will fail."

The neighborhood-school concept and the *decentralization of power* have the outward appearance of clarity and principle, but inwardly they are hampered by the same old semantic confusion. One of the conflicts that must be resolved is: What is meant by the neighborhood school? Professor John Coons of Northwestern University School of Law challenges the traditional concept:

Neighborhood schools do not exist in many of the crowded areas of Chicago, unless the requirements of that concept are satisfied by the mere existence of a building called a "neighborhood." If the school is not adequate to serve the needs of a neighborhood, it is playing with words to label it a neighborhood school. The most serious charge against the administration seems to be that in many areas it has not been operating a neighborhood school system, but has acted as if it were. [Silberman, 1964, p. 292.]

FIXED NEIGHBORHOOD

There is no such thing as a "fixed" neighborhood which is based on school attendance records. Boards of education determine the boundaries of neighborhoods. These authorities build schools "to accommodate" youngsters, and they include or exclude a particular street from a zone. Racial and ethnic composition can be ignored or manipulated to fit the needs of the board. Examination of legal decisions reveals that it has been most difficult to bring a conviction of gerrymandering against a school system. It is an illegal practice, but it is difficult to fit the intentions of a board together with their performance about school administration. Thus, many broadly stipulate that they are "preserving the Constitution," "providing for the security of our children," or maintaining a right to "freedom of choice." If these generalized phrases serve to relegate children to segregated schools, championing the cause of the "neighborhood school" does not offer any change in the concept of segregation.

When a "neighborhood school" becomes improperly exclusive in fact or in spirit, when it is viewed as being reserved for certain community groups, or when its effect is to create or continue a ghetto type situation, it does not serve the purpose of democratic education. [State Education Department, 1963, p. 3.]

When the neighborhood school merely helps to emphasize and confirm an all-black area in an urban setting, a geographical condition surrounding the black area emerges which is commonly called a "white noose." White individuals desperately attempt to hold black individuals within the confines of the expanding center of the urban area. Blacks in the inner city increase in number, and their needs and demands compel them to push against the geographic "white noose" that seems to strangle them. It is difficult to describe the social-psychological impact on a community of adult blacks who are surrounded by the majority race of white citizens. Isolated in the ghetto, black separatists have called upon Washington officials for massive federal aid— with no white strings attached. Even though black members in the inner cities recognize their limited resources, they ridicule any attempt at integration as fantasy and the white man's method of maintaining dominance. Continuing to emphasize the "within" ghetto enrichment, however, may merely bring about the "embalming" of the ghetto, as Kenneth Clark describes it.

In March, 1970, President Nixon promulgated the decision of his administration that it is not for forced integration by busing but favors protecting the concept of the neighborhood school. Children would be permitted and encouraged to attend the school closest to their homes. In February, 1971, a Supreme Court decision is expected to rule on the issue of forced integration by *extensive busing* plans.

MAJORITY NEGRO DISTRICTS

In many communities of the South there are majority black school districts. A survey in 1969 identified 242 majority black districts in seven southern states. One of the most serious effects of desegregation in the majority Negro districts during 1969–1970 has been the high proportion of black students and faculty (sometimes 70–80%) and the disproportionate number of white students. Nevertheless, the schools are controlled by white administrators. How long the conflict over power to administrate the schools will remain is a challenging question. Some similarity between the community-school movement and transfer of power in majority Negro districts seems evident.

FATE CONTROL

One of the chief characteristics of the black separatists' psychology in educating their children is the concept of "fate control." Black separatists argue strongly for controlling their own destinies, their own schools, and their total politico-social lives. If the racial majority dictates "what should be done," the minority race of blacks will never obtain the inner control of their lives. The path that Mayor Carl Stokes of Cleveland and Mayor

Richard Hatcher of Gary, Indiana, have taken is frowned upon by large numbers of the black community. Black leaders should tend black people. Pettigrew (1969) points up the interesting data of the Coleman report (Coleman et al., 1966) supporting the fact that levels of fate control among black children were found (by Coleman) to be significantly higher in interracial schools than in all-black schools.

Even though black separatists assert that the all-black schools we are talking about today are not the model of tomorrow's black schools, the data we now possess support the interracial type of school as the guarantee of "fate control." Separatism, it should be remembered, appeals to a small number of blacks (Campbell & Schuman, 1968, p. 5):

"Separatism" appeals to from five to eighteen percent of the Negro sample, depending on the question, with the largest appeal involving black ownership of stores and black administration of schools in Negro neighborhoods, and the smallest appeal to the rejection of whites as friends or in other informal contacts. Even on questions having the largest appeal, however, more than three-quarters of the Negro sample indicate a clear preference for integration.

DETERIORATION OF THE SELF-CONCEPT

No greater disadvantage can be observed in separatism or in segregation than the harmful effect of the poor self-concept of young children in the racial minority. The Supreme Court, in 1954, pointed to the damage to the personality of minority-type students which would possibly result from segregated educational institutions. Students isolated within the ghetto and students outside the ghetto receive only a limited view of the world. Fourth-, fifth-, and sixth-grade deprived black students in a segregated rural area of Georgia (Powell & White, 1969), and in one all-black school in Atlanta (Richmond & White, in press) maintained well-defined negative self-concepts. There have been instances, however, in numerous Follow Through programs indicating that economically deprived black first- and second-grade students in integrated classrooms have positive, healthy self-concepts. Other studies (Soares & Soares, 1969) report evidence of higher self-esteem among deprived children than among advantaged children, but the negative self-concept is certainly found much more frequently among segregated poverty-stricken black children. The inadequate feeling about self seems to dominate the entire school life of deprived black, Mexican, and Puerto Rican children who are kept in the isolation of the "minority image."

The child with a negative view of self is a child who will not be able to profit adequately from school. Once a child is convinced he cannot learn in school, the task of educators becomes almost impossible. He may well make trouble for his classmates, his teachers, and himself. A negative self-concept is just as crippling and just as hard to overcome as any physical handicap. In fact, a negative self-image may be even more crippling, because it is often hidden from the view of the naïve or untrained observer.[*]

Disadvantaged children do not necessarily reflect more negative self-perceptions or lower self-esteem than advantaged children. Soares and Soares (1969) compared the self-perceptions of disadvantaged black, Puerto Rican, and white children with those of advantaged children in grades 4 to 8 of the Bridgeport, Connecticut, school system. Results indicated more positive self-concept measures for economically deprived children ($N = 229$) than for the more advantaged children ($N = 285$) of the Bridgeport area. Although disadvantaged girls had lower self-perceptions than advantaged girls, the deprived boys maintained a higher self-esteem than the comparison sample of advantaged boys. The important conclusion from this small study in Bridgeport is that disadvantaged children, despite their economic handicap (annual family income below $4,000), do not necessarily suffer from a lower self-esteem and a lower sense of personal worth.

Many complex factors have been found to determine the concept of self in students. It would be erroneous to maintain a set

[*] *From* **Negro self-concept,** *by* **W. Kvaraceus et al., 1965.** *Used with permission of McGraw-Hill Book Company.*

that all deprived children have a poor self-sentiment formation. The situation is always critical and must be examined in discussing self-concepts of disadvantaged children. Stable identification figures, community spirit, and even nutrition determine feelings about self. Being poor does not mean low self-concept, nor does being wealthy guarantee a high positive ego strength. Effective teaching, adequate instructional materials, and a low teacher/ pupil ratio can make a difference among deprived children. There is a certain amount of pity that must be attributed to those well-meaning individuals who believe that desegregation produces some miraculous adjustment of deprived black children's personalities. If desegregation is only a numbers game of mixing a ratio of white and black students and faculty, the racial issue will still be there with all its ugly effects. Daily one reads in the newspapers of numbers of black children being transported to white schools. When seven or eight black children attend a junior high school with hundreds of white children, the self-concept of the black children most likely will be worse than it was while they attended a predominantly black school. Desegregation, whether it includes pairing of certain grades in black schools or using freedom-of-choice plans to accomplish goals, must consider the effect on the academic and emotional lives of the students. It is the social-emotional lives of individuals that become the terminal objectives in education and not the numerical ratio of blacks to whites. The numbers game may very well make matters worse. The self-concept of youngsters in any school system will depend upon the *meaning*, both cognitive and affective, of desegregation in that locale, not on proportionate population numbers.

Most educators and psychologists today admit that desegregation is an "indispensable first step in the reconstitution of Negro personality—especially since the school is the most strategically placed social institution for effecting rapid change both in ego structure and in social status" (Ausubel & Ausubel, 1963, p. 10). The major expression that is being heard today, however, is that big-city school systems in the North are becoming more and more segregated, with more blacks attending all-black schools and fewer blacks attending white schools. Segregation is more pronounced today than it was in 1954, when the courts rendered illicit any system of segregation.

SCHOOL DESEGREGATION—NORTH AND SOUTH

More school desegregation is taking place in the South than in the big Northern and Western communities. The South is moving from a status of no desegregation to some kind of segregation, but the large Northern cities are being crippled by growing inner-city problems. The dramatic change in the metropolitan areas maximizes the problem and stifles any significant gains in de-segregation. In the post-World War II days, hundreds of thousands of deprived people, especially blacks, poured into the large cities, migrating from the rural areas, particularly the South. For years, white families have been shifting to the suburban areas, leaving the inner city inhabited by poor black families. Three out of every four black elementary students attend school in seventy-five major cities in which 90 percent or more of the population are blacks. With the segregated ghetto schools, severe overcrowding, old buildings, inadequate teaching materials, and inexperienced teachers add to the crisis. The racial separation of city and suburb is no more dramatically evinced than in the District of Columbia, where 94 percent of the school registration is black, while only 4 percent of the school population in sur-rounding Montgomery County is black. Black enrollment in public schools is rapidly rising in all major cities:

Atlanta	62%	District of Columbia	94%
Baltimore	64%	Indianapolis	33%
Boston	26%	New York *	30%
Buffalo	35%	Newark	74%
Chicago	52%	Philadelphia	58%
Cincinnati	42%	Pittsburgh	38%
Cleveland	58%	Rochester	27%
Detroit	58%	St. Louis	63%

* *New York also has 22 percent Puerto Rican population.*

The massive school crisis in desegregating the pockets of blacks in the large communities prompted busing programs throughout the country.

INTEGRATION VIA BUSING

When schools opened in September, 1969, in Boston, 1,125 black children boarded buses to attend classes in the suburbs. In Hartford, 750 inner-city children waited for buses to transfer them to area schools outside the city limits. Berkeley, with a school population of 41 percent black children, began moving 2,000 white children to the black-dominated areas and 2,000 blacks out to the white section for a "pairing" type of school plan. In Rochester, New York, where the first busing program to a suburb began in 1965, 630 inner-city children were transported into seven Rochester suburban communities. But the busing plan is not catching on. The argument for busing is, in most communities, not supported by sufficient research. The Bannockburn Elementary School in Bethesda, Maryland, reported that the seventeen inner-city children transported to the suburbs made about normal school progress. Studies in Boston supported the hypothesis that inner-city children make better than average progress in spelling, reading, and vocabulary work. Earlier studies in Rochester had noted that academic gains of students transferred from the city to the suburbs were greater than those of students remaining in the black area of Rochester. Children in the primary grades in Hartford who were transported achieved significantly higher than those who remained, but in the fourth and fifth grades the children in the inner-city area of Hartford performed better. In all these studies, however, busing was on a voluntary basis. No one has controlled for the motivational variable of those desiring to leave the city. Results in all the studies suffer from a serious experimental difficulty in that the children who may want to transfer are more highly motivated to learn than those who remain.

Four major objections hamper the effectiveness of the busing program and have reduced its hope for the future in the issue of race and power: (1) black militancy, (2) cost of transportation, (3) poor condition of black schools to which the white students are to be transported, (4) amount of valuable time used in bus trips.

With *black pride* and *separatism* increasing, support for busing is now dwindling. In Rochester, New York, for example, the blacks objected to the fact that 630 black children were the only ones being used. A total integration plan was demanded, in which an equal number of white children would attend black schools. When schools are committed to a ratio plan, there is some guarantee that both black and white children will be bused. The black critics complain that present busing plans only skim away the cream of the black community. Although there is much intense criticism over the busing plans, in Rochester, Hartford, and Boston long waiting lists of black children can be observed. There is no question about the fact that a great many black parents want their children to attend the schools which have better facilities.

The cost of busing children in various communities ranges from $250 to $400 per pupil. In addition, most programs pay a full tuition costing about $100 per child when children are bused into neighboring school systems. When free lunches, teacher aides, and specialists are involved, costs for transporting a pupil range from $1,000 to $1,500. In many Southern communities, less than $500 a year is spent annually to educate each child.

The poor condition of integrated schools which have housed black children angers white middle class parents. Frequently, white parents want their children to grow and develop in a racially mixed society but are horrified at the conditions of black schools. Lacking equipment, certified teachers, and a clean, orderly environment, many black schools in the South are terrifying images for white parents. At least one thing is worthwhile in these trying times. Middle class white parents are becoming aware of the tragedy of the black schools, i.e., their poor facilities and buildings and their inadequate allotment of state and local money.

MORE, NOT LESS, SEGREGATION

Continuous migration of white families from the centers of large cities to suburban areas and the entry of nonwhites to take their place in the inner city are the most important reasons why segregation in large Northern cities is greater than it was in 1954. The solution to such a concentration of race in large cities cannot be found in racial balance. Quality education for each child, no matter what his race, would be a better approach to the problem of race and power.

Louisville, St. Louis, Pittsburgh, and Chicago offer examples of more rather than less segregation (Hill, 1966). Louisville and St. Louis had desegregation plans within a year after the 1954 court decision. The percentage of blacks attending the all-black schools in the inner-city area has increased steadily over the years. In the 1960s, St. Louis gained 3,300 black pupils each year and lost 1,000 white children. The elementary-school population is now more than 66 percent black, and half the faculty are black teachers. The cities of Pittsburgh and Chicago follow similar patterns. Although serious attempts have been made toward desegregation, there are more blacks attending substantially black schools each year. In 1966, black pupils in predominantly black elementary schools of Chicago numbered 188,000. More than 90 percent of Chicago's black children attended all-black schools. The percentage is continuing to change in the direction of more segregation. Many educators are observant enough to note that the situation is not a great deal different from the status of 1954. In large cities, school populations located in the inner areas are all black. Busing does not seem to be working. There are not enough white students in the inner city to bus, and busing with outside systems needs the cooperation of the suburban community. Since each community is an established educational system protected by state laws, taxpayers in each system have enough responsibility caring for their own children. The cost of the transfer (busing and tuition) also makes it prohibitive. No real solution can be accomplished without quality education for each child.

The courts are surfeited with suits contesting the busing of students to a school in another neighborhood or school system. The State of Georgia was brought to court by the Justice Department, which insisted that the state was responsible for the integration of its school systems. Georgia has argued that it does not have such legal power over individual school systems throughout the state. Schools in the South have been integrating slowly. Hill (1966) gives the example of Nashville, Tennessee, as an indication of slow but successful integration. In compliance with a court order, Nashville desegregated one grade each year, accomplishing a full integration of twelve grades by 1967.

The metropolitan school system currently enrolls 90,000 children. The Negro enrollment has increased from 18,496 a year ago to 19,442 during the current year, and the number of public schools with both races represented has increased from forty to seventy-three. The number of Negroes attending school with white children rose from 1,801 or 9.7 per cent of the Negro scholastics, in 1964–65 to 3,405, or 17.5 per cent of the Negro enrollment, in 1965–66. In addition, nineteen white children are currently attending Negro schools, compared with three whites last year. [Hill, 1966, p. 301.]

As the debate over the meaning of desegregation continues, it is unfortunate that those public schools of substantially all-black or all-white populations have to be labeled unfair, unequal, or racially prejudiced. An all-black school can have quality education. Able black teachers and principals *can* carry out sound educational programs in substantially all-black schools. An all-white school is not necessarily un-American. The question of integration should not be a numbers game but should be interpreted from the viewpoint of psychological health. Integration must bring about an equal chance to learn cognitively and affectively in coping with the environment. Anything short of this is not worth the conflict in our social systems.

eight

Improving language skills of children with deprived backgrounds

Maintaining intellectual and emotional growth in economically deprived children depends upon several factors, but one factor seems to predominate our thinking about cognitive and affective development: the skills in the use of language. The amount and variety of patterned stimulation provided by the environment determine the kind of language development. If children are exposed to a limited language experience, they will not communicate as well and will fail to respond in the same way as children from more advantaged backgrounds. The rural, isolated child and the ghetto-bound child have not had the opportunities of "learning to listen" to complex grammar, have not been exposed to extensive vocabulary, and have not been consistently rewarded for verbal behavior. Defects in auditory discrimination contribute further to the failure of poor children to perform well in the English language skills promoted by schools. The one outstanding cause of the slowness of deprived children to perform well on written work and in oral language is poor verbal mediation.

Rural deprived children seldom leave their immediate geographic area; inner-city children become localized to the dull, drab, tenement areas. Just as books, magazines, and newspapers are seldom seen in the homes of abject poverty, stimulating and divergent toys are absent in the homes of the poor. Advantaged children engage in a highly verbal type of role playing with the toys, costumes, and books which their parents have purchased. The museums, zoos, movie theaters, sports events, and large stores with numerous items to stimulate the imagination add tremendously to the verbal stimulation of advantaged youngsters. So frequently, deprived children lack the experiences which, in their more advantaged peers build meaning for the sounds and symbols of language. The question for all parents and teachers dealing with disadvantaged children is how to overcome the initial deficit of verbal mediation (one to five years of age) and the cumulative-deficit effect of verbal and conceptual output (six years to adolescence). To deal effectively with the improvement of language skills at those crucial periods requires a consideration of two language forms: standard English (school language) and the language of the culture from which the children emerge.

NONSTANDARD VERSUS STANDARD ENGLISH

Although too many economically deprived children come to school with a highly developed communications system (a great deal of it on the vocal level), they suffer defeat because they are not verbally adequate. Differences between nonstandard dialects and standard English have been strongly emphasized since Colonial times. Our schools are textbook schools, which attempt to transmit cultural knowledge and attitudes through the standard English language. Any serious deviation is considered almost "un-American" or, at least, as foreign to the public school way of teaching. It has been consistently reported that the most frequent sources of error in the nonstandard language are the violation of subject-verb agreement, substitution of present for past tense, use of *got* for *have,* wide use of *ain't,* and a poor use of the verb *to be* (Cazden, 1968; Loban, 1963). Other errors that become quite noticeable are the use of double negatives and the wrong forms of the personal pronoun.

Teachers find it difficult to approve non-standard usage if it detracts from the reverence and authority of standard English in the classroom. Nonstandard English is a social liability and prevents both children and adults from accomplishing status and self-esteem. Just what specific features of nonstandard English are looked upon as objectionable or are negatively evaluated in language appraisal is difficult to demonstrate (Cazden, 1968). Generally, small points and relatively insignificant word and grammar errors characterize nonstandard English as "bad English" or "low-level talk." A powerful politico-social line is drawn between those who "have it" and those who do not have competence in the English (standard) language. The image established by the "correct" use of the standard English language determines the behavioral expectancy in the classroom.

Children who use a nonstandard dialect also may have difficulty comprehending denotatively and connotatively what the teacher is saying in standard English and what the textbook is supposed to be communicating. In a classroom of disadvantaged children, serious harm could result if the teacher forced a total communication in standard English. Nonstandard English would be frowned upon and considered inferior and low-level. Any child's identity with such a language form would be classified as inferior. The tactfulness of a sensitive teacher of deprived children permits both language forms as acceptable and worthwhile. Neither language is rated as better, but situations are described in which each language form is more appropriate. A number of years ago, Fries (1940, p. 287) observed that the only striking difference between the two language forms is in the limited use of resources in the nonstandard English:

It appeared that the differences between the language of the educated and that of those with little education did not lie primarily in the fact that the former used one set of forms and the latter an entirely different set. In fact, in most cases, the actual deviation of the language of the uneducated from Standard English grammar seemed much less than is usually assumed. . . . The most striking difference between the language of the two groups lay in the fact that Vulgar English seems essentially poverty stricken. It uses less of the resources of the language, and a few norms are used very frequently.

We know very little about dialect differences between lower socioeconomic and middle class societies, but research is continuing on ways of categorizing the functions that language serves in various socioeconomic levels (Cazden, 1968). If there is to be a widespread change in the verbal ability and conceptualization process of economically deprived children, the subcultural functions of language must be respected and used as a vehicle of communication. Stamping out the nonstandard English as a worthless caricature that must be discarded will merely predict a greater negative self-concept among deprived children.

THE READING READINESS PROBLEM

Mastering the complex task of deriving meaning from the pages of books is the formula for success in schools. Disadvantaged youngsters acquire this skill too slowly or not at all. The curriculum, teaching strategies, and instructional materials for preparing three-, four-, and five-year-old children to read are being developed in various experimental programs. A few early-education models have proposed that a highly formal, phonetic reading program be introduced at the five-year level, e.g., the University of Georgia Research and Development Center program. If the phonetic reading program is introduced at the kindergarten level, it is very likely to be preceded by a highly structured oral language readiness curriculum emphasizing labeling, discrimination, and generalization. The structured lesson plans for three- and four-year-olds permit children to move from level to level in verbal skills and cognitive styles of thinking (Mason et al., 1969; Taylor, 1969). The principles and procedures in highly structured cognitive programs are supported by the structural linguists, who insist that the children master complex syntax before they come to school in a first-grade program. Those who have insisted on a strong sound-symbol readiness program in pre-kindergarten and especially in kindergarten have demonstrated the effectiveness of such an early-childhood program with advantaged children. Many are experimenting with economically deprived children in federally sponsored programs.

For the disadvantaged child, deficit in verbal mediation points up the serious problem in any kind of readiness programs. Oral language and conceptual development are the assets that advantaged children will use in working out problems in readiness programs. Deprived children do not function in the same way. Typical basal reading readiness programs among deprived children sometimes require three to four times as much time as with "average" children (Ware, 1964). Prekindergarten schools for deprived children, therefore, will have to direct their major thrust toward the development of oral skills and the building of concrete experiences to be associated with verbal labels. Oral language is the key—"talk, talk, talk" in small groups (about five or six pupils), in which there are plenty of opportunities to speak and to be heard. Meaningful equipment which can be touched and changed in shape and form must also be provided. Deprived children must be taken to stimulating places and exposed to the world of signs, symbols, and relationships. Directors of early-childhood programs must be challenged by the possibilities of "making up" for the difference in verbal stimulation between an advantaged and a disadvantaged home.

MATRIX GAMES

One of the most effective ways of developing verbal ability and concept formation among three-, four-, and five-year-old deprived youngsters is the use of a games approach, particularly matrix games (Gotkin, 1967). Since the game is played in groups of five or six, opportunity for dialogue is greatly facilitated. The verbal emphasis in asking children to pick up various shapes and colors and place them upon highly discriminating pictures generates the labeling, discrimination, and generalization that prepares for reading. The verbal interaction in dealing with generalizations (i.e., the common elements in a row or column) lays the groundwork for a classificatory conceptual system in the learner. Intensive work with matrix games speeds up the verbal process among prekindergarten children and develops the warehouse of word associations to bring about abstract functioning.

COMPREHENSIVE SERVICES

It would be presumptuous to attempt to change the cognitive lives of deprived children without being concerned about medical-dental, nutritional, psychological, and social services. No matter how stimulating a classroom might be, an economically handicapped child has physical requisites which must be satisfied before a stable cognitive gain can be expected. Tissue needs of hunger and thirst, as well as safety needs, demand attention before needs of self-fulfillment. In economically depressed areas, the total child has to be considered. Merely thinking of a child's interaction in a classroom is narrow and foolhardy.

THE UNGRADED PRIMARY AND INDIVIDUALIZED INSTRUCTION

The graded school system is based on the principle that there is an identifiable curriculum which almost all children can master during specific periods of time, e.g., first grade, second grade, and third grade. Deprived children have not been able to assimilate the curriculum during those specific periods. Data consistently reveal that economically deprived children generally fall back two to three years in the curricula by the time they reach the fourth grade. As a group, economically deprived youngsters are significantly different from advantaged children in verbal mediation. To expect poverty children to move through complex learning tasks at the same *rate* as advantaged children is recognized as mystical jibberish. Principals in schools are beginning to realize that when a large part of their student population is economically deprived, some other system must be developed if reading levels are to be maintained among deprived children. Children differ widely in the *application* of reading skills and in the *rate* at which they acquire them. Since public school children are expected to achieve the basic reading skills by the beginning of fourth grade, why can't we establish the specific sequence of skills for each child? Why is it that all children (deprived and advantaged) have to learn in terms of the commercial materials to which they are exposed?

The sequence of basic primary reading skills appears to be better accomplished in ungraded schools. In traditional, graded school systems, the criterion for promotion and advancement is a locked-step pattern and pace modeled after "the average advantaged student." The initial concern of all those teachers attempting to teach reading to deprived students is the continuing diagnosis of the skills of each learner as he progresses through a sequence of more and more complex behaviors. As he is programmed through a sequence of basic skills, each motivational step and each production become self-reinforcing agents. Teaching reading is primarily a job of setting the conditions for each child to proceed at his own rate and, at the same time, intermittently reinforcing the successful steps in the program. The problem for the teacher is to present a large variety of interesting tasks. To keep the lesson interesting and novel for each reader demands that the teacher and the paraprofessional be very well informed of the level of each child's functioning and what reading events would be most interesting and novel to the young reader. The ungraded primary, in which focus is on the individual rather than his grade level, is much more effective in developing reading skills among disadvantaged children.

STRUCTURED SEQUENCE OF READING SKILLS

The important direction for developing initial reading skills in most disadvantaged youngsters is to diagnose each child's present perceptual and verbal abilities and then bring him along step by step in a behavioral sequence of sound-symbol relationships. If the deprived child is permitted to slip and miss a basic skill along the way, it is not long before his total reading program is in jeopardy. One of the reasons for the importance of avoiding the omission of even one sequential step in a deprived child is that it is very unlikely that the phonetic problem will be noted at home. Very little assistance with phonics can be expected outside the classroom. Generally, advantaged children will receive a great deal of reinforcement in phonetic problems during the home hours. The important issue with deprived children is that they should not be permitted to have gaps in learning processes. Teaching children a relatively high number of associations before they move on to more complex structural skills will bring about a higher level of competence in each child.

It may be that behavioral sequences develop a cognitive set or style in the beginning reader and are the best predictor of accomplishing reading skills. Gotkin (1969) suggests that programmed reading is extremely important for disadvantaged learners because too much is going on and children are unable to focus on relevant dimensions. Learning theorists have been advocating this position for years. The first step in learning is motivation: get the attention of the subject and remove competing stimulation so that the subject can attend to the specific stimuli. In the beginning stages of reading, effective strategy is to remove the competing environment and reinforce strongly the structured, simple steps in sequence.

Gotkin, McSweeney, and Richardson (1969) demonstrated the value of an empirically derived sequence for the acquisition of analytical skills. During a three-year research project for the Office of Education in cooperation with the Institute for Developmental Studies (New York University), five-year-old children from economically deprived backgrounds were taught an interrelated hierarchy of beginning reading skills. Programmed instruction provided the vehicle of presentation, specifying in behavioral terms the steps to reading proficiency. The approach to teaching the structural skill sequence involved teaching a few sounds (e.g., *m*, *p*, *o*), combining them in pairs (e.g., *mo*, *po*), and then presenting them in three-letter words (e.g., *mop*). The skills were developed from anagrams, bigrams, and then trigrams; blending of the letter sounds became the crucial question in the progression of skill sequence. Students were tracked at regular, frequent intervals, and teachers were continually fed back information about each child's performance and development. Results over three years were most promising and support Gotkin's contention that large proportions of disadvantaged children are rapid learners but that the standard curriculum of schools has failed to permit them to demonstrate how capable in learning they are.

PERFORMANCE AIDS IN TEACHING READING

Aids in teaching reading by a programmed method range from simple manuals to sophisticated electronic equipment. Gotkin, McSweeney, and Richardson (1969) have developed a materials engineering approach to teaching reading which has great potential for the parents, tutors, paraprofessionals, and reading specialists. The *Performance Aids in Teaching* (PAT) differ from commercially produced manuals, for they provide a general framework which includes a wide range of stimuli that can be presented to "average students" and a wide range of expected responses from students. Basically, the aids are merely broad descriptions of what ought to be done rather than prescriptions of what each child should do. McSweeney feels that commercial materials are passive guides, therefore, as opposed to the active guidance that PAT presents to the agent's performance.

Analogous to machine programming, every word or image to be presented to the child is specified and controlled. The sequence of events dealing with the interaction of teacher and pupil is highly programmed. Although it is impossible to specify every stimulus with every behavioral event, PAT tends toward an exhaustive specification for a prescribed population. Presently, PAT materials are being used in Newark, New Jersey; Plainfield, New Jersey; Atlanta, Georgia; and New York City. Although PAT can take a variety of forms, a book form has proved to be economical and flexible. The instrumental agent (teacher or paraprofessional) reads the left page while the child is encouraged to look at the right page. The essential feature is that the program actively prescribes all the necessary words and signs which are meant to elicit responses from children.

The benefit of the PAT materials in an early-childhood program for economically deprived children is that they permit paraprofessionals (and professional teachers) to teach complex beginning reading skills with a limited amount of pretraining (Gotkin, 1969). Early results in the Atlanta Follow Through program using PAT materials point up two important conclusions: (1) there is a heavy need for diagnosis of each student's ability, and (2) children using PAT have learned how to learn, i.e., have developed a cognitive style for solving beginning reading tasks.

PROGRAMMED STRATEGY AND THE CREATIVE PROCESS

Programmed instruction avoids the abrupt conclusion in the educational process. When activities are planned so that one step leads to another, there are no stops in the learning process. Each solved problem only serves to raise more questions and to motivate children toward continuous learning. Knowledge should not be gathered together in a pile, in a drawer, or on a bookshelf; it should be the stimulant to further knowledge.

The learning process is analogous to the three stages in the Saturn V rocket, which presents us with the notion of tremendous blast-off and the successive steps, each setting off new bursts of motion toward an objective. Each cluster of learned behavior should present a divergent approach to the complex business of learning. It is pretty difficult to imagine human learning confined to a Skinner box. Because of environmental deficits, children from economically deprived homes must be guided carefully along a pathway into new situations and new worlds of thought. Most often, the disadvantaged child has a background of disorder, lack of logical planning, and a world determined more by emotion than by thinking. He cannot be permitted the luxury of failure. He needs discipline and self-control as well as ordered flexibility which can be achieved only in a scientifically ordered program.

Critics of programmed instruction refer to the emphasis on programs to the near exclusion of everything else. A tendency to use programmed instruction as the *only* approach to cognitive learning results from those educators who are overwhelmed by missionary zeal for behavioral analysis and programming and feel obliged to use this method. There are many scholars who do not agree with the total emphasis upon programmed strategies among the disadvantaged because they believe that with this approach the creative process in each child becomes stifled and the sensitivity to problems, the making of guesses, the testing and modifying of solutions, and the communication of the process to others are heavily limited. Those educators and psychologists who propose *discovery methods* and *inquiry approaches* have concluded that most children have lost their inquisitiveness, which is so fundamental to the scientific method, by the time they finish elementary school.

In applying theory (or strategies) to reading, proponents of *behavioral analysis* (i.e., modification of behavior, programmed instruction, etc.) and leaders of the *creative approach* (i.e., the inquiry method, discovery, creative-aesthetic strategies) would have us believe that there is no middle ground. Those interested in teaching reading would either control the stimulus features rigidly, externally reinforce for correct solutions, and shape behavior by small steps *or* present a variety of stimuli, encourage children to ask questions, test their best guesses, and receive reinforcement from their own solutions and products. With economically deprived children, both theories and strategies are presently being employed in early-childhood intervention programs. What should be kept in mind is that, in itself, there is no one theory or one set of strategies that is best or that precludes other theories. The child's abilities and skills should determine the kind of processes and strategies to be employed. In beginning reading, a phonics approach with tight control over stimulus and response characteristics can still present a variety of experiences and the novelty of new reading material. Children can still be allowed to ask as many questions as they are expected to answer. At some levels of development, especially in the initial learning of a task, reinforcement should be given every time. Later on, as the child experiences success and moves forward in the learning sequence, he does not need to be reinforced every time but is intrinsically reinforced by his own accomplishment. To vigorously program every component in learning would be boring and hypnotizing. To present a variety of stimuli and ask for a number of different solutions adds to motivation and brings sensitivity to problem solving.

The PAT materials are aimed in the direction of asking the child to use problem-solving skills rather than store facts about letters. The facts that are stored are products of trying-out processes. Expected reading levels for the first grade, second grade, and third grade are replaced by mastery levels of skills in terms of processing information. Observing and testing become more important in the teaching strategies than the end product. With the emphasis on *process* in the programmed instruction and on creative approaches to reading, the disadvantaged child is going to learn to read. Both theories and many different strategies can be used effectively with those learners with limited experience. With the heavy emphasis on verbal mediation, programmed reading, and a games approach, it should not be construed that there are no adequate basal reading series with which the disadvantaged can learn to read. The Open Highway Program by Scott Forsman Company and the 360 Reader (1969) by the Ginn Publishing Company have been used successfully with the disadvantaged. The Open Highway program begins with the first grade and continues on up through the grades in sequential learning tasks. Materials other than books assist the teacher in developing the ability to read. The 360 Reader begins with ten basic steps or stages of sequential development in learning to read. Concern for creativity in reading is dispersed throughout the whole program. When school systems are in a position to provide effective teachers with a low teacher/pupil ratio and with comprehensive services to the deprived children, reading programs in the Open Highway series or the 360 Reader can be most promising.

CLINICAL DIAGNOSIS AND THE READING SPECIALIST

The regular primary-school teacher, as well as teachers in the elementary school, are not expected to be reading specialists. Specialists can discuss characteristics of reading successes and failures with teachers and propose plans for overcoming failures. With a background of many cases in which technical skills have been used to correct reading difficulties, the reading specialist provides diagnostic aids and treatment suggestions for behavioral problems.

Above all, a clinic staff with reading specialists, psychologists, physicians, and social workers should provide a complete profile and prognosis of each child referred for evaluation. Clinics can provide the means for discriminating the mentally retarded from children who have reading difficulties because of verbal deprivation. Those children who have organic dysfunction can be identified, and the most promising therapy can be provided. When all professional resource personnel come together and evaluate a particular child's performance and try to get at the causes of the lowered performance level, much more confidence can be placed in the diagnosis and suggested treatment.

Many school systems have "traveling clinics," in which psychologists and educational specialists arrive in mobile trailers and work up clinical indices about referred students to be presented and evaluated at the regular staff meetings. Individualized instruction (about forty-five minutes) is a universal outgrowth of such diagnosis. Individual attention at the earliest sign of deficit will serve to prevent a host of failures at the fourth-grade level.

Teachers can be assigned to reading clinics and gain valuable in-service training with realistic clinic experience. Not only the teacher of a particular child who is being evaluated but also teachers assigned to the clinic learn a great deal in the clinic setting which can be translated into more efficient teaching of reading.

REDUCTION OF THE CLASS SIZE AND SMALL-GROUP PROCESS

The importance of the reduced teacher/pupil ratio was described in Chapter 5, but in any discussion of reading problems, the size of the class and the student/teacher ratio must be determined by the effectiveness of the teacher in maintaining a high percentage of reading success. *Paraprofessionals must occupy every class-*

room with deprived children. The paraprofessional is needed as an image for identification and as a means by which subgroups in a classroom can focus on different tasks or at different levels of the same task. The intensive work with deprived children necessitates a careful pacing in each individual. "Being left behind" is the kiss of intellectual death. To be so concerned about each individual's progress, to chart each child's course with him, and to track information about each individual step in learning require the small-group concept in the total learning process. The affective life of the disadvantaged child (i.e., the emotional, the attitudinal, the feeling dimension) is important because it determines so much of his behavior. If increased emotions of fear and hopelessness result from failing at academic tasks, the total child is harmed much more deeply than among more advantaged children. Stable emotional support cannot be predicted as well as in the advantaged homes. The most important objective in a classroom of deprived children is to reduce the indices of fear and hopelessness and bring about better "feelings" of hope, joy, and security. Schools for the deprived *must be schools without failure.* Research has been building strong evidence over the past five years that the self-concept and the achievement motive of deprived children predict scholastic achievement. (Epps, 1970; White, Bashaw, Moore, in press.)

Small groups allow for more physical, verbal, and emotional contacts. Paraprofessionals not only reduce the teacher/pupil ratio and present additional identification figures in the classroom but offer opportunities to touch and be touched and become involved in the emotional lives of the children. Perhaps the ideal classroom would have three teachers (one lead teacher and two assistant teachers). The various styles and individual reinforcement which each teacher provides in the classroom add to the variety of stimuli and the broadening of experiences.

READING MATERIALS

During the 1960s there was much competitive dialogue about the basal reading series, especially in programs for disadvantaged children. First of all, there continues to be disagreement about the advantages of using one basal reading series compared with those of having a multiseries program. Advocates of one basal reading program hold that mobility of pupils in deprived areas is very high (at least 50 percent). Unless schools in metropolitan areas use common reading materials in the primary grades and unless there is a transmission of school records, the child will be lost in the maze of an undefined academic environment. If the school remains a traditional classroom, with the "grade criterion," a new child entering a class would not be continuing in a sequential development of reading skills but would be placed in the milieu of the grade level defined by that particular reading series at that school.

With a relatively high teacher turnover, common materials provide more consistency in the teaching of reading throughout the primary system. In-service programs can be stimulated and monitored much more easily if common materials are used at the early education levels. Multiseries does provide for more generalization among the better readers and extends opportunities for the more highly motivated. Many who advocate multireading series insist that multiseries prevents the "memorizing" of one system and assists the student in general reading ability. With disadvantaged children, it might be best to advocate one system of beginning reading and one series but add different types of readers for those who can adequately deal with them.

The content of the basal readers has always been a problem for disadvantaged children. The experiences of the characters in the basal readers are supposed to be "average American children." The child in an economically depressed area frequently finds the story characters foreign to his own identity. Merely placing pictures of black protagonists in the stories of a book is not going to help; the content and experiences of black people will have to be presented. Otherwise, the white, upper-middle class image is just as abstract as sophisticated statistical formulas. The economically deprived child must "see his kind" in books if the content of books is going to be motivating.

The titles of books in language arts place them in such categories as "grade 7" or "grade 8," but they really turn out to be fifth- or sixth-grade reading materials in terms of difficulty and interest. With disadvantaged children, the conflict is even greater. As deprived children grow older, the difference between advantaged and disadvantaged children becomes greater. The difference in experiences becomes more pronounced. Language arts programs for the disadvantaged become no more than remedial reading programs.

Based on work with a population of disadvantaged children in New York City, a programmed reading series called *Building Reading Power* was established for children at the fifth-grade level. Three separate dimensions of context clues, structural analysis, and comprehension constitute the programmed series. The content of the series is current and has application among disadvantaged children. The series advances communications skills at a pace fitting the limited experience of deprived children.

ACCOUNTABILITY IN READING

No matter what reading program or system is used in teaching deprived children reading skills, the key to the entire educational enterprise is accountability. School systems should be made accountable for the reading ability of the children in each class. Programs which are using state or federal money to upgrade reading levels should be placed under educational audit. In March, 1970, President Nixon revealed that Head Start and Title I projects had not made a measurable change in the reading abilities of economically deprived children. Nineteen percent of the children in those programs did gain in reading skills, while 13 percent of the children did not even gain the pretest score (they even regressed). The remainder of the children in the remedial reading programs (68 percent) did not change their level of reading ability. Anyone who spends a year in a remedial reading program and does not improve must be considered a failure.

There are three comments to be made regarding these data on the Head Start and Title I reading projects: (1) There is a tendency of scores to regress to the mean; i.e., some programs may have accomplished great feats of helping children, but other programs, which accomplished little or no gains, pulled the gains of the better programs to a lower mean level. There were some very fine Head Start and Title I projects, but their gains were obscured by the poor programs. (2) Emphasis in many of those programs was not upon information feedback and evaluation. Many programs feigned evaluation. Money was given "on faith," as if money makes a difference. The teacher learning process can make a difference, but money alone does not make a difference. (3) Frequently, standardized test scores are more of an indication of performance than of learning. So frequently the economically deprived are not motivated to perform on standardized tests. Poor performance results from poor motivation.

Perhaps the concern for performance bonds and educational audit will be prevalent during the 1970s. When programs are given funds to improve children's reading levels and are not refunded if evaluations show a poor program, education will be moved forward. When the worth of a reading program is measured and judged as contributing to the skills of children, the state and federal governments have a responsibility to financially support the program. Throughout the country, the emphasis in the last few years has been upon readiness to read. With the multimillion-dollar concern each year for building readiness for first grade, accountability must serve as the guide for worth and effectiveness. If schools became more business-oriented, they would be more efficient schools.

One of the serious criticisms of accountability and educational audit in reading is that "cold, machinelike methods" would prevail in the classroom. Children would become machines, and teachers would be on an assembly line. Performance would be more important than the child. These remarks emerge from the defense mechanisms of teachers who are anxious about their own abilities. There is no incongruity between teachers' (and administrators') evaluations and their love of children. They are most compatible. The problem will surface if teachers are not made part of the evaluation team and allowed to contribute to the decisions regarding criteria of effectiveness. The teacher who wants "to see" children improve their reading levels is desirous of knowing if he (or she) is doing a good job. When children do not succeed, teachers want to know why they are not advancing. Frequently, in economically deprived areas, the inability of a child to learn cannot be remedied in the classroom. Outside professional help is essential. Educational audit can point to this serious responsibility. Teachers of reading are not "gods" in the educational enterprise. Other professional help is required to make children succeed in learning. The major variable in all the learning is the teacher. He or she must be informed and must be part of the decision-making processes in all matters of reading. If there is a true teamlike effort toward improving language skills among the economically deprived, internal educational audit will be welcomed as a system. There are some schools and some projects which evaluate and feed back information on the entire reading process. If emphasis is on an effective way to help children to read and not merely on evaluation, teachers will not be threatened. More people will be aware of the tremendous job teachers of reading are doing with deprived youngsters.

nine

Information-systems approach in programs for the deprived

One of the greatest problems in the varied experimental programs for economically deprived children has been the limited flow of information and the total lack of feedback to the classroom teachers. There is no greater disappointment than the fact that data, whenever they are collected, never seem to get back to the teachers. There are a large number of compensatory education programs which collect different kinds and amounts of information about teachers and students, but this information is often designed, obtained, and recorded by a group of individuals known as the "research team." Frequently, educational psychologists are hired to decide on what data are important, what standardized tests should be administered, and what analysis will be applied in interpreting the data. The teachers are supposed to do the teaching, and the researchers are expected to do the researching. If the research personnel are very capable, a printed report will contain a multitude of tables and various statistical procedures that will help to demonstrate that a particular funded program was worth the money. Information about the program frequently becomes rooted in random verbal dialogue among the staff and in standardized test scores (about a year late), which are difficult to interpret with disadvantaged youth.

In relatively sophisticated school systems, the instructional service decision and the research and development department will be capably administered, but it will be most unusual if there is a total information exchange between the two divisions. The instructional service personnel will be spending most of their time in deciding upon existing commercial curriculum materials and developing their own materials and procedures, with a strong emphasis upon in-service training. The research division will be exhibiting great fervor in writing proposals to compete for federal and state funds, as well as in auditing many budgets of ongoing programs. There is nothing illicit about these approaches, but the need for continuous feedback to everyone involved in the teacher-learner process is essential. Then, too, a warehouse of information should be continuously tracked and maintained for evaluation purposes.

The problem in educational programs is the need to operationally define what is being done for children and then to measure the effectiveness of what is being done against the criterion of what is considered to be a good program. Information about what is being done and how well it is being accomplished should be continuously available to all those who have responsibility in the program. Merely having data at the end of a program (or months afterward) is not enough for effective pedagogy. An information system which stores its data into a high-speed computer (hardware) in such a way that it is quickly available for analysis is called an *information-retrieval system*. Ideally, an information-retrieval system should be available in every experimental program for disadvantaged children in which more than 150 children are involved. The word *system* means that two or more parts are functioning as one. The many components and their subcomponents, with huge numbers of categories and characteristics, can be effective only when all the parts are working together as one variable. The system provides the communications link among all the people and among all the variables in the program. Every person in the program does not need to receive all the information each day the program is operating. The amount of information and the manner (including the time—

e.g., each week) in which the information is exchanged determine the accuracy, validity, and worth of the particular system.

UPDATING AND COMPUTATION

To the millions of us who watched the Apollo 11 launch and the moon landing, the carefully guided spacecraft performance gave us a magnificent demonstration of a guidance and navigation system. It was remarkable enough to note that a vehicle with 8.7 million parts built by 300,000 people and packaged into the familiar-looking 363-foot-high Saturn rocket (Figure 9-1) was

FIGURE 9-1   *The Apollo 11 trip to the moon carrying astronauts Neil A. Armstrong, Michael Collins, and Edwin E. Aldrin, Jr., July 16, 1969. (Courtesy of National Aeronautics and Space Administration.)*

on its way toward a moving target 230 million miles away, but the onboard computer (1 cubic foot in size and weighing only 65 pounds) performed the phenomenal task of navigating that huge craft in its flight to the moon. The onboard computer actually did the guidance and navigation. Ground control, with its banks of machinery, merely kept sending up to the spacecraft an occasional updating to correct what was on board (Paquette, 1969). If it had been required, the onboard computer could have gone the trip alone.

Accurate timekeeping and precise mathematical calculations were the two important navigational requirements on that historic journey:

A spacecraft on the way to the moon travels at speeds as high as seven miles a second. The moon is also moving at a rate of one-half mile a second with respect to the earth. Thus, a small error in the clock can result directly in significant errors in position. [Bratten, Dec. 21, 1968.]

Without the constant updating of information and computation, the navigation to the moon would continually have deteriorated. "Without the availability of modern high-speed digital computers, the required calculations could not be performed rapidly enough to keep pace with the Apollo voyage." (Bratten, Dec. 21, 1968.) The entire navigational task of Apollo was the measuring, predicting, and correcting of the spacecraft's trip to the moon and return (Figure 9-2). On the basis of receiving, storing, and quickly analyzing information from many sources, the mission was accomplished. An analogy can be drawn to goals in education. The many different professionals and educational agencies, together with the high number of behavioral inputs in the teacher-learner process, demand that systems analysis be adopted by all scientifically oriented school programs. The goals of educating our children must be as carefully planned and controlled as the Apollo 11 trip to the moon. The success of any special-education program directed toward improving the level of disadvantaged children will depend upon a *systems analysis*, i.e., thinking in a special way about a big objective and about each step toward that objective. Information must be fed back quickly and analyzed for improvement in future performances.

SYSTEMS ANALYSIS

There are various ways to describe a systems analysis. One of the interesting characteristics of a systems analysis is that each system turns out to be a subsystem of the large system which is operating; the larger system is also a subsystem of a much larger system. When a systems approach to an educational problem is being built, therefore, the whole idea is to break big problems down into smaller and smaller tasks. The process of breaking down big educational problems so that they can be analyzed has been greatly helped by the use of computers. Many schools have access to computer time and hire programmers to assist them in

FIGURE 9-2 *High-speed digital computer in the Apollo 11 mission helped receive, store, and analyze information throughout the flight.* (*Courtesy of* SDC Magazine.)

preparing information for the computer. Probably the best thing
that has happened to school systems which use computer-based
facilities is that the computer demands a quantitative input and
avoids mystical phraseology. School officials have been forced to
"think out" their problems and define them in operational terminology.

SUBSYSTEMS IN PROGRAMS FOR THE DISADVANTAGED

The number and kinds of subsystems in educational programs
for the disadvantaged will depend upon the terminal objectives
of the educational program.

If there is to be positive educational change among disadvantaged youngsters, a special program with the special emphasis
that has been given in the preceding chapters must be applied to
the general goals of helping deprived children. The specificity
of the behaviors that are expected at the end of the program will
determine the kind of system that is developed. Let us take a
hypothetical example of a Follow Through (FT) program. There
is a definite philosophy and psychological theory in the FT program. Comprehensive services, an instructional early-childhood
model in addition to existing programs in the school system,
parental involvement, and a reduced teacher/pupil ratio would
determine the systems model for the experimental program.
Major emphasis would be upon the educational improvement of
deprived children.

Collecting information about students   Students in FT programs must
fulfill the guidelines of the poverty index if they are going to
receive the total services established in all FT programs. Criteria
selection is generally made at the time of registration for school.
One of the major sources of data is the *confidential-information
sheet* (Figure 9-3), which gives the parents' income and number
of individuals in the family. A well-controlled system maintains
complete confidentiality over the data. Although children are
placed in a Title I program on the basis of the financial state-

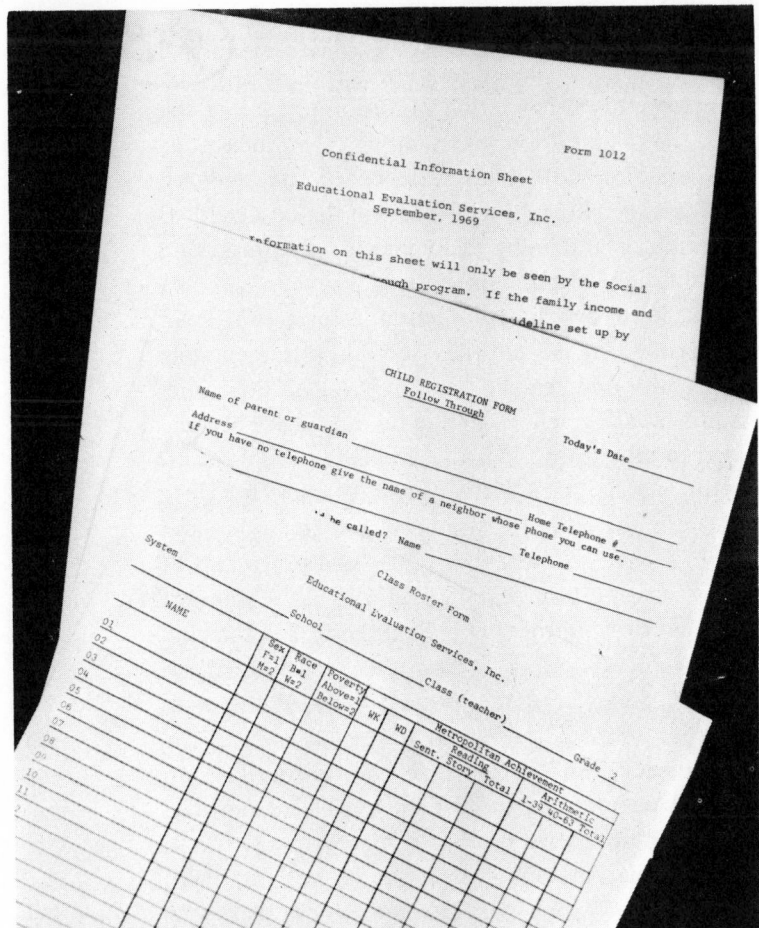

FIGURE 9-3   *Confidential information sheet, child registration form, and class roster form.*

ment, no one but the social worker (if the parent has agreed by signature) will view the original statement. Children selected by such a process are eligible for the FT program.

Another source of information is the *registration form* (Figure 9-3), in which basic data are compiled. The general rule for the entire system, which should protect every parent and child, is that *no information should be verbally asked for more than once.* If information is maintained on one instrument or form, similar or identical questions can be placed on new forms, but the recorder must complete this information before approaching the child or parent. The registration form provides valuable discrimination-type data and can quickly be recorded and analyzed by computer facilities. Sensitized forms provide the best method for avoiding the handling of data by many persons and for saving money and time through keypunching.

When base-line data from the confidential-information form and registration form are obtained, they should be immediately punched on data cards and readied for analysis. At this time, individual ID numbers are given to each child, and these become the numbers used in all future reporting on each child, protecting his identity by name. Class roster forms (Figure 9-3) are quickly generated from existing ID numbers, and sex, race, and poverty code are indexed. Teachers receive the class roster sheet and check out the existing information and all scores from an instrument such as the Metropolitan Readiness Test or the Metropolitan Achievement Test. Data from the class roster form are quickly recorded and placed in the data bank of the computer. The teacher is immediately given information from the total data base for each child in his own class as well as an analysis of the total population in the program (local norms), e.g., 800 children with thirty-two teachers, thirty-two aides, and eight lead teachers. Comparisons can be made with national norms or regional norms which will help to discuss programs other than local ones.

SUBSYSTEMS IN A HYPOTHETICAL FT PROGRAM

Figure 9-4 presents various subsystems in a model FT program. Arrows pointing to and from each component indicate the information exchange for the various subsystems and their components. All data are channeled through the research and development department and its agent for information processing, e.g., Educational Evaluation Services, Inc. or some similar infor-

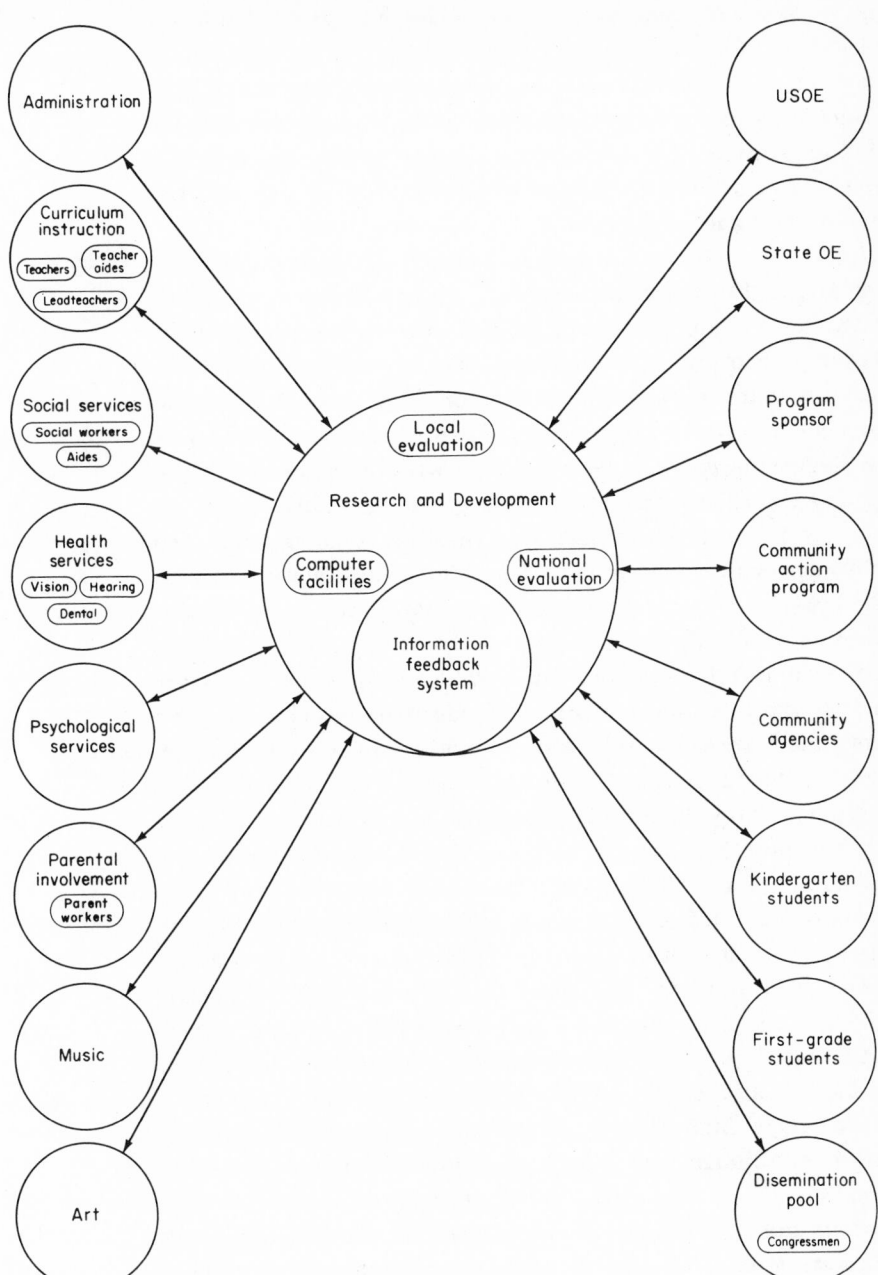

FIGURE 9-4   *Subsystems in a hypothetical Follow Through model.*

mation feedback systems approach. Each subsystem should receive at regular intervals information pertinent to an effective program. An entire book would be required to describe the instruments and the modules (units) in each subsystem. Therefore, only three subsystems are projected here to describe the effect and capability of feedback into the total system working for disadvantaged children.

Medical-dental (health services) subsystem   Teachers are as interested in the total health of a child as they are concerned about his classroom learning. If a child is farsighted, for example, he is certainly going to have difficulty in working at his table. Most teachers are aware of the fact that the Snellen Chart only assists in diagnosing nearsightedness. In early-childhood programs, such as the FT program, the child's language ability greatly influences the visual acuity measures. Disadvantaged children need full diagnosis and treatment. If a child has auditory or visual problems, his classroom responses will show limited achievement levels. Not only do teachers want to know whether a child has been examined by a dentist, but they also want to know what is the health of the child's mouth and what treatment is being given over time. Consistent monitoring should be made on immunizations and blood analysis. The anemic child or one with sickle-cell deficiency will exhibit fatigue levels in the classroom that will deprive him of an opportunity to perform. Figure 9-5 gives a partial list of the hundreds of variables that can be tracked repeatedly (four or five times a year), placed in the data bank, and retrieved in a matter of moments. Information about immunizations, blood analysis, visual and hearing levels can be quickly analyzed for individuals, classes, and schools. Health coordinators can quickly pinpoint schools which have severe or mild medical problems. When the incidence of dental caries is extremely high in one school area, it is much easier to control the budget and place extra time and money into that area.

Collecting medical-dental data is difficult in large programs since every home must be visited for completing the form. Data should be collected at least four times a year. Depending upon the language in the medical-dental form used and the amount of training given to the interviewers, paraprofessionals (e.g., parent workers) could obtain the information with a high degree of reliability. Information about dental and medical examinations as well as visits by the nurse should be kept in personal files in each school. Therefore, two sets of data are kept on each child. One form is in the data bank and is quickly retrievable, and the other data form is the official record signed by qualified personnel. If specific information with open-ended responses and sophisticated medical language is required, the official record can provide such information. The role of the computer-based part of the system is to keep the staff and teachers consistently informed about the major medical-dental variables. So frequently, health records are maintained by a health nurse and are placed in files that require the memory of the nurse to keep the information readily retrievable. The health component in programs for the disadvantaged is too important to be buried in the myriad of folders in the health office.

Instructional-curriculum subsystem   The teachers, program sponsors, research personnel, and staff generate the kind and amount of information required to fulfill the cognitive classroom goals. Generally, pretests and posttests of standardized achievement measures are placed into the feedback system. There is always debate about what kind of standardized achievement tests should be employed, but some kind of comparison is demanded if deprived children are to have an equal opportunity for jobs, scholarships, and awards in later life. If the Metropolitan Readiness Test or Metropolitan Achievement Tests are employed as instruments, scores should be analyzed quickly and returned standardized to the teachers and entire staff. Frequently, mental-ability measures are used to assess general scholastic ability. Some programs use the Stanford-Binet Intelligence Test for an IQ score, while others frequently use the Peabody Picture Vocabulary Test as an index of verbal ability. Scores on pretests in September are most often compared with posttest scores in May. Beyond the global IQ scores, there are a number of verbal and conceptual measures that can be assessed in an early-childhood model and interpreted for teacher-pupil behavior. Some investigators have looked for the effect of experimental treatment on verbalizations during

FIGURE 9-5 *Partial checklist for monitoring the medical-dental variables in Follow Through programs.*

Form 1022

Educational Evaluation Services, Inc.
Medical–Dental Component

ID _____   Date _____ _____ _____

                                         Mo.   Day   Yr.

Immunizations:

1. DPT (Diphtheria, Pertussis, Tetanus)
   1. ___ Has never been immunized for DPT
   2. ___ Has received at least one dose of DPT but is not fully immunized for DPT
   3. ___ Is fully immunized for DPT
   4. ___ Has unknown immunization for DPT

2. Smallpox
   Had this child received a smallpox vaccination during the current FT program?
   1. ___ NO
   2. ___ NO, because of recent vaccination
   3. ___ YES, because he had not recently been vaccinated
   4. ___ YES, because he had never previously been vaccinated
   5. ___ Immunization unknown

3. Hearing
   Had this child received a test of hearing in the FT program?

4. IF result of test was abnormal
   1. ___ Has had no further evaluation
   2. ___ Has been retested
   3. ___ Is receiving treatment
   4. ___ UNKNOWN follow-up status

5. Poliomyelitis
   1. ___ Has never been immunized for polio
   2. ___ Has received at least one dose, but not fully immunized
   3. ___ Is fully immunized for polio
   4. ___ Has unknown immunization for polio

6. Measles
   Had this child received
   measles vaccine during the
   current FT program?
   1. ___ NO
   2. ___ NO, because he
      had already had
      measles vaccine
   3. ___ NO, because he
      already had
      measles
   4. ___ YES
   5. ___ Measles immu-
      nization status
      unknown

7. Vision
   Had this child received a
   test of visual acuity in
   present FT program?
   1. ___ NO
   2. ___ Yes, result
      normal
   3. ___ YES, result ab-
      normal
   4. ___ YES, child not
      testable
   5. ___ NOT KNOWN

8. IF result is abnormal
   1. ___ Has had no fur-
      ther evaluation
   2. ___ Has been fully
      evaluated
   3. ___ Is now wearing
      glasses

9. Height and Weight
   Date of measurement

   _____ _____ _____
   Month   Day   Year

10. Height _____ (inches)

11. Weight _____ (pounds)

play. The speech of deprived children during play can be compared with that of advantaged children by monitoring the following five criteria adapted from Smilansky (1968):

  1. *Fluency:* the average number of words uttered in fifteen
minutes
  2. *Length of utterance:* the average number of words in an
utterance
  3. *Length of sentence:* the average number of words in a sentence
  4. *Contextual speech:* the average number of words uttered in
fifteen minutes if all speech not relevant to play is excluded
  5. *Range of vocabulary: the average number of words uttered in*
fifteen minutes, repetitions excluded

Speech samples included in the verbalizations of deprived children can be classified and analyzed. Knowledge about the speech patterns of each deprived child, or of groups of children, could be checked numerous times during the year. Data could be sent to the central *educational audit*, and an analysis could be returned to each teacher as often as desired.

Many experimental programs provide a *music specialist*, an *art specialist*, and *a speech and hearing specialist*. The laudatory plan of placing highly trained professionals in elementary schools invariably involves a disappointment. There are always too many children or too many classrooms which need the educational specialist. More and more, the specialist is obliged to consider the teacher her student rather than the 500 or 700 children that may be in the program. Some balance must be arranged between working on a 1-to-1 relationship, as in referrals, and working with the teacher and groups of children. I have observed frequently that when the music specialist enters the classroom, the teacher feels she has some free time to write lesson plans, complete reports, etc. Teachers will have to become involved with the educational specialist if any large and lasting gains are to be realized.

Specialists can place many criteria into the information system that will assist them in communicating with teachers and involving them in specialized instruction. For example, a specialist in art might enter the classroom with a brief checklist of specific skills—such as holding a crayon, pressure on the crayon, holding scissors—and ask the teacher to check the information on the checklist as the specialist is carrying out the instruction for the day. Data from the checklist completed by the teacher and teacher aides can be discussed and related to goals in art education and could be placed in a data bank and returned with an analysis of comparisons with other groups.

Reading   If reading is an important curriculum variable in an FT program, the type of diagnosis and the continuous evaluative measures will depend upon the theory and objectives of the total reading program. There are voluminous scales that can assist teachers and specialists in diagnosing individual readiness or reading characteristics and in comparing group levels of abilities and disabilities. There are many tests which could be used as components of the reading subsystem. Since written and oral language improvement are the most important needs among disadvantaged children, the following instruments are suggested as selective criteria in an instructional subsystem:

I. Oral Reading Tests
    A. Informal Reading Inventory
        The IRI is a series of graded paragraphs from selected basal readers and is designed to establish the levels on which a pupil may be instructed. In oral reading, the instructional level is the highest level at which a pupil can read 95 percent of the words without errors and can answer correctly 75 percent of the comprehension questions. The independent level is the highest level at which the pupil attains 99 percent word recognition and 59 percent comprehension.
    B. Durrell Analysis of Difficulty
        The Durrell is a series of tests designed to measure reading ability from the nonreader to the sixth-grade level and to pinpoint specific competencies and difficulties. The oral test consists of a series of paragraphs of ascending difficulty which the pupil is asked to read. Questions which measure comprehension follow each selection. A checklist for recording reading habits and observations made by the examiner is provided. Norms provide estimates for a timed grade placement (a graded measure of reading rate). The basal level is that level at which a paragraph is read without errors.
    C. Spache Diagnostic Reading Scales
        The oral reading test in this battery contains twenty-two reading passages of graduated difficulty from 1.6-grade placement to 8.5-grade placement. The oral performance, in terms of errors and comprehension, provides an estimate of the pupil's instructional level. Norms are provided for the number of word-recognition and comprehension errors to be allowed for each paragraph.

D. Gray Oral Reading Test

The Gray is a series of timed passages constructed to give a measure of oral reading skill. The test provides for the establishment of a basal level (that level at which no word-recognition errors are committed) and a timed grade placement (calculated on the basis of the number of word-recognition errors and the time taken to read the selection orally). The types of errors are recorded so that insights into the kinds of instruction needed may be gained. The questions accompanying each selection are not designed to measure comprehension; they are designed to determine the extent of understanding at the simplest level.

II. Silent Reading Tests

A. Informal reading instructional level is the highest level at which the pupil attains 75 percent comprehension.

B. Durrell Analysis of Difficulty

The silent reading test consists of graded paragraphs to be read silently. Norms provide graded estimates of a pupil's ability to recall the selection just read, as well as graded estimates of silent reading rate.

C. Spache Diagnostic Reading Scales

The silent reading test of the Spache is designed to identify the level at which a pupil can read independently with a 75 percent comprehension.

D. Stroud-Hieronymus Primary Profiles

This battery consists of five tests (1) aptitude for reading, a measure of the pupil's capacity for learning to read; (2) auditory association, a test of the pupil's ability to make the proper association between the initial sound of a word represented by a picture and the letter or letters that stand for that sound; (3) word recognition, a test of the pupil's ability to recognize the printed forms of words; (4) word attack, a test of the pupil's ability to use both context and auditory clues; and (5) reading comprehension. A composite score is provided to give an overall measure of reading achievement, emphasizing the ability to read with understanding.

III. Word-analysis Skills
  A. Nonsense-words (Phonics) Test
      This test consists of a series of nonsense words or syllables which do not appear as words in our current sight vocabulary. The child is asked to pronounce these letter combinations in order to evaluate his ability to use phonics as a means of word recognition. Sections are provided which stress all the phonic skills and principles introduced in the Scott-Foresman basal readers through the third grade. The specific sounds or elements are grouped according to the level at which they are introduced in order to determine at which level retraining should begin.
  B. Spache Diagnostic Reading Scale Phonics Tests
      There are six supplementary phonics tests, each devised to measure a specific phonic skill. These tests help to determine a pupil's need for retraining in the recognition and use of (1) consonant sounds, (2) vowel sounds, (3) consonant blends, (4) common syllables, (5) blends, and (6) letter sounds.
  C. Durrell Analysis of Reading Difficulty
      1. *Word-analysis test:* The word-analysis test is a word list which is used to assess the pupil's ability to correctly analyze words not immediately recognized. Observations provide insights into the pupil's phonic and analysis skills. Norms provide an estimated grade placement.
      2. *Visual-memory test:* The test of visual memory is divided into two levels, the primary and the intermediate. The primary test has a range of from non-reader to third-grade reading level, while the intermediate test has a range of from fourth- to sixth-grade reading level. In using the

primary test, isolated letters and words are presented for several seconds. Then the pupil is asked to choose the word or letter he saw from a list of several words and letters provided in the record booklet. Norms are provided to indicate the level at which a pupil successfully codes in and remembers visual stimuli. In using the intermediate test, isolated words are presented for several seconds, after which the child is directed to write them from memory. Norms provide estimated grade placements calculated on the basis of the number of words reproduced correctly.

3. *Hearing sounds in words:* This is a primary-level test for children whose reading level is grade 3 or below. The test requires the child to notice the separate sounds in spoken words and then indicate in the record booklet words which begin, end, or begin and end like the words pronounced.

D. Silent Reading Diagnostic Test (Bond-Clymer-Hoyt)
The SRDT is composed of the following subtests constructed to evaluate a pupil's functional level in word-recognition skills:

1. *Recognition of words in context:* This test measures the pupil's ability to use context clues in recognizing words.

2. *Recognition of reversible words in context:* This test reveals reversal tendencies.

3. *Locating elements:* This test measures the ability to locate parts of words which are useful in word recognition.

4. *Syllabication:* This test measures the ability to divide words into parts.

5. *Locating root words:* This test indicates a pupil's ability to locate root words.

6. *Word elements:* This test measures knowledge of word elements.

7. *Beginning sounds:* This test is a measure of

auditory and visual discrimination of word beginnings.

8. *Rhyming sounds:* This test measures auditory and visual discrimination of endings.

9. *Letter sounds:* This test measures a pupil's knowledge of letter sounds essential to mastery of the relation between symbol and sound.

10. *Word synthesis:* This test measures the ability to blend words together visually and phonetically.

E. Harrison-Stroud Reading Readiness Test

This is a test administered to pupils to determine whether or not they are ready for reading. Subtests are:

1. *Using symbols:* This test measures the pupil's ability to understand the meaningful use of symbols to represent familiar ideas symbolized by pictures.

2. *Making visual discriminations:* This tests the pupil's ability to make visual discriminations of words common to primary reading vocabulary, those embodying common visual discrimination difficulties, and those frequently reversed. The test is divided into two sections: in part *a*, the teacher controls the pupil's attention to each item; in part *b*, the attention span is uncontrolled.

3. *Using the context:* The ability to use context before actual reading begins is measured through the pupil's use of context given orally by the tester. The pupil is asked to choose and mark one of three pictures which best supplies an element that is missing in the oral context.

4. *Making auditory discrimination:* This test measures ability to discriminate between spoken words which do or do not begin with identical initial consonant sounds. The child is asked to indicate which of several pictured objects begin with

the same initial consonant as that in a word pronounced by the examiner.

5. *Using context and auditory clues:* In this test the pupil listens to oral context which suggests two possible responses illustrated in a group of three pictures. From an auditory clue supplied, he selects the one picture representing the only choice which is right for both context and auditory clues.

6. *Giving the names of the letters:* The pupil is asked to name letters presented on a card.

IV. Sight Vocabulary

A. Dolch Basic Sight Word List

This word list is made up of 220 words, basic to most reading through the third grade. Recognition of 80 percent of these words is the criterion for adequacy.

B. Durrell Analysis Flash Word List

A graded word list is tachistoscopically administered in order to determine the extent of the pupil's sight vocabulary. Norms provide estimated grade placements according to the number of words called correctly during this flashed presentation.

C. Spache Diagnostic Reading Scale

The word lists are used to test the pupil's skills in word recognition and analysis and to determine the level at which he should be introduced to the reading passages. Each of the three lists is standardized and graduated in difficulty.

D. Betts Individual Word Recognition Lists

The Betts test is composed of separate word lists from preprimer level to ninth-grade level. The forms are designed to give two complete and separate tests. The lists may be administered with a tachistoscope and flashed in order to obtain a sight vocabulary level. The lists may also be administered by untimed exposures in order to assess the pupil's skill at analyzing words.

E. SRDT Recognition of Words in Isolation

This test assesses sight vocabulary and indicates visual habits in recognizing words.

V.   Sight Test

The Keystone Visual Survey Tests are tests of usable binocular vision. They are used for screening purposes only. The tests were not designed to give diagnostic data and cannot be compared test by test with clinical findings in the doctor's office. They should not be considered separately but should rather be taken as a whole. The records of these tests will generally give a reliable picture of the subject's visual efficiency.

VI. Hearing Test

The Audiometer Sweep Check is a survey tool for measuring auditory acuity.

VII. Listening Skills (Potential Reading Level)

A.   Durrell Analysis of Listening Skills

The listening comprehension test consists of graded paragraphs to be read to the child and questions designed to measure his comprehension of what he has heard. Listening comprehension is estimated as being on the level where not more than one question in seven is missed.

B.   Spache Diagnostic Reading Scale Listening Skills

Paragraphs are read to the pupil, and comprehension questions are asked. The potential level is the highest level at which he can answer correctly the number of questions normed for that selection. The potential level indicates the pupil's expected reading capacity at the time the test is given.

VIII. Other Tests

A.   Wepman Auditory Discrimination Test

This test is designed to indicate discrimination weaknesses in hearing vowel and consonant sounds in various positions within a word. The pupil listens to the examiner say two words for each test item. He is then asked to determine whether he heard the same sound twice or whether the examiner gave two different sounds (words). The sounds which he fails to discriminate efficiently will be noted in the school report so that the classroom teacher will know with what sounds the pupil needs help.

B. Iowa Test of Basic Skills

This test is administered to determine whether the pupil has the major skills necessary for effective use of reference materials at his current grade level.

C. California Arithmetic Test (Fundamentals)

The arithmetic fundamentals section is administered in order to see how well the pupil can function in an academic subject requiring a minimum of reading skill.

D. Winter Haven Visual Perception Test
Bender Motor Gestalt Test

These tests provide a graphic presentation of a pupil's visual perception skills. The pupil is directed to draw stimuli presented on cards. The drawings are then rated according to normed scales of performance. Accurate perception is seeing correctly that which is presented. Focusing the pupil's attention on his perceptual errors is essential to the corrective program since the pupil *does not realize* that he is not seeing that which is presented as he should see it. The Winter Haven gives a numerical score. Scores below 60 are considered unsatisfactory. The Bender gives a developmental age.

E. The Frostig Developmental Test of
Visual Perception

This test is administered when serious perceptual problems are indicated on the preceding tests. This test seeks to measure five operationally defined perceptual skills: (1) eye-motor coordination, (2) figure-ground perception, (3) constancy of shape, (4) position in space, and (5) spatial relationships.

A splendid example of a reading criterion test was developed for the Follow Through program in Atlanta, Georgia. Based upon a beginning reading program developed by Gotkin, McSweeney, and Richardson (1969), anagrams, bigrams, trigrams, and blending were analyzed for each child at various stages in the program. The diagnostic value of the criterion test in assessing basic reading skills for each individual as well as for groups and subgroups has been demonstrated in the Follow Through program.

Parent-involvement subsystem   There are many different objectives in involving parents in programs. Some parents in large metropolitan areas feel strongly that they should administer their own community schools, i.e., that parents "should run the schools." Any educational program for economically deprived children must bring parents closer to their children and make them more motivated to the goals of public education and the ongoing process in the classroom.

Parent educators, who spend half their time in classrooms and the remainder visiting homes, provide communication between school and home and bring some instructional strategies into the homes. The frequency of visits to the home by teachers or parent workers can easily be recorded. The number of telephone conversations made to the homes or made by parents to the school can be consistently tracked and examined. Parents are always invited to meetings; attendance can always be registered.

Some educational models directed toward disadvantaged children attempt to train parents for teacher-aide jobs. It is this training of the parents as teacher aides which seems to be the crucial variable. Information on how this training takes place would be the essential material for the parent-involvement subsystem. The system would require checking on the parent workers at various periods of time to determine whether the parents have learned sufficient facts, acquired instructional skills at a competent level, and developed the necessary attitudes for working efficiently with parents of poor children. Two examples help to emphasize this point. Parent workers in Atlanta's Follow Through program (1968) remained full time in the classroom as aides for three months prior to spending full time in visiting homes. Some observers felt that the parent workers should have been working with parents in homes earlier and more substantively. But this proved to be the best mistake Atlanta made. The parent workers had learned so many skills in actually teaching the children and had obtained so much information in the in-service training that they were extremely confident and competent when they visited parents. They knew about matrix games, language lotto games, and reading variables, and they communicated and demonstrated this knowledge to parents in an admirable way. Evaluation reports of parental comments supported the preparedness of the parent workers.

The following year (1969) new parent workers were anxious to visit homes as quickly as those who had been in the program for a year. Staff members noted a high level of anxiety among the new parent workers and a very ineffectual skill development. Even the attitudes about teaching others seemed to be disappointing. The parent-involvement coordinator was quick to sense the problem of "too much, too soon." It takes time to become acquainted with the many processes in the classroom, and it takes a great deal of time to modify and develop attitudes. Checklists on skill development and positive attitude attainment can be placed into the subsystem and can be carefully analyzed over time.

Information for social workers is also a necessary part of a retrieval system. Besides demographic data, information about referrals to social agencies becomes a valuable asset in the total program. It is always important to know *who* referred a child to *which* social service personnel, and *when* the referral was made, and *who* did something, and *when* it was done. Progress in solving basic social service problems is also a most desirable index for computer-based systems. Frequently, when educational programs provide a competent professional social worker to work with family and community problems, the responsibilities are so numerous that the social worker must keep "in her head" and in her classified file drawers mountains of data, which are difficult to pull together for program information. Putting the information in more quantifiable form and placing it in a computer data bank monitors the program more efficiently, cuts down on errors, and contributes to creative solutions to social problems early in the school year. Continuous refinement of forms according to changing variables in each locale will prevent an outdated assessment of social service (Figure 9-6).

FIGURE 9-6 *Part of a parent questionnaire for a Follow Through program in a typical public school system.*

Parent Questionnaire

Form 1081

Child's Name _____   I.D.# _____
Child's Teacher: _____

Please answer all questions.
1. Check which person is completing this questionnaire:
      Mother   (   )
      Father   (   )
      Guardian   (   )
      Other   (   )
2. Check which grade your *youngest* child in Follow Through is in:
      Kindergarten (   )
      First Grade   (   )
3. Do you have *more than one child* in the Follow Through program?
      Yes   (   )
      No   (   )
4. Is this the first year you have had a child in school?
      Yes   (   )
      No   (   )
5. Are *both* of this child's parents living together in the home?
      Yes   (   )
      No   (   )
6. Do any of the child's grandparents live in the home?
      Yes   (   )
      No   (   )
7. How long have you lived in this neighborhood?
      _____ years and/or _____ months
8. Do you have a child 16 years old or older who helps you by looking after your other children when you need to go out?
      Yes   (   )
      No   (   )

INFORMATION THEORY AND EVALUATION

One of the greatest problems in education has been the evaluation of programs. Educational evaluation has developed into a formidable factor in programs funded with federal money. The Elementary and Secondary School Act (1965), especially in the Title I and Title III programs, made the administrators and proposal writers significantly aware of the evaluation component in educational programs. In 1970, the Nixon administration introduced the word *accountability* into the instructional aspect of federal programs in addition to the budget component in applications for federal money. With the emphasis on accountability came the performance achievement bond, in which industrial firms were given contracts to raise the reading and mathematics scores of a specified number of children. In 1970, the Office of Economic Opportunity contracted with six commercial firms to enact performance achievement contracts in twenty metropolitan areas. Evaluation, accountability, and visibility were components that were no longer appended as issues separate from instruction. Proposals were now written in which evaluation and instruction, or treatment, were intertwined throughout the entire proposal and were to be a continuous ongoing part of every educational program. Debate about the nature of evaluation will be intense in the 1970s and will center on the information-systems approach to educational problems.

A new look at evaluation theory and application is being taken which provides some hope for those who have been discouraged with the fact that models of evaluation have insisted on experimental and control groups. In the past, educators trying to locate control groups for purposes of comparison and "to find their significant differences" sought some school (or schools) which had a relative similarity to the experimental school and then "forced'" the school to give a number of standardized tests which had little or nothing to do with that school's own objectives. Most of the time, the data were collected cursorily, with varying administrative procedures. In almost every case the organizational variance in the control group was nothing like the variance in the control group. The variance within each structure was usually greater than that between groups. Population variance has always been a serious problem in "experimental" situations. Recently, a new theory has appeared which makes the information-retrieval system a must in programs for the disadvantaged.

What appears to be happening is that evaluation is being either defined as or related to the providing of information for decision making. This interpretation causes evaluation to move from the act of making a judgment itself as in the past (good-bad, effective-ineffective, pass-failure) over to providing the person who has to make such judgments or decisions with the information needed to make them. Thus, the evaluation escapes the value question. [Cook, 1970, p. 14.]

When we consider the emphasis on information theory in recent writing about evaluation, it is not clearly recognized that there has been a long history of models for evaluation which point to the retrieval of data, interpretation of data, and the character of decision making as the essence of optimal evaluation. Business and industry have used this model successfully for a number of decades. Basically, an information model is a management control type of model. Many teachers and administrators have felt guilty about regarding the teacher as a business manager. In today's pedagogy, however, we are seeing individualized instruction, small-group processes, the use of consultants, communication of instructional materials to the home, and the use of paraprofessional and special service personnel. These functions bring the role of the teacher into perspective as a manager of classroom activity. Many people now share the responsibility of teaching. Emphasis can be placed correctly on information in the decision-making process. In management control theory, we understand the setting of objectives, the establishment of criteria to identify the reaching of the objectives, measures of behavior toward the goals, and identification of deviations from acceptable performance together with the decisions to return to correct performance toward expected goals.

Feedback or cybernetics-control system   The control over a system is maintained by information and decision. For a system to be self-regulatory and efficient, data are required. Generally, large amounts of data are required from a number and variety of subsystems, and these data need interpretation to various personnel at various levels of explanation. The interpretation of the data (information) should be regularized; i.e., feedback reports should be consistent, well planned, and on schedule. Feedback reports in the Atlanta public schools Follow Through program are regularized at four specific periods in each scholastic year. Information is provided continuously to various personnel, but it is presented in an integrated, collective way four times a year. *Cybernetics* can be defined as a science of communications and control (Beer, 1959). Cybernetics control is a mechanical way of obtaining information for regulating behavior. Feedback is the key to a cybernetics type of model.

In programs for the disadvantaged, the information feedback model is extremely important. One of the reasons for this is that using feedback, the goals of a program can be changed. So frequently we study or report about programs which stipulated their objectives clearly enough but in which evaluation was merely checking on pretest and posttest scores to discover "the significant difference." An information system which is identified by excellent cybernetics control would supply information consistently which might bring about a change in goals during the year. Above all, knowledge about what is happening or has happened would not be left to the end of the year, when the program has terminated. This is the severe criticism in evaluations of Projects Head Start and Follow Through. Information is received too late for decision making. Frequently, information is reduced to minimal criteria on a pretest-posttest basis. The variables that are identified do not have a great deal to do with an experimental model, but above all, they do nothing to modify the program.

Function of evaluation in education   Education is concerned with the total child and not merely with standardized test scores in reading and mathematics. Concern for evaluation in education should be toward the total process of learning and each of the many components in a comprehensive program. Evaluation should be looked upon as an information system which will:

1.   Identify what each component of a total program is trying to do.
2.   Monitor measurable performance in each of those components.
3.   Feed information back at regularized periods to every person in the program, although in different modes.
4.   Identify deviations in performance toward objectives.
5.   Provide opportunities for decisions to restore system to reach stated objectives, or change objectives for new approaches. Continuous monitoring of decisions will keep program on a critical path toward positive goals.
6.   Consistently re-aim and reassess results and provide an open system in which data permit more efficient decision making.

ten

Preservice and in-service training for teaching disadvantaged children

There seems to be only one cardinal rule in preparing teachers to teach disadvantaged children: teachers who are to fulfill the specialized role of teaching deprived children must be trained in a very different way from teachers in general education. So much improvement is needed, however, in preparing teachers for directing classroom learning among advantaged children and in the development of in-service training for those who are already teaching that it makes the task of preparing teachers for the instruction of the disadvantaged even that much more of a problem. Before anyone can teach the disadvantaged, he (or she) must elect to teach economically deprived youngsters or must be assigned to such a task even though it might not be desired. The assignment gives the mandate to teach, but the reason for the assignment may have nothing to do with criteria for effective teaching. Although there is not very much experimental evidence, it can be stated with confidence that most teachers consider it "second best" to be assigned to an economically deprived group of children. This does not mean that the majority of teachers *compelled* to teach disadvantaged children do not have a real love for poor children or that those teachers are actually second-rate teachers. Probably the most important reason for the negative attitude toward teaching the disadvantaged results from the deep frustrations involved. The large, overcrowded classroom, the poor equipment, the disinterest of school board members in supporting a worthwhile attack on the effects of poverty, the cumulative cognitive deficit in many deprived children, and other sociological variables stifle and restrict any teacher enthusiasm for helping poor children to become as able (mentally and emotionally) as economically advantaged children. Whether teachers choose to teach deprived children or are "forced" into the task, something drastic must be done to change the image and make the job more operationally sound. If teachers can be taught specifically what it means to teach the deprived and if teachers are given the resources to do those specific teaching tasks, education will jump forward at least a hundred years. The first crucial question that preservice and in-service personnel must resolve is: What specific teacher-learner behaviors are you talking about when you speak of "teaching deprived children"? The second question is: "Are you preparing (preservice) young men and women to fulfill the defined teacher role, and are the expected behaviors on the job being successfully implemented (in-service) in the daily events of the classroom?" If there is going to be a serious, scientific effort to develop an effective teacher training program for disadvantaged children, systems analysis of the complete teacher-role behavior must be defined and monitored over time and situations. Instead of building a systems approach to teaching in the ghettos and in rural, isolated poverty areas, most colleges of education have been adding new courses about "the disadvantaged learner" to the overburdened teacher education curriculum. A larger number of schools are not even preparing special courses in the curriculum but are leaving it up to college instructors to "bring in" references to deprived groups in lectures and laboratory exercises. The ideal program for teacher training for disadvantaged children will have to be a systems approach, a competency- skill-based program, operationally defining each individual task and skill used on the job.

SYSTEMS ANALYSIS OF TEACHER TRAINING

Major emphasis in any systems approach must be directed to the goals and objectives of the total program. Goals for teaching disadvantaged children certainly overlap with those for teaching advantaged children, but there are significantly different immediate, intermediate, and final goals. Theoretically, the terminal educational goals of all American youth are the same. Although great divergency is permitted in the skills that are developed individually, the "ability to cope with the environment" and the "pursuit of happiness" seem to be universal goals. The immediate objectives and those behaviorally defined goals that are two or three years distant from the immediate goals seem to be hardest for teachers and educators to define and agree upon. The background for these objectives demands a scientific knowledge of the nature of the learner—his knowledge, skills, attitudes, emotions, health, and family background. Objectives relating to teacher-pupil interaction within the classrooms would depend upon knowledge about prior research with cognitive and affective variables in the classroom. Once objectives have been behaviorally defined, i.e., fulfilling social criteria, describing observable patterns in the nature of learner, etc., specific behaviors in the job of teaching the disadvantaged can be identified. The development of specifications for the preservice and in-service programs would follow an information flow chart similar to that in Figure 10-1.

EXPECTED TEACHER BEHAVIOR: JOB ANALYSIS

The expected teaching behaviors constitute the role behavior which research has indicated is most likely to cause the optimum learning of deprived students. Based upon what we know from

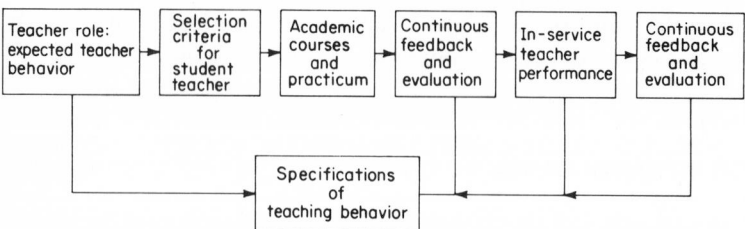

FIGURE 10-1 *Systems flow chart for preservice and in-service programs among teachers of the disadvantaged.*

such programs as Head Start and Follow Through, the teacher role would include both the professional teacher and paraprofessionals, i.e., teaching assistants, teacher aides, and secretaries. Activities of professional teachers (PT) can be described as (1) *instructional behavior* in the presence of the children and (2) *preparatory and evaluation activity* that is not in the presence of children. When instructional activities of the PT are described, it seems logical that these activities be broken down into other subsystems: prekindergarten, kindergarten to the third grade, fourth to sixth grades, junior high school years, and senior high school period.

Let us examine some of the PT expected behaviors during the kindergarten through the third grade:

PT Instructional Activities with the Class

1. Helping students to learn the physical handling of classroom equipment, e.g., crayon, paper, pencil, pen.
2. Reducing anxiety and defensiveness in the learner by providing an acceptable and desirable identification figure for each child.
3. Assisting children in the acquisition of labels.
4. Developing in each child the ability to generalize and to discriminate.
5. Developing in each child the skill of making abstract volitional shifts, i.e., of shifting from the concrete to the abstract in tasks defined for grade level.
6. Helping each child to develop a positive self-concept emerging from success experiences in the classroom.
7. Initiating the development of observational skills related to each grade level and achievement level.

8. Helping students learn independent behavior in solving academic tasks, in handling classroom tools, and in social settings where leadership is desired.
9. Developing in each child writing and listening skills.
10. Assisting each child in developing an interpersonal maturity (etc.).

PT Preparatory and Evaluation Activities

1. Structuring the specific information or skills to be learned each day.
2. Preparing concrete empirical props in learning, i.e., the charts, the books, audio-visual materials, and games material.
3. Continuous reading about new approaches to early childhood teaching.
4. Consulting with instructional specialists and research consultants.
5. Preparing evaluation criteria for assessing whether a child has learned basic curriculum concepts or has developed specific attitudes or skills that relate to classroom behavior, etc.

If we have learned anything about early-childhood instruction in the past five years, we recognize the need for teacher aides (TA) or paraprofessionals in prekindergarten, kindergarten, and the primary grades. The job description of the TA depends largely upon the instructional model within the early-childhood focus, but the TA in most programs, at least, reduces the teacher/pupil ratio and provides essential help in the instructional responsibilities. If a TA is not being used for instructional activities in the classroom or if there is poor communication or limited interaction between the professional teacher and the teacher aide, the contribution of a teacher-aide program is questionable. The primary motive for hiring aides is to provide assistance in the teacher-learner process. Anything short of this goal is probably not worth the money. Statements below provide some suggested role behavior of the teacher aide:

TA Instructional Activities with the Class

1. Working with small groups of children, reinforcing acceptable behavior and attempting the extinction of behavior harmful to the individual and society.

2. Assisting children in their learning skills with crayons, scissors, paintbrushes, puzzle games, etc.
3. Directing singing, dancing, and organized physical exercise.
4. Reading to students.
5. Using matrix games, language lotto games, and puzzle games to bring about language development, etc.

TA Preparatory and Evaluation Activities for the Class

1. Keeping records of attendance, health, and research data.
2. Collecting money for the lunch program.
3. Supervising children to and from the bus stops.
4. Assisting children in putting on and taking off clothes and boots.
5. Assisting in feeding children snacks and lunch.
6. Arranging blackboard and bulletin boards.
7. Assisting in transitional periods between various curricula.
8. Monitoring playground behavior.
9. Duplicating materials, etc.

Another subsystem in the instructional component of early-childhood education relates to the job analysis of the program specialists. The role of the specialist is to develop instructional competence in teachers as well as in teacher aides. Using new and innovative methods in the teacher-learner process, the specialist demonstrates and reinforces the procedures of effective learning of behaviorally defined goals. Introducing techniques with small groups or presenting new materials, the program specialist assists the teacher in becoming more competent in various skills. A music specialist, for example, might demonstrate to teachers and students the ways to identify and develop tone discrimination, rhythm, and "music appreciation." Frequently, teachers are not well trained in music and lack sufficient skills to develop the important criteria in music for elementary-school years. The role of the specialist has to be defined since modern pedagogy does not expect the teacher to be the "end-all" of instruction. Specialists are as essential in working with economically deprived children as the classroom teachers. Among deprived children, we are finding out that significantly less tone discrimination can be expected. Perhaps this factor supports the auditory-discrimination deficit that Cynthia Deutsch (1964) observed among many disadvantaged youth. The high incidence of ear infections may also have some effect on hearing and, therefore, on discrimination of sounds. Young black deprived children have a significantly greater skill in rhythm than other children their own age. This rhythm ability, however, has limitations and a structure that needs to be examined. Perhaps the clapping of hands and the beating of objects with wooden sticks have facilitated this unique rhythm quality, but it could be a serious error to conclude that very young black children have rhythm and, therefore, fail to develop this initial skill. Specialists are needed to assist the teacher in the intensification of learning in various areas. Teachers and specialists must know what specific behavior is expected of each of them. This requires a job analysis of the specialist as interacting with the teacher.

The analysis of the expected behavior of teachers, teacher aides, and program specialists for teaching the disadvantaged has not been completed. Many schools, such as Michigan State University, the University of Georgia, and the University of Florida, have been developing systems approaches toward their teacher education programs. The Georgia Education Model (1968) appears to be an excellent beginning toward elementary-school instruction, but the model must be applied and tested. In the meantime, a specific systems approach for teaching disadvantaged youngsters is greatly needed.

Specific criteria for student teachers (preservice)　　Specifications of those who would be effective in the special task of teaching the disadvantaged have not been publicly defined. If we could summarize the prevalent attitudes toward teaching the disadvantaged, they could be identified by the familiar statement, "Anyone who can teach, can teach the disadvantaged." I doubt if there is a more foolish attitude in our educational enterprise. Not everyone can teach deprived children in an effective way. It demands special preparation and a careful selection of personnel for fulfillment of goals in the classroom of deprived children. Specifications of admission criteria and of teacher performance are the two most pressing needs in building a systems approach to the teaching of the disadvantaged. Figure 10-2 shows a sample diagram of the specifications for selection of students for preservice teacher education.

Application Criteria   The most important component in the application materials should be the letter of intent or the desire to teach disadvantaged children. The letter, and the teacher education program, will have little importance if the role of teaching the disadvantaged has not been considered a "special assignment," with status and attractive rewards. When the job of teaching and doing research with disadvantaged children is characterized as a *scientific, specialist's task,* the letter seeking entrance to the program will express motives of changing the cognitive and affective qualities of youngsters toward desirable ends. The more careful the selection procedure and the more detailed the criteria for the job of teaching the disadvantaged, the less frequently will letters express weak and anemic motives for teaching the poor.

Application criteria should focus on records of high school achievement and on special projects and skills which could provide indications of predicting success in teaching deprived children.

Selection Criteria   In the specifications for selection to a teacher education program for the disadvantaged, both cognitive and affective criteria have to be developed. The difficult problem in making statements about criteria is that there is a continuous need to update and improve the criteria. Consistent feedback on the effectiveness of teachers in the field should be related to the

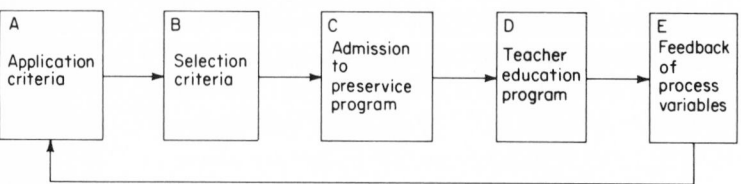

FIGURE 10-2   *Specifications of selection for preservice teacher education.*

criteria. Some criteria must be changed over time. New variables will be added, while others will fade away as relatively unimportant in predicting the effectiveness of teaching the disadvantaged.

Two *cognitive* requisites that could be part of the preprofessional program are verbal ability and quantitative ability as measured on the College Entrance Examination Board test or the Scholastic Aptitude Test. Perhaps a minimum verbal score of 500 on the standardized achievement test would be an acceptable criterion together with a numerical or quantitative score of at least 500. Constant comparison of effective teaching among disadvantaged children could provide the basis for lowering or increasing the general scholastic achievement levels of those choosing to teach the deprived. Minimum scores of 500 on the verbal or quantitative sections of the Scholastic Aptitude Test may be somewhat high. At least there is nothing magical about the criterion of 500. The range of scores predictive of effective teaching of culturally depressed students has yet to be determined. It would seem to be an unfortunate decision if some educators felt that "it really doesn't matter—with the deprived. The big thing is to get a warm body in that classroom." Disadvantaged children should not be given intellectually inferior teachers. High scholastic achievement and teacher competence should not be given solely to advantaged children. All children should be taught by effective teachers.

Another essential component of the selection criteria relates to *affective* structures—personality, interests, and self-concept. Many of the emotional and attitudinal variables could be examined in interview situations, but the supporting information from standardized tests could make the decision of accepting or rejecting a student more valid. The Sixteen Personality Factor Questionnaire (16PF) provides first- and second-order factor scores inferring certain characteristics of personality behavior (as perceived by Raymond Cattell). Norms could be developed over time to identify effective and noneffective teachers. The Strong Vocational Interest Blank (SVIB) could provide supporting measures of interest in teaching children. Needless to say, norms must be developed continually to compare scores of a particular individual with those of the total group of preprofessional teachers and teachers who have been working for a long time with disadvantaged children. If a particular candidate's scores are 1 standard deviation below the mean on any of the sixteen primary factors of the 16PF, counseling and clinical examination should be given the teacher candidate before he (or she) is accepted. There are numerous self-concept instruments that can be used as general measures of feelings about self. In time, general measures of self and normative data for teachers of the disadvantaged will be developed and standardized. Presently, Dr. Ira Gordon's *How I See Myself* can be used. One can also administer a form of the semantic differential in which the concept of "self" and the concept of "others" can be measured by twelve adjective pairs that have been used in numerous studies (White, 1969). It would be hard to justify the view that a negative self-concept and narrow and hostile feelings about others could be acceptable for teaching the disadvantaged. Although negative feelings should not prevent a student from taking preservice training, modification toward positive, healthy attitudes about self would have to be initiated. In order to develop an adequate personality, the teacher of the disadvantaged will have to acknowledge, accept, and deal appropriately with his (or her) own emotions, feelings, and attitudes. No one can determine children's behavior toward the fulfillment of social, psychological, and physical needs if he himself lacks an integrated personality behavior.

Based upon data from personality inventories and interview records, ratings of *sensitivity* and *identification* with problems of the poor should become a high-priority affective criterion. No matter where one goes in discussing the characteristics of the disadvantaged, a quality that is consistently and firmly attributed to the "good" teacher of the disadvantaged is *compassion* or *warmth*. It seems very difficult to operationally define such a term, but so many teachers in the ghettos or in rural, isolated areas use the term that some hypotheses about compassion, love, or warmth in teachers of the poor must be tested. Reissman (1967) is not too certain that effective teachers of the disadvantaged must be healthy and well adjusted. Many personality types seem to function effectively with economically deprived youngsters. For example, the "compulsive type," who teaches things

over and over again with order and structure, can be very effective with poor children. Reissman refers to another teacher type
as the "maverick" because that kind of teacher upsets everything.
He (the teacher) apparently identifies strongly with young and
eager students. The "maverick" is continually stirring people up
over new ideas. "He is as surprised and curious as they (the students), at each turn of mind, each new discovery, and it is this
fresh quality that comes through to them." (Reissman, 1967, p.
331.) Such a style is different from the "coach," who is informal,
earthy, and physically expressive in conducting his dialogue with
the class. The personality characteristics of the "compulsives,"
the "mavericks," and the "coaches" can be behaviorally identified and can be related to various types of teachers of disadvantaged children. Reissman's (1967) feelings about effective
teacher styles and teacher types can be subjected to analyses.
The insightful contribution of Reissman toward determining the
emotional and attitudinal characteristics of effective teacher
styles is that he raises questions about "nonhealthy" components
of teachers of the disadvantaged. It may well be that the desire
to obtain effective teachers for deprived children motivates many
individuals to look for "too much of an ideal" and not enough
effective criteria. There seem to be many teacher types that can
and would be effective with teaching assignments to economically
deprived areas. Teachers, researchers, and administrators must
work together to test the "hypotheses of types" in various situations. Before excluding anyone from admission to preservice programs for the disadvantaged, we had better be sure we have evidence for our decisions. Above all, using audio and video tapes
and observational methods, teacher preparation in preservice programs should provide the opportunity for student teachers to try
out various roles in practice situations so that each student
teacher can develop his own style which will blend with his own
personality.

In a very recent report by Faunce (1970), effective teachers
of the culturally disadvantaged were found to hold attitudes
which differed from the attitudes of teachers who were not effective with the disadvantaged. Effective teachers tended to accept
the fact that the disadvantaged suffer from physical and material
deprivations which other children do not experience. Another

factor that predicted effective teaching was the belief that disadvantaged youth have been discriminated against. The extent to which teachers of the disadvantaged stereotype poor children determines their effectiveness. Faunce suggests that the stereotyping factor points to the heredity-environment controversy. Noneffective teachers were inclined to perceive blacks as lazy and poor children mostly because of their appearance. Nine factors discriminated the effective teachers of the disadvantaged from those who were not effective. Attitudes of teachers have a powerful influence on what is learned in the classroom. Continuous testing of hypotheses about the attitudes of teachers of economically deprived children can help to show educators and politicians that the teachers must be carefully selected. Merely placing teachers in a black/white ratio plan is contrary to the research on teacher attitudes. Although some basic control over integration is necessary, the attitudes of teachers of the deprived children must be considered. It makes a difference.

Specifications of teacher performance   Specifications which describe a particular behavioral competency are the observable activities which the teacher of disadvantaged children should perform in order to operate at optimum effectiveness in teacher-learner situations. Descriptions of the specifications would be the determiners of preservice and in-service education programs. Students who are preparing for teaching the deprived would follow a program that would develop those specific skills.

The system of classification of the specifications could be generated from many theoretical bases. The Georgia Educational Model (1968) used the *Taxonomy of Educational Objectives* in categorizing the cognitive domain: (a) knowledge, (b) comprehension, (c) application, (d) analysis, (e) synthesis, and (f) evaluation (Bloom, 1956) and the Krathwohl, Bloom, and Masia (1956) taxonomy of the affective domain to classify the attitudinal, interest, and emotional specifications of elementary-school teacher behavior: (a) receiving, (b) responding, (c) valuing, (d) organization, and (e) characterization. Optimum performance of teachers in specific classroom situations would depend upon how the teacher-learner behaviors had been operationally defined and classified.

A classificatory system I have been developing for teachers of the disadvantaged in early-childhood programs is as follows:

Cognitive		*Affective*		*Psychomotor*	
(a)	Knowledge	(a)	Attitude	(a)	Strength
(b)	Generalization	(b)	Interest	(b)	Speed
(c)	Application	(c)	Emotion	(c)	Precision
				(d)	Coordination
				(e)	Flexibility

An example of specifications of teacher behavior that could be used in both preservice and in-service training programs for teaching the disadvantaged might focus on dimensions of learning:

Learning			*Cognitive*	*Affective*	*Psychomotor*
2.10	0.01	Theories about learning	(a)	(a)	
2.10	0.02	Pavlovian concepts of conditioning applied to primary-school classrooms	(a)(b)(c)		
2.10	0.03	Concept of association by contiguity	(a)(b)(c)	(a)(c)	
2.10	0.04	Extinction in the classroom	(a)(b)(c)	(a)(c)	
2.10	0.05	Principle of generalizations	(a)(b)(c)		
2.10	0.06	Principle of discrimination	(a)(c)	(a)(c)	
2.10	0.07	History of Thorndike's theory	(a)		
2.10	0.08	Principle of reinforcement	(a)(b)(c)	(a)	
2.10	0.09	Immediacy of reinforcement	(a)(b)(c)	(a)	
2.10	0.10	Effect of negative reinforcement	(a)(b)(c)	(a)	
2.10	0.11	Punishment in the classroom	(a)(b)(c)	(a)(c)	
2.10	0.12	Teach someone something by reinforcement	(a)(b)(c)	(a)(c)	

PRESERVICE TRAINING AND THE PRACTICUM

There is probably nothing more important in preparing to teach the economically deprived child than a well-balanced practicum which lasts long enough and in which student-teachers have a substantive sharing in the job of teacher. Much has been said about the worth and generalizability of certain teacher education programs, but not a great deal of research information is available. Robert Strom (1965) suggested that school administrators bring newly hired teachers for deprived areas to the school one month earlier than the beginning of the school year. Each new teacher would attend workshops on classroom management and the behavioral problems of frustrated children, interaction of area professionals (i.e., psychologists, social workers, public health officers), and community resources. Films about conditions in the area as well as field trips into the community would help some teachers to overcome the "culture shock" that is a frequent experience for young advantaged women assigned to inner-city schools.

In preparing to meet the needs of the economically deprived child and his community, student teachers must be given more accurate knowledge about behavioral patterns of the poor. Living, thinking, and feeling in severely depressed areas are different from the logic, emotional control, and freedom representative of advantaged homes. To learn about the different modes of thinking, feeling, and valuing requires more than a textbook of verbal explanations by scholarly professors. Those preparing for careers as physicians realize how important it is to have an extensive clinical internship. Lawyers know only too well the value of debating clubs and moot courts during their study of law. Those who are to be professional teachers, competent to change the cognitive and affective lives of poor children, must have an extensive and meaningful internship. How long an internship, how well defined, and in what intensity are certainly much debated questions.

There are a number of educational psychologists who would support the program in which a student teacher participates as an aide in the summer sessions between the junior and senior years. Head Start, Follow Through, remedial reading programs under Title I and Title III, and a host of other summer projects could provide the bases for the beginning of practicum experience. Although there are a phenomenal number of problems, a continuing internship from October to May in the senior year (two classes a day) would provide an excellent preparation for teaching the poor.

DIFFERING VALUE SYSTEMS AND INTEGRATION

Probably there is no greater classroom problem for teachers of the disadvantaged than "discipline." Of course, what one teacher calls a discipline problem another will speak about as a conflict of values. All teachers discussing discipline will include in their definitions a control over the class or an individual child. There seem to be too many naïve young women and men emerging from our teacher training programs with the belief that the basic needs and goals of fifth- and sixth-graders are generally the same. The level of deprivation is a significant determiner of the needs of children and of the methods used to control those needs. In economically deprived neighborhoods, parents or parent surrogates use much more verbal and physical aggression in maintaining control than is employed in more advantaged homes. Even the parent identification models are different by reason of social class characteristics. In a large number of depressed black homes, the young black male fails to identify with his father. If the father is in the home and has any stability in obtaining a job, employment generally ends up as a seasonal job or as such a menial, low-paying job that the adult black male becomes a sad image for young black sons to emulate. Many young black males in severely deprived areas in both the North and the South will identify more strongly with their mothers or with male peers than with their fathers.

Integration has not caused the problem of value differences, but it has certainly highlighted the black-white, poor-advantaged behavioral differences. When poor black children are bused into an advantaged white school, the differing value systems become quickly apparent. Teachers must know the value systems of the children they teach. Educators trying to keep the old clichés and the traditional methods in dealing with the deprived are doomed to failure. Searching to mold a class into a homogeneous value system merely puts our education practice further back in scientifically dealing with deprivation problems. As integration becomes more pronounced, principals, teachers, and board members are going to realize that the traditional and conventional classrooms are frustrating and ineffective for disadvantaged children. Teachers will have to be trained in *small-group processes, ungraded schools,* and *individually prescribed programs* if they are going to be effective in teaching the disadvantaged. If advantaged white administrators and teachers maintain the attitude that "these poor kids" are going to fit into *our* school system, inadequate teaching will continue. Poor children and their values are not the only variables that must change. The young teacher who faces economically deprived children with the attitude that "they must change" and adopt "my goals, my attitudes, and my values" can never be very effective with the economically deprived. When two different value systems are integrated among interacting children, a total change will take place. Advantaged children can learn worthwhile things from disadvantaged children.

VIDEO-TAPING OF TEACHER PERFORMANCE

There has been so much success with video-taping of classroom activities that it is difficult to imagine future teacher training programs without the use of video tapes (Salomon & McDonald, 1969; Fuller, 1969; Fuller, Veldman, & Richek, 1966). Student teachers need to observe the skillful teaching tactics of master teachers. Young, inexperienced teachers also gain tremendously by observing their own performance in the classroom. When teachers examine their own behaviors on video-tape replay and analyze strategies and their effects with experienced, professional teachers, improvements in teacher behavior are bound to take place. Video tapes also record behavior so that professional supervisors can examine classroom performance at convenient times. During interviews with the teacher candidate, tapes can be presented to exemplify and support some of the personal observations made by critical observers.

AUDIO-TAPING AND INTERACTION ANALYSIS

Student teachers would gain much more effectiveness in their teaching styles if audio tapes were used to provide the data base for a modified Flanders scale or an Ober scale (cf. Chapter 2). In the preservice as well as the in-service program, having teachers "learning the system" and measure their own performance generates a more indirect teacher style. When young men and women are not forced to make changes but are encouraged to evaluate their own performance, great progress is made. The important result of audio-taping preservice performance is not the data but the teacher's knowledge of verbal interaction in the classroom and concern for self-appraisal.

IN-SERVICE PROGRAMS

The progress of teacher training during in-service programs in the 1970s will depend upon the working together of university personnel, private and local government agencies, and teachers and administrators in developing better ways of teaching disadvantaged children. The one outstanding characteristic of successful in-service programs for teachers in lower socioeconomic areas will be the scientific approach toward teaching strategies. Teachers will be looking for consistent improvement in the learner's performance. Scientific methods will stimulate teachers to test hypotheses, gather data, and evaluate their own performance as well as that of their students. Teachers will be communicating in more objective terminology and will be measuring what they are doing in the classroom. As a subsystem in the larger system of teacher training, the in-service program should be patterned upon the specifications of teacher-learner behavior in the system. Constantly appraising the teacher role, continuously modifying various styles and content, tomorrow's teachers will be better informed and more amenable to change. The attitudes and personal values and constructs of student teachers have been significantly modified through training programs (Mazer, 1969).

UNIVERSITY PERSONNEL

Specialists on university campuses should share part of their professional time in the in-service programs. Teams consisting of university personnel, private agencies, and teachers and administrators would maintain a total educational unit. The in-service benefits would affect university teachers and researchers as well as the teachers in the field centers and school districts. The communication and sharing of ideas about the characteristics of the economically deprived and teaching strategies would make the in-service programs a scientific enterprise. Research would have an applied value since it would be relegated to existing problems. Innovations in the classroom of the disadvantaged would be a cooperative effort. Above all, researchers would not be doing the research while teachers did the teaching. Teachers would be caught up in the excitement of testing hypotheses, while researchers would share the difficult task of working with deprived children. Above all, the researcher would not come to the school to do "his" research and leave after he has minimally explained the conclusions of "his" study. The human-engineering approach to classroom teaching (i.e., to do better tomorrow what you accomplished satisfactorily today) can be accomplished only when teachers and research personnel *consistently* and over a *long period of time* work together in modifying existing performances based on scientific methods.

NEW YORK UNIVERSITY IN-SERVICE TRAINING PROGRAM

New York University has demonstrated a new way of organizing academic resources and of stimulating interaction among school systems, private agencies, and the university. The major part of the program is funded by federal antipoverty money. Consultants are drawn from the faculties of various schools on the New York University campus as well as from among directors of day-care centers, nursery schools, and community agencies. The men and women on these consultant teams work 1½ days a week as technical assistants in various projects. The unique organizational factor is that each faculty member is assigned to a specified agency (e.g., Head Start) for work in a specific geographic area. In the New York in-service training program (Ginsberg & Greenhill, 1968), sixteen areas have been defined and provide a working basis through which communication between agencies can be facilitated and resources from many institutions can be shared.

The program advances a strong model for institutional interaction. There is bound to be interaction within the university when members of all disciplines work together instead of each college, or discipline, struggling to obtain grants to justify a righteous concern for the poor. A common cause in solving human relations problems will bring institutions of higher learning into a cooperative effort.

SELF-EVALUATIONS OF TEACHING STYLE

More than anything else, teachers need to examine themselves and the total climate in which they are working. In-service programs can provide the basis for observing interacting patterns of teacher and student. Moskowitz (1967) and Bentley and Miller (1969) found that the training of teachers in interaction analysis (e.g., the modified Flanders model) made marked changes in the way teachers taught. Emphasis was placed not on "indirect" or "direct" scores on the Flanders or the Ober scales but upon examining one's teaching style. When teachers are not threatened by the scores on verbal interaction scales, they will be inclined to style much of their teaching after student-initiated talk. Teacher attitudes and skills will be patterned closely in the direction of student motivation. General teaching effectiveness will be increased since teachers will be concerned about the intercommunication in the classroom and its effect on learning processes. If in-service training could provide the vehicle for cooperative effort between university personnel and elementary or secondary school teachers in carrying out a self-evaluation study, improvement in teacher strategies and children's learning should be highly predictive.

NURTURING CREATIVE TALENT

In-service programs should provide a vehicle for nurturing divergent skills among teachers as well as instructing teachers in developing creative abilities in the children they teach. More attention should be given to the development of teacher abilities, not merely giving teachers information. Flanders (1963) described the typical in-service programs:

> At its worst, in-service training is a gigantic spectator sport for teachers costing at least twenty million dollars annually. As spectators, teachers gather to hear speeches, usually choosing seats in the rear of the room. They play a passive role in which their own ideas and questions are not adequately considered. They react as one does to any performing art and are more impressed or disappointed by the quality of the performance than with how much they have learned. [Flanders, 1963, p. 26.]

In-service training for teachers should be appraised much as the training children receive is evaluated. The index of a successful in-service program is that teachers act differently as a result of training. Unless teachers learn to teach better, the worth of time spent on in-service is questionable. Teachers can be trained to be more divergent, seeking alternate solutions to the problems and consistently testing new hypotheses. Creative teachers are not a luxury; they are a necessity. If teachers can become more original, flexible, fluent, and elaborative, their students stand a better chance of being creative.

THE NEED FOR A NEW IMAGE

Tomorrow's teacher of the disadvantaged should reflect high status in the teaching profession as well as superiority in scientific inquiry. More often than not, teachers of the economically deprived are regarded as "just like any other kind of teacher." Very few administrators pay teachers of the disadvantaged more money, although it is a more difficult job than teaching advantaged youngsters. It seems to require more effort to teach deprived children, a different teaching style, and highly developed skills. Teachers of deprived children will have to be regarded as specialists, working with a special kind of child. The measure of success in teaching disadvantaged children will be in the image of teachers in deprived areas. Teachers themselves will have to be more scientific in speeding up the learning processes of children limited by a variety of experiences. The "new look" of teachers of economically poor children will depend on how well the teacher observes and analyzes behavior in the classroom.

If old methods are not working, new methods must be created and implemented so that children born and raised in poverty can be successful in school. All curricula and methods should be open to revision. It will take outstanding teachers, with new ideas and unprecedented zeal, to lead the way in preparing the school situation for poor children to master. Tomorrow's teacher of the disadvantaged will have to be more scientifically oriented and more skilled in dealing with psychosocial variables than teachers in the last decade. The attitudes, interests, and emotions of children must be given tremendous importance. With their skill in determining the academic independence and the interpersonal and emotional maturity of boys and girls from poor homes, teachers of deprived children will be a select group of professionals. Instead of fearing to stand before children in economically depressed areas, young student teachers will be pleading to enter careers of teaching the disadvantaged. With success in teaching the deprived will come the pride of being different.

Bibliography

AHR, A. E.: The development of a group preschool screening test of early school entrance potential, *Psychology in the Schools*, 4 (1): 59–63, 1967.

ALLINSMITH, W., and G. W. GOETHALS: Cultural factors in mental health: An anthropological perspective, *Review of Educational Research*, 26: 433–438, 1956.

AMIDON, E. J., and N. A. FLANDERS: *The role of the teacher in the classroom: A manual for understanding and improving teachers' classroom behavior*, P. S. Amidon, Minneapolis, 1963.

———, PEGGY AMIDON, and B. ROSENSHINE: *Skill development in teaching work manual*, Association for Productive Teaching, Minneapolis, Minn., 1969.

——— and J. B. HOUGH: *Interaction analysis: Theory, research, and application*, Addison-Wesley, Reading, Mass., 1967.

——— and ELIZABETH HUNTER: *Improving teaching*, Holt, Rinehart and Winston, New York, 1966.

——— and ———: Interaction analysis: Recent developments, in E. Amidon and J. Hough (eds.), *Interaction analysis: Theory, research, and application*, Addison-Wesley, Reading, Mass., 1967.

ANASTASI, ANNE: *Differential psychology*, Macmillan, New York, 1958.

ANDERSON, H. E., W. F. WHITE, and J. A. WASH: Generalized effects of praise and reproof, *Journal of Educational Psychology*, 57: 169–173, 1966.

ANDERSON, H. H.: Domination and integration in the social behavior of young children in an experimental play situation. *Genetic Psychological Monographs* 19: 341–408, 1937.

AUSUBEL, D. P.: A teaching strategy for culturally deprived pupils: Cognitive and motivational considerations, *The School Review,* 71: 454–463, 1963.

————: How reversible are the cognitive and motivational effects of cultural deprivation? Implications for teaching the culturally deprived child, *Urban Education,* 1: 16–38, 1964.

————: The effects of cultural deprivation on learning patterns, *Audiovisual Instruction,* 10: 10–12, 1965.

———— and PEARL AUSUBEL: Ego development among segregated Negro children, in A. Harry Passow (ed.), *Education in depressed areas,* Bureau of Publications, Teachers College, Columbia University, New York, 1963, pp. 109–141.

BALES, R. F.: Interaction process analysis: A model for the study of small groups, Addison-Wesley, Cambridge, Mass., 1950.

BANDURA, A., and CAROL KUPERS: Transmission of patterns of self-reinforcement through modeling, *Journal of Abnormal and Social Psychology,* 69: 1–9, 1964.

———— and R.H. WALTERS: *Social learning and personality development,* Holt, Rinehart and Winston, New York, 1963.

BECKER, W. C., and S. ENGLEMAN: *The University of Illinois Follow Through approach,* paper presented at Follow Through meeting, Atlanta, Ga., 1968.

BEER, S.: *Cybernetics and management,* John Wiley and Sons, New York, 1959.

BELCHER, LEON H., and JOEL T. CAMPBELL: An exploratory study of work associations of Negro college students, *Psychological Reports,* 68: 195–201, 1968.

BENTLEY, E. L., and EDITH MILLER: *Systematic observation,* Supplementary Educational Center, Atlanta, Ga., 1969.

BEREITER, C., ROBBIE CASE, and VALERIE ANDERSON: Steps toward full intellectual functioning, *Journal of Research and Development in Education,* 1: 70–79, 1968.

BERNSTEIN, B.: Some sociological determinants of perception: An enquiry into sub-cultural differences, *British Journal of Sociology,* 9: 159–174, 1958.

BLACKMAN, L. S., and P. HEINTZ: The mentally retarded, *Review of Educational Research,* 36: 5–36, 1966.

BLOOM, B. S. (ed.): *Taxonomy of educational objectives: The classification of educational goals: Handbook I: Cognitive domain,* David McKay, New York, 1956.

————, A. DAVIS and R. HESS: *Compensatory education for cultural deprivation,* Holt, Rinehart and Winston, New York, 1965.

BOGUR, J. H.: An experimental study of the effects of perceptual training on group $T2$ scores of elementary pupils in rural ungraded schools, *Journal of Education Research,* 46: 43–52, 1952.

BORMUTH, JOHN R.: Comparable Cloze and Multiple Choice Comprehension Test Scores, *Journal of Reading,* 5: 291–299, 1967.

BOWER, E. M.: *Early identification of emotionally handicapped children in school,* Charles C Thomas, Springfield, Ill., 1960.

—— and NADINE M. LAMBERT: *A process for in-school screening of children with emotional handicaps,* Educational Testing Service, Princeton, N.J., 1962.

BRATTEN, R.: Apollo 11 Flight. *New York Times,* December 21, 1968.

Brown v. Board of Education of Topeka, 347 U.S. 483 (1954).

BUGELSKI, R. B.: *The psychology of learning applied to teaching,* Bobbs-Merrill, Indianapolis, 1964.

BUSHELL, D.: *Behavior analysis: A research approach to Follow Through,* paper presented to Follow Through meeting, Atlanta, Ga., 1968.

——, P. A. WROBEL, and M. L. MICHAELIS: Applying "group" contingencies to the classroom study behavior of preschool children, *Journal of Applied Behavior Analysis,* 1: 55–61, 1968.

BUTTS, R. F. A.: *A cultural history of western education,* McGraw-Hill, New York, 1955.

CALDWELL, BETTYE M.: *The Preschool Inventory,* Educational Testing Service, Princeton, N.J., 1967.

CALHOUN, LILLIAN S.: New: Schools and power—whose, *Integrated Education,* 7: 11–35, 1969.

CAMPBELL, A., and H. SCHUMAN: Racial attitudes in fifteen American cities, in the National Advisory Commission on Civil Disorders, *Supplemental Studies,* U.S. Government Printing Office, 1968.

CATTELL, R. B.: Concepts and methods in the measurement of group syntality, *Psychological Review,* 55: 48–63, 1948.

CAZDEN, COURTNEY B.: Subcultural differences in child language: An interdisciplinary review, in J. Hellmuth (ed.), *Disadvantaged child,* vol. 2, Brunner-Mazel, New York, 1968, pp. 219–256.

CLARK, A. D. B., and A. A. CLARK: Recovery from the effects of deprivation, *Acta Psychologia,* 16: 137–144, 1959.

CLARK, C., and H. WALBERG: The influence of massive rewards on reading achievement in potential urban school dropouts, *American Educational Research Journal,* 5:305–310, 1968.

CLARKE, K. B., and M. P. CLARK: Racial identification and preference in Negro children, in Newcomb and Hartley (eds.), *Readings in social psychology,* Holt, Rinehart and Winston, New York, 1947, pp. 169–178.

COAN, R. W., and R. B. CATTELL: *The Early School Personality Questionnaire,* Institute for Personality and Ability Testing, Champaign, Ill., 1961.

COLEMAN, J. S., E. Q. CAMPBELL, C. J. HOBSON, J. McPARLAND, A. M. MOOD, F. D. WEINFIELD, and R. L. YORK: *Equality of educational opportunity,* U.S. Government Printing Office, 1966.

COOK, D. L.: Management control theory as the context for educational evaluation, *Journal of Research and Development in Education,* 3: 13–26, 1970.

DAVIS, A.: *Social class influences upon learning,* Harvard University Press, Cambridge, Mass., 1948.

DEUTSCH, CYNTHIA: Auditory discrimination and learning: Social factors, *Merrill Palmer Quarterly*, 10: 277–296, 1964.

DEUTSCH, M.: The disadvantaged child and the learning process, in E. H. Passow, (ed.), *Education in depressed areas*, Teachers College, Columbia University, New York, 1963.

———: Facilitating development in the pre-school child: Social and psychological perspectives, *Merrill-Palmer Quarterly*, 10: 249–264, 1964.

———: Some psychological aspects of learning in the disadvantaged, *Teachers College Record*, 67: 260–265, 1966.

——— et al.: Communication of information in the elementary school classroom, *Cooperative Research Project* 908, Institute for Developmental Studies, Department of Psychiatry, New York Medical College, New York, 1964.

DI VESTA, F. J.: A developmental study of the semantic structures of children, *Journal of Verbal Learning and Verbal Behavior*, 5: 249–259, 1966.

DOLL, E. A.: *Measurement of social competence*, Educational Testing Bureau, Educational Publishers, 1953.

DUNN, L. H.: *Peabody Picture Vocabulary Test*, American Guidance Service, Minneapolis, 1965.

Early Childhood Inventory Project, Institute for Developmental Studies, New York, 1967.

ENGLEMANN, S.: *Conceptual learning*, Dimensions Publishing, San Rafael, Calif., 1969.

ENTWISLE, DORIS R.: Developmental sociolinguistics: Inner city children, *American Journal of Sociology*, 74, 1968.

——— and ELLEN GREENBERGER: *Differences in the language of Negro and white grade-school children 1, 2*, Johns Hopkins University, Baltimore, 1968.

EPPS, E. G.: Interpersonal relations and motivation: Implications for teachers of disadvantaged children, *Journal of Negro Education*, 39: 14–25, 1970.

FAUNCE, R. W.: *Attitudes and characteristics of effective and not effective teachers of culturally disadvantaged children*, paper presented to American Educational Research Association, Minneapolis, 1970.

FELDHUSEN, HAZEL, ROSE LAMB, and JOHN FELDHUSEN: Prediction of reading achievement under programmed and traditional instruction, *The Reading Teacher*, 23: 446–450, 1970.

FLANDERS, N. A.: Intent, action, and feedback: a preparation for teaching, *Journal of Teacher Education*, 14: 251–260, 1963.

FORTSON, LAURA R.: A creative-aesthetic approach to readiness and beginning reading and mathematics in the kindergarten, unpublished doctoral dissertation, University of Georgia, Athens, Ga., 1969.

FRIES, C. C.: *American English grammar*, Appleton-Century-Crofts, New York, 1940.

FROST, J. L., and O. R. KING: Educating disadvantaged children, *Journal of Arkansas Education*, 11: 6–28, 1964.

FULLER, FRANCES F. (ed.): *Effects of personalized feedback during teacher preparation on teacher personality and teaching behavior,* R. & D. Report Series 4, final report of Project 5-0811, Grant OE 3-10-032, *Personality, Teacher Education and Teaching Behavior,* 1969.

———: D. J. VELDMAN, and H. G. RICHEK: Tape recordings, feedback and prospective teachers' self evaluation, *Alberta Journal of Educational Research,* 12: 301–307, 1966.

GAGNE, R. M. (ed.): *Learning and individual differences,* Charles E. Merrill Books, Columbus, Ohio, 1967.

GALLAGHER, J. J., and M. J. ASCHNER: A preliminary report on analyses of classroom interaction, *Merrill-Palmer Quarterly of Behavior and Development,* 9: 183–194, 1963.

———, and J. T. HUNT (eds.): Education of exceptional children, *Review of Educational Research,* 36: 202 pp., 1966.

Georgia educational model specifications for the preparation of elementary teachers, final report of Project 809024 Grant OEC-0-089024-3311 (010), USOE, 1968.

GILKESON, ELIZABETH: The Bank Street College approach to Follow Through, *Focus on Follow Through,* USOE, January, 1970.

GINSBERG, SUSAN, and MURIEL GREENHILL: New York City Head Start: Pluralism innovation and institutional change, in J. Hellmuth (ed.), *Disadvantaged child: vol. 2,* Brunner-Mazel, New York, 1968, pp. 399–420.

GLASSER, W.: *Schools without failure,* Harper & Row, New York, 1969.

GOLDBERG, MIRIAM: Adapting teacher style to pupil differences: Teachers for disadvantaged children, *Merrill-Palmer Quarterly,* 11: 161–178, 1964.

GORDON, E. W., and D. A. WILKERSON: *Compensatory education for the disadvantaged,* College Entrance Examination Board, New York, 1966.

GORDON, I. J.: *The Florida parent education Follow Through approach,* paper presented at Follow Through meeting, in Atlanta, Ga., 1968.

GOTKIN, L. G.: *Teacher's introduction to matrix games,* Appleton-Century-Crofts, New York, 1967.

———: *The development of a beginning reading program,* Institute for Developmental Studies, New York, 1969.

———, J. F. McSWEENEY, and E. RICHARDSON: *The development of a beginning reading program,* New York University, Institute for Developmental Studies, New York, 1969.

GRUSEC, JOAN, and U. MISCHELS Model's characteristics as determinants of social learning, *Journal of Personality and Social Psychology,* 4: 211–215, 1966.

GUILFORD, J. P., and W. ZIMMERMAN: *Guilford-Zimmerman Temperament Survey,* Sheridan Supply Co., Los Angeles, Calif., 1949.

HANSEN, C. F.: The scholastic performance of Negro and white pupils in the integrated public schools of the District of Columbia, *Harvard Educational Review,* 30: 216–236, 1960.

HARLEM YOUTH OPPORTUNITIES UNLIMITED, INC.: *Youth in the ghetto: A study of the consequences of powerlessness and a blueprint for change,* New York, 1964.

HARRINGTON, M.: *The other American,* Macmillan, New York, 1962.

HAVIGHURST, R. J.: Who are the socially disadvantaged? *The Journal of Negro Education,* 210–217, 1964.

HEIL, L. M., M. POWELL, and I. FEIFER: *Characteristics of teacher behavior related to the achievement of children in several elementary grades,* Office of Education, Cooperative Research Branch, U.S. Department of Health, Education, and Welfare, 1960.

HESS, R. D., and VIRGINIA SHIPMAN: Early experience and the socialization of cognitive modes in children, *Child Development,* 36: 869–886, 1965.

HILDRETH, G. H., N. L. GRIFFITHS, and M. E. McGAUVRAN: *Metropolitan readiness tests,* Harcourt, Brace & World, New York, 1964.

HILL, H. H.: School desegregation North and South: It will take time, *Saturday Review,* 7: 54–71, 1966.

HOLMES, J. A., and H. SINGER, The substrata-factor theory: Substrata-factor differences underlying reading ability in known groups at the high school level. Cr. 538 and 538A. U.S. Department of Health, Education, and Welfare, 1961.

HORTON, C. P., and E. P. CRUMP.: Growth and development: XI. Descriptive analysis of the background of 76 Negro children whose scores are above or below average on the *Merrill-Palmer Scale of Mental Tests* at three years of age, *Journal of Genetic Psychology,* 33: 813–822, 1962.

HOUGHTON, A.: The case for intelligence testing, *Phi Delta Kappan,* 46: 106–108, 1964.

HUNT, J. McV.: The psychological basis for using pre-school enrichment as an antidote for cultural deprivation, *Merrill-Palmer Quarterly,* 10: 209–248, 1964.

INSKO, C. A., and J. E. ROBINSON: Belief similarity versus race as determinants or reactions to Negroes by southern white adolescents: A further test of Rokeach's theory, *Journal of Personality and Social Psychology,* 7: 216–221, 1967.

JAMES, W.: *Talks to teachers,* Norton, New York, 1958.

JENSEN, A. R.: Social class, race, and genetics: Implications for education, *American Educational Research Journal,* 5: 1–42, 1968.

JOHN, VERA P.: A brief survey of research on the characteristics of children from low-income backgrounds, *Urban Education,* 1: 215–222, 1965.

JOSEPH, S. M.: *The me nobody knows,* Avon, New York, 1969.

KATZ, PHYLLIS A., and M. DEUTSCH: Reduction of auditory-visual shifting to reading achievement, *Perceptual and Motor Skills,* 17: 323–332, 1963.

KENNEDY, W. A., VIRGINIA VAN DE RIET, and J. C. WHITE: A normative sample of intelligence and achievement of Negro elementary school children in the southeastern United States, *Monographs of the Society for Research in Child Development,* ser. 90, vol. 28, no. 6, 1963.

KIM, Y., H. E. ANDERSON, and W. L. BASHAW: The simple structure of social maturity at the second grade, *Educational and Psychological Measurement*, 28: 145–154, 1968.

KIMBLE, G. A., and N. GARMEZY: *Principles of general psychology*, Ronald, New York, 1963.

KINGSTON, A. J., and W. F. WHITE: Semantic meaning of a protagonist as determined by the concept of self and personality factors, *Reading Research*, 2: 107–116, 1967.

KIRK, S. A., J. J. McCARTHY, and W. D. KIRK: *Illinois Test of Psycholinguistic Abilities*, University of Illinois Press, Urbana, Ill., 1968.

KLINEBERG, O.: Negro-white differences in intelligence test performance: A new look at an old problem, *American Psychologist*, 18: 198–203, 1963.

———: Life is fun in a smiling, fair-skinned world, *Saturday Review*, 2: 75–76, 1963.

KRATHWOHL, D. R., B. S. BLOOM, and B. B. MASIA: *Taxonomy of educational goals: Handbook II: Affective domain*, David McKay, New York, 1956.

KVARACEUS, W., et al., *Negro self-concept: Implications for school and community*, McGraw-Hill, New York, 1965.

LEE, J. M., and W. W. CLARK: *Lee-Clark Reading Readiness Test*, California Test Bureau, Monterey, Calif., 1962.

LESSER, C. S.: Mental abilities of children from different social class and culture groups, *Monographs of the Society for Research in Child Developments*, 34 (102): 115, 1965.

LEWIN, K., R. LIPPITT, and R. K. WHITE: Patterns of "aggressive" behavior in experimentally created "social climates," *Journal of Social Psychology*, 10: 271–299, 1939.

LICHTER, J. H., and JOHNSON, D. W.: Changes in attitudes toward Negroes of White elementary school students after use of multi-ethnic readers, *Journal of Educational Psychology*, 60: 148–152, 1969.

LOBAN, W. D.: *The language of elementary school children*, National Council of Teachers of English, Champaign, Ill., 1963.

LORETAN, J. O., and S. UMANO: *Teaching the disadvantaged*, Teachers College Press, New York, 1966.

MACKLER, B., and M. GIDDINGS: Cultural deprivation, *Teachers College Record*, 66: 608, 613, 1965.

MADSEN, C., W. BECKER, and T. DON: Rules, praise, and ignoring: Elements of elementary classroom control, *Journal of Applied Behavioral Analysis*, 1: 139–150, 1968.

MASLOW, A. H.: The instinctoid nature of basic needs, *Journal of Personality*, 22: 326–347, 1954.

MASON, G. E., et al.: *Written language: Level A*, Research and Development Center in Educational Stimulation, University of Georgia, Athens, Ga., 1969.

MAZER, G. E.: Attitude and personality change in student teachers of disadvantaged youth, *Journal of Educational Research*, 63: 116–120, 1969.

McCANDLESS, B. R.: Predictor variables of school success for slum children, presidential address for Division 16, American Psychological Association meeting, San Francisco, 1968.

McKEACHIE, W. J.: Procedures and techniques of teaching: A survey of experimental studies, in N. Sandord (ed.), *The American College*, Wiley, New York, 1962.

MEDLEY, D. M., and L. H. SMITH: *Instructions for recording behavior with OSCAR. A continuation of the CRAFT project*: Comparing reading approaches with disadvantaged urban Negro children in the primary grades, Division of Teacher Educaiton in the City of New York, Cooperative Research Project 5-0570-2-12-1, New York, 1968.

MILLER, G. A.: The magical number seven, plus or minus two: Some limits on our capacity to process information, *Psychological Review*, 63: 81–97, 1956.

———: Communication and information as limiting factors in group formation, in L. C. Kobb (ed.), *Communication, values, influence, and group structure*, Walter Reed Army Institute of Research, Washington.

MORENO, J. L.: *Who shall survive?* Nervous and Mental Disease Publishing Company, Washington, 1934.

MOSKOWITZ, GERTRUDE: The attitudes and teaching patterns of cooperating teachers and student teachers trained in interaction analysis, in N. A. Flanders and R. Hough (eds.), *Interaction Analysis*, Addison-Wesley, Reading, Mass., 1967, pp. 271–282.

MOWRER, O. H.: *Learning theory and behavior*, Wiley, New York, 1960.

———: *Learning theory and the symbolic processes*, Wiley, New York, 1960.

MUSSEN, P. H.: Some antecedents and consequents of masculine sex typing in adolescent boys, *Psychological Monography*, 75 (2, whole no. 506), 1961.

———, J. CONGER, and J. KAGAN: *Child development and personality*, Harper and Row, New York, 1969.

NIMNICHT, G.: The autotelic-discovery Follow Through approach, paper presented at Follow Through meeting, Atlanta, Ga., 1968.

OBER, R. L.: Predicting student teacher behavior, unpublished doctoral dissertation, Ohio State University, Columbus, Ohio, 1966.

———: The nature of interaction analysis, *The High School Journal*, 51: 7–16, 1967.

O'LEARY, K. D., and W. C. BECKER: The effects of the intensity of a teacher's reprimands on children's behavior, *Journal of School Psychology*, 7: 8–11, 1969.

OLIM, E. G., R. D. HESS, and VIRGINIA C. SKIPMAN: *Relationship between mother's language styles and cognitive styles of urban preschool children*, paper presented to the Society for Research in Child Development, 1965, Urban Child Study Center, Chicago, Ill., 1965.

OREM, REGINALD C., and MARIE MONTESSORI: *A Montessori Handbook*, Putnam, New York, 1966.

OSGOOD, C. E.: The nature and measurement, *Psychological Bulletin,* 49: 197–237, 1952.

PASSOW, A. T. (ed.): *Developing programs for the educationally disadvantaged,* Teachers College Press, New York, 1968.

———, MIRIAM L. GOLDBERG, and A. J. TANNENBAUM, (eds.): *Education of the disadvantaged,* Holt, Rinehart and Winston, New York, 1967.

PAQUETTE, R.: Apollo: The giant leap, *SDC Magazine,* 12: 1–21, 1969.

PETTIGREW, T. F.: *A profile of the Negro American,* Van Nostrand, Princeton, N.J., 1964.

———: Race and equal educational opportunity, *Harvard Educational Review,* 38: 66–76, 1968.

———: Racially separate or together? *Integrated Education,* 7: 36–56, 1969.

PINKO, CELMA: Five major themes of the Montessori method, in R. C. Orem (ed.), *Montessori for the disadvantaged,* Capricorn Books, New York, 1967.

PORTER, R. B., and R. B. CATTELL: *Handbook for the IPAT Children's Personality Questionnaire,* Institute for Personality and Ability Testing, Champaign, Ill., 1959.

POWELL, E. R., and W. F. WHITE: Peer-concept ratings in rural children, *Psychological Reports,* 24: 461–462, 1969.

REES, HELEN E.: *Deprivation and compensatory education,* Houghton Mifflin, Boston, 1968.

REISSMAN, F.: *The culturally deprived child,* Harper & Row, New York, 1962.

———: Teachers of the poor: A five-point plan, *Journal of Teacher Education,* Fall, 1967, pp. 326–336.

RENTSCH, G. J.: Open enrollment, unpublished doctoral dissertation, State University of New York at Buffalo, 1966.

RENTZ, R. R.: A theoretical and empirical validation of a multivariate interrelational affective model for describing group structure, unpublished doctoral dissertation, University of Georgia, Athens, Ga., 1969.

———, E. FEARS, and W. F. WHITE: Similarity of the group's perception of its interrelational structure with group member's personality, *Journal of Psychology,* 70: 163–167, 1968.

———, and NORINNE A. OLSON: *A multivariate method for the description of group structure using semantic differential data,* paper presented at the National Council on Measurement in Education, Chicago, Ill., 1968.

———, and W. F. WHITE: Congruence of the dimensions of self-as-object and self-as-process, *Journal of Psychology,* 67: 277–285, 1967.

Report of the Council of Economic Advisers, Washington, 1964.

RICHMOND, B. O., and W. F. WHITE: Sociometric predictors of the self concept among fifth and sixth grade children, *Journal of Educational Research,* In press.

ROACH, E. G., and N. C. KEPHART: *The Purdue Perceptual-Motor Survey,* Charles E. Merrill Books, Columbus, Ohio, 1966.

Rock, W. C., H. R. Goldberg, T. R. Knapp, and Joanne Lang: *An interim report on a fifteen point plan to reduce racial isolation and provide quality integrated education*, Rochester City School District, Rochester, N.Y., 1968.

Rokeach, M., and G. Rothman: The principle of belief congruence and the congruity principle as models of cognitive interaction, *Psychological Review*, 72: 128–142, 1965.

Rosenshine, B.: Evaluation of classroom instruction, *Review of Educational Research*, 40: 279–300, 1970.

Ross, Dorothea: Relationship between dependency, intentional learning, and incidental learning in preschool children, *Journal of Personality and Social Psychology*, 4: 374–381, 1966.

Ryans, D. G.: Some validity extension data from empirically derived predictors of teacher behavior, *Educational and Psychological Measurement*, 18: 355–370, 1958.

———: Some validity extension data from empirically derived predictors of teacher behavior, *Educational and Psychological Review*, 72: 128–142, 1965.

———: *Characteristics of teachers: Their description, comparison and appraisal*, American Council on Education, Washington, 1960.

Saloman, G., and F. J. McDonald: Pre- and post-test reactions to self-viewing one's teaching performance on videotape, *Research and Development Memo* 44, Stanford Center for Research and Development in Teaching, Stanford University, Stanford, Calif., March, 1969.

Samuels, S. J.: Effects of pictures on learning to read, comprehension and attitudes, *Review of Educational Research*, 40: 397–407, 1970.

Schaeffer, E. S., and M. Aaronson: *Classroom Behavior Inventory*, form for preschool to early primary, National Institute of Mental Health, 1966.

Schmuck, Richard: Some aspects of classroom social climate, *Psychology in the Schools*, 3: 59–65, 1966.

Sears, P.: Child rearing factor relating to playing sex and typed roles, *American Psychologist*, 8: 431 (abstract), 1953.

Seligman, B. B.: *Permanent poverty*, Quadrangle, Chicago, 1968.

Segel, I. E.: How intelligence tests limit understanding of intelligence, *Merrill-Palmer Quarterly*, 9: 37–39, 1963.

Silberman, C.: *Crises in black and white*, Random House, New York, 1964.

Skinner, B. F.: Operant conditioning, *American Psychologist*, 18: 503–515, 1963.

———: The machine that man is, *Psychology Today*, 2: 20–25, 1969.

Smilansky, Sara: *The effects of sociodramatic play on disadvantaged pre-school children*, Wiley, New York, 1968.

Smith, B. O., M. Meux, et al.: *A study of the logic of thinking, III*, Bureau of Educational Research, Urbana, Ill., 1963.

Smith Carole R., L. Williams, and R. H. Willis: Race, sex, and belief as determinants of friendship acceptance, *Journal of Personality and Social Psychology*, 5: 127–137, 1967.

Smith, L. M., and W. Geoggrey: *The complexities of an urban classroom*, Holt, Rinehart and Winston, New York, 1968.

Smith, R. M.: The relationship of creativity to social class, *Cooperative Research Project* 2250, School of Education, University of Pittsburgh, Pittsburgh, Pa., 1965.

Snider, J. G., and C. E. Osgood: *Semantic differential technique*, Aldine, Chicago, 1969.

Soares, A. T., and Louise M. Soares: Self perceptions of culturally disadvantaged children, *American Educational Research Journal*, 6: 21–45, 1969.

Spivack, G., and M. Swift: Patterns of disturbed classroom behavior: *The nature and measurement of academically related problem behavior*, Deveraux Foundation, Devon, Pa., 1968, ERIC ed. 012, p. 545.

Stallings, F. H.: Atlanta and Washington racial differences in academic achievement, *Southern Regional Council Report* L-16, Southern Regional Council, Atlanta, Ga., 1960.

Starkweather, E. K.: Studies of the creative potential of young children, in F. E. Williams, *Creativity at home and in school*, Macalester College, St. Paul, Minn., 1968.

State Education Department: *Guiding principles for securing racial balance in public schools*, The University of the State of New York, Albany, N.Y., 1963.

———: *Closing the gap*, The University of the State of New York, Albany, N.Y., 1968.

Stein, D. D.: The influence of belief systems on interpersonal preference: A validation study of Rokeach's theory of prejudice, *Psychological Monographs*, 80 (616): 1–29, 1966.

Stoffer, D. L.: Investigation of positive behavioral change as a function of genuineness, nonpossessive warmth, and empathic understanding, *Journal of Educational Research*, 63: 225–228, 1970.

Stott, D. H., and Emily G. Sykes: *Bristol Social Adjustment Guides*, Educational and Industrious Testing Service, San Diego, Calif., 1967.

Strom, R. D.: *The inner-city classroom: Teacher behaviors*, Charles E. Merrill Books, Columbus, Ohio, 1960.

———: *Teaching in the slum school*, Charles E. Merrill Books, Columbus, Ohio, 1965.

———: *Psychology for the classroom*, Prentice-Hall, Englewood Cliffs, N.J., 1969.

Strong, Ruth: *Reading*, Dimensions Publishing, San Rafael, Calif., 1969.

Taba, Hilda, and Deborah Elkins: *Teaching strategies for the culturally disadvantaged*, Rand McNally, Chicago, 1966.

Taylor, Jane C.: *Language stimulation*, Education Improvement Program, Durham, N.C., 1969.

Thomas, D. R.: Oral language, sentence structure and vocabulary of kindergarten children living in low socio-economic urban areas, unpublished doctoral dissertation, Wayne State University, Detroit, Mich., 1962.

THORNDIKE, E. L.: *Animal intelligence*, Macmillan, New York, 1911.

THORPE, L. P., W. W. CLARK, and E. W. TRIGS: *California Test of Personality*, California Test Bureau, Los Angeles, 1953.

TORRANCE, E. P.: *Education and the creative potential*, University of Minnesota Press, Minneapolis, Minn., 1963.

———: Must pre-primary educational stimulation be incompatible with creative development? in F. E. Williams (ed.), *Creativity at home and in school*, Macalester College, St. Paul, Minn., 1968.

———: Peer influences on preschool children's willingness to try difficult tasks, *Journal of Psychology*, 1969.

——— and LAURA R. FORTSON: Creativity among young children and the creative-aesthetic approach, *Education*, 16: 1–4, 1968.

———, ———, and CAROLYN DIENER: Creative-aesthetic ways of developing intellectual skills among five year olds, *Journal of Research and Development in Education*, 1: 58–69, 1968.

——— and M. H. FREEMAN: Group size and question asking performance of pre-primary children, *Research and Development Center in Educational Stimulation Bulletin*, Athens, Ga., 1969.

———: Encouraging creativity in the classroom, Wm. C. Brown, Dubuque, Iowa, 1970.

TRIANDIS, H. C., and E. E. DAVIS: Race and belief as determinants of behavioral intentions, *Journal of Personality and Social Psychology*, 2: 715–725, 1965.

USDAN, M. D.: The preparation of teachers for the disadvantaged, in Jerome Hellmuth (ed.), *Disadvantaged child, I*, Brunner-Mazel, New York, 1967, pp. 225–253.

VAN DE RIET, V., HANI VAN DE RIET, and H. SPRIGLE: The effectiveness of a new sequential learning program with culturally disadvantaged preschool children, *Journal of School Psychology*, 7: 5–15, 1969.

VERNON, M. D.: The value of pictorial illustration, *British Journal of Educational Psychology*, 23: 180–187, 1953.

WARE, KAY: Ways to develop reading skills and interests of culturally different youth in large cities, in J. Jewett, J. Mersand, and Doris Gunderson (eds.), *Improving English of culturally different youth in large cities*, U.S. Dept. of Health, Education, and Welfare, 1964.

WAYSON, W. W.: Expressed motive of teachers in slum schools, *Urban Education*, 1: 223–238, 1965.

WHITE, R.: Motivation reconsidered: The concept of competence, *Psychological Review*, 66: 297–333, 1959.

WHITE, W. F.: *Psychosocial principles applied to the classroom*, McGraw-Hill, New York, 1969.

——— and R. AARON: Non-verbal cues as determinants of reading comprehension, *Journal of Reading Behavior*, 1969.

———, W. L. BASHAW, and G. R. MOORE: Congruent expectations of children's classroom performance by teachers and paraprofessionals, *Journal of Teacher Education*, In press.

————, and B. O. RICHMOND: Perception of self and peers by economically deprived black and advantaged white fifth graders. *Psychological Reports*, 30: 533–534, 1970.

WHITE, E. F., and J. A. WASH: Perception of teacher effectiveness as a function of the student's need for social approval, *Perceptual and Motor Skills*, 23: 717–723, 1966.

————, W. W. WEAVER, and A. J. KINGSTON: Affective correlates of reading comprehension, *Journal of Psychology*, 68: 87–95, 1968.

WITT, G.: *The life enrichment activity program*, a private paper, 1968.

WOOCK, R. R.: Community operated schools: A way out? *Urban Education*, 3: 132–142, 1968.

YOURMAN, J.: The case against group I.Q. testing in schools with culturally disadvantaged pupils, *Phi Delta Kappan*, 3: 108–110, 1964.

ZAHORI, J. A.: Teacher verbal feedback and content development, paper presented to the American Educational Research Association, University of Wisconsin, Milwaukee, Wis., 1969.

Indexes

Name Index

Subject Index